Essential Tort Law for SQE1

Essential Tort Law for SQE1 explains the key principles of tort law in a clear, easy-to-follow style. Principles are introduced and illustrated with reference to practical examples. The book demonstrates the skill of client case analysis, taking a clear and structured approach to analysing the facts of a client's case and then applying the relevant principles. It also includes a range of supportive features:

- Revision points: Each chapter concludes with a concise list of key revision points.
- Problem questions: To test understanding and analytical skills applied to practical scenarios. A companion website also provides suggested answers.
- Multiple choice questions: Each section of the book provides multiple choice questions following the SQE1 question format (with answers to enable you to test your knowledge). Further multiple choice questions and answers are also provided on the companion website.

The first in a series of books aimed at those preparing for SQE1, this concise and accessible text provides a clear understanding of the tort element of SQE1 and enables you to test your assessment skills.

Wendy Laws was a litigation solicitor for 14 years, before moving to work in higher education for the last 21 years, variously as a senior lecturer, course designer, and problem-based learning tutor writing study materials for GDL, LLB, LPC, QLTS, and SQE.

Essential Law for SQE1

Series editor: Wendy Laws

Essential Law for SQE1 is a series of concise textbooks aligned to the latest SQE1 curriculum. Providing candidates with an accessible summary of the core principles in each area of law, the style of each book is precise, with bullet-point lists summarizing key information and revision points concluding each chapter. The books also feature multiple choice questions with answers and example problem questions and a glossary of key cases, while a companion website provides further multiple choice questions and example outline answers to the problem questions.

For more information about this series, please visit: www.routledge.com/Essential-Law-for-SQE1/book-series/SQE1

Essential Tort Law for SQE1
Wendy Laws

Essential Tort Law for SQE1

Wendy Laws

Routledge
Taylor & Francis Group
LONDON AND NEW YORK

First published 2022
by Routledge
2 Park Square, Milton Park, Abingdon, Oxon OX14 4RN

and by Routledge
52 Vanderbilt Avenue, New York, NY 10017

Routledge is an imprint of the Taylor & Francis Group, an informa business

© 2022 Wendy Laws

The right of Wendy Laws to be identified as author of this work has been asserted by her in accordance with sections 77 and 78 of the Copyright, Designs and Patents Act 1988.

All rights reserved. No part of this book may be reprinted or reproduced or utilised in any form or by any electronic, mechanical, or other means, now known or hereafter invented, including photocopying and recording, or in any information storage or retrieval system, without permission in writing from the publishers.

Trademark notice: Product or corporate names may be trademarks or registered trademarks, and are used only for identification and explanation without intent to infringe.

British Library Cataloguing-in-Publication Data
A catalogue record for this book is available from the British Library

Library of Congress Cataloging-in-Publication Data
Names: Laws, Wendy (Law teacher), author.
Title: Essential tort for SQE1 / Wendy Laws.
Other titles: Essential tort for Solicitors Qualifying Examination 1
Description: Abingdon, Oxon ; New York, NY : Routledge, 2022. |
   Series: Essential law for SQE1 | Includes bibliographical references and index.
Identifiers: LCCN 2021009085 (print) | LCCN 2021009086 (ebook) |
   ISBN 9780367679903 (hardback) | ISBN 9780367679767 (paperback) |
   ISBN 9781003133698 (ebook)
Subjects: LCSH: Torts—England—Examinations, questions, etc. |
   LCGFT: Study guides.
Classification: LCC KD1949.6 .L39 2022 (print) | LCC KD1949.6 (ebook) |
   DDC 346.4203—dc23
LC record available at https://lccn.loc.gov/2021009085
LC ebook record available at https://lccn.loc.gov/2021009086

ISBN: 978-0-367-67990-3 (hbk)
ISBN: 978-0-367-67976-7 (pbk)
ISBN: 978-1-003-13369-8 (ebk)

Typeset in The Sans
by Apex CoVantage, LLC

DOI: 10.4324/9781003133698

Visit the companion website: www.routledge.com/cw/sqe

Contents

Table of cases	xv
Table of statutes	xix
Introduction	1

Part 1: Introduction to claims and remedies in tort — 5

1 Harms, remedies, and client case analysis — 7
- 1.1 Chapter overview — 7
- 1.2 Introduction to the range of torts — 7
- 1.3 Introduction to remedies in tort — 10
- 1.4 Client case analysis in tort — 12
  - 1.4.1 Identifying the relevant tort — 12
  - 1.4.2 Identifying the parties to the claim — 14
  - 1.4.3 Establishing the elements of the claim — 15
  - 1.4.4 Client case analysis as the foundation for litigation — 16
  - 1.4.5 Further development of client case analysis skills — 17
- Chapter 1 revision points — 17

Part 2: Trespass to land and to the person — 19

2 Trespass to land — 21
- 2.1 Chapter overview — 21
- 2.2 Overview of trespass — 21
  - 2.2.1 Trespass actionable per se — 21
- 2.3 Introduction to trespass to land — 22
- 2.4 Definition and elements — 22
  - 2.4.1 Possession — 22
  - 2.4.2 Land — 23
  - 2.4.3 Interference — 23
- 2.5 Defences to trespass to land — 25
  - 2.5.1 Licence (permission) — 25
  - 2.5.2 Necessity — 25
  - 2.5.3 Other lawful justification — 25

	2.6	Remedies for trespass to land	25
		2.6.1 Declaration	25
		2.6.2 Injunction	26
		2.6.3 Damages	26
		2.6.4 Order for possession of land	26
		Chapter 2 revision points	27
3		**Trespass to the person**	**29**
	3.1	Chapter overview	29
	3.2	Introduction	29
	3.3	Battery	30
	3.4	Assault	32
	3.5	False imprisonment	33
	3.6	Defences to trespass to the person	34
		3.6.1 Consent	34
		3.6.2 Necessity	34
		3.6.3 Self-defence	35
		3.6.4 Lawful arrest	35
	3.7	Remedies for trespass to the person	36
		Chapter 3 revision points	36
		Multiple choice questions for Part 2	**37**

Part 3: Negligence — 39

4		**Negligence: duty of care**	**41**
	4.1	Chapter overview	41
	4.2	The tort of negligence – overview	41
	4.3	Established duty situations	42
		4.3.1 Situations in which case law establishes that no duty is owed	42
		4.3.2 Summary	43
	4.4	Novel duty situations	44
		4.4.1 Foreseeability	44
		4.4.2 Proximity	45
		4.4.3 Fair, just and reasonable	45
		4.4.4 Summary	46
		Chapter 4 revision points	46
5		**Negligence: breach of duty**	**47**
	5.1	Chapter overview	47
	5.2	The standard of reasonable care	47
		5.2.1 Reasonable person – objective standard	47
		5.2.2 Level of risk	48
		5.2.3 Reasonable precautions	49
	5.3	Under-skilled defendants	49

	5.4	Defendants exercising special skills	50
	5.5	Child defendants	51
	5.6	Proving breach of duty	51
		5.6.1 *Res ipsa loquitur*	52
		Chapter 5 revision points	53
6	**Negligence: causation of damage and remoteness**		**55**
	6.1	Chapter overview	55
	6.2	Introduction to causation	55
	6.3	The 'but for' test for causation	56
	6.4	Multiple causes	58
		6.4.1 Material contribution to harm	59
		6.4.2 Material increase in the risk of harm	60
	6.5	Contribution between tortfeasors	62
	6.6	Intervening acts	62
		6.6.1 Acts of a third party	63
		6.6.2 Acts of the claimant	64
	6.7	Remoteness of damage	64
		6.7.1 Reasonable foreseeability	65
		6.7.2 The 'egg shell skull' rule	65
		6.7.3 The 'similar in type' rule	66
	6.8	Causation and quantifying damages	66
		Chapter 6 revision points	68
	Multiple choice questions for Part 3		**69**
Part 4: General defences			**75**
7	**General defences**		**77**
	7.1	Chapter overview	77
	7.2	Introduction: analysing defences in negligence claims	77
	7.3	Contributory negligence	78
		7.3.1 Claimant's lack of care for their own safety	78
		7.3.2 Contributing to the harm suffered	78
		7.3.3 Reduction in damages	79
		7.3.4 Children	79
	7.4	Limitation of actions	79
	7.5	Exclusion of liability	80
		7.5.1 Effective notice	80
		7.5.2 Statutory controls	81
	7.6	Voluntary assumption of risk	82
		7.6.1 Distinguished from consent	82
	7.7	Illegality	83
		Chapter 7 revision points	84
	Multiple choice questions for Part 4		**85**

Part 5: Negligence: limited duty situations — 89

8 Negligence: limited duty situations – economic loss — 91
- 8.1 Chapter overview — 91
- 8.2 Distinguishing pure economic loss from consequential economic loss — 91
- 8.3 Damage to a defective product acquired by the claimant — 92
- 8.4 Damage to property which does not belong to the claimant — 93
- 8.5 Financial loss which is not caused by damage to property (statements/services) — 93
- 8.6 Breach of duty and causation of damage — 95
- Chapter 8 revision points — 95

9 Negligence: limited duty situations – psychiatric harm — 97
- 9.1 Chapter overview — 97
- 9.2 Distinguishing pure psychiatric harm from consequential psychiatric harm — 97
- 9.3 Primary and secondary victims — 98
- 9.4 Medically recognised condition and sudden shock — 98
  - 9.4.1 Medically recognised condition — 98
  - 9.4.2 Sudden shock — 99
- 9.5 Primary victims — 100
- 9.6 Secondary victims — 100
  - 9.6.1 Reasonable foreseeability of psychiatric harm — 101
  - 9.6.2 Close ties of love and affection with the immediate victim — 101
  - 9.6.3 Proximity to the accident — 101
  - 9.6.4 Direct perception by sight or hearing — 102
- 9.7 Rescuers — 102
- 9.8 Breach of duty and causation of damage — 103
- Chapter 9 revision points — 103

Multiple choice questions for Part 5 — 104
Summary overview of negligence — 105
Overview of the tort of negligence — 106

Part 6: Remedies in tort — 109

10 Remedies — 111
- 10.1 Chapter overview — 111
- 10.2 Introduction to damages — 111
  - 10.2.1 Damage to property — 112
- 10.3 Damages for personal injury – living claimant — 113
  - 10.3.1 Non-financial losses – pain, suffering, and loss of amenity — 113
  - 10.3.2 Financial losses — 113
  - 10.3.3 Terminology – special and general damages — 116

10.4	Damages on death	116
	10.4.1 The effect of death on liability in tort	116
	10.4.2 Deceased victim's own cause of action surviving death	117
	10.4.3 Damages for loss of dependency and for bereavement	118
10.5	Injunctions	120
10.6	Causes of action other than claims in tort	121
	Chapter 10 revision points	121

Multiple choice questions for Part 6 — 122

Part 7: Employers' liability and vicarious liability — 125

11 Employers' liability — 127
- 11.1 Chapter overview — 127
- 11.2 Duty of care — 127
  - 11.2.1 Non-delegable duty — 129
- 11.3 Breach of duty — 129
- 11.4 Causation of damage and defences — 130
- 11.5 Other claims by employees — 130
- Chapter 11 revision points — 130

12 Vicarious liability — 133
- 12.1 Chapter overview — 133
- 12.2 Introduction to vicarious liability — 133
- 12.3 Tort — 134
- 12.4 Relationship – employment or 'akin' to employment — 134
  - 12.4.1 Independent contractors — 136
- 12.5 Close connection/course of employment — 137
- Chapter 12 revision points — 140

Multiple choice questions for Part 7 — 141

Part 8: Occupiers' liability — 145

13 Occupiers' liability: visitors — 147
- 13.1 Chapter overview — 147
- 13.2 Introduction to occupiers' liability — 147
- 13.3 Liability to visitors – introduction — 148
- 13.4 Liability for the state of the premises — 149
  - 13.4.1 Premises — 149
  - 13.4.2 State of the premises, not activities on premises — 149
- 13.5 Who is a visitor? — 149
  - 13.5.1 Visitors who enter pursuant to a contract — 149
- 13.6 Who is an occupier? — 150

13.7	The occupier's duty of care to visitors	150
	13.7.1 Discharging the duty	151
13.8	Causation of damage	153
13.9	Defences	154
	13.9.1 Contributory negligence	154
	13.9.2 Exclusion of liability	154
	13.9.3 Voluntary assumption of risk	155
	Chapter 13 revision points	155

14 Occupiers' liability: trespassers — 157
- 14.1 Chapter overview — 157
- 14.2 Liability to trespassers – introduction — 157
- 14.3 Occupiers and premises — 158
- 14.4 The limited duty of care — 158
  - 14.4.1 When is a duty owed? — 159
  - 14.4.2 What is the scope of the duty? — 159
- 14.5 Causation of damage — 160
- 14.6 Defences — 160
  - 14.6.1 Contributory negligence — 160
  - 14.6.2 Exclusion of liability — 161
  - 14.6.3 Voluntary assumption of risk — 161
  - 14.6.4 Illegality — 161
  - Chapter 14 revision points — 161

Multiple choice questions for Part 8 — 163

Part 9: Product liability — 165

15 Product liability — 167
- 15.1 Chapter overview — 167
- 15.2 Why claim in tort rather than in contract? — 167
- 15.3 Claims in negligence — 168
- 15.4 *Consumer Protection Act 1987* – strict liability — 170
  - 15.4.1 Who may claim? — 170
  - 15.4.2 Who is the claim against? — 170
  - 15.4.3 Strict liability for defective products — 170
  - 15.4.4 Meaning of damage — 171
  - 15.4.5 Defences — 171
- 15.5 Which claim to bring? — 173
- Chapter 15 revision points — 173

Multiple choice questions for Part 9 — 174

Part 10: Nuisance — 177

16 Private nuisance — 179
- 16.1 Chapter overview — 179
- 16.2 Introduction to private nuisance — 179

	16.3	Who may sue for private nuisance?	180
	16.4	Who may be sued?	181
		16.4.1 The creator of the nuisance	181
		16.4.2 The occupier of the land where the nuisance occurs	181
		16.4.3 Landlords	183
	16.5	Continuing state of affairs	183
	16.6	Intangible damage – interference with amenity	183
		16.6.1 Reasonableness factors	184
		16.6.2 Factors which do not excuse a nuisance	186
		16.6.3 Proof of damage	187
	16.7	Tangible damage and encroachment	187
		16.7.1 Proof of damage	188
	16.8	Causation and remoteness of damage	188
	16.9	Defences to nuisance	188
		16.9.1 Consent	189
		16.9.2 Statutory authority	189
		16.9.3 Prescription	189
	16.10	Remedies for private nuisance	190
		16.10.1 Damages	190
		16.10.2 Injunctions	190
		16.10.3 Abatement	191
	16.11	Nuisance, trespass, and negligence – which claim to bring?	192
		Chapter 16 revision points	193
17	**The rule in *Rylands v Fletcher***		**195**
	17.1	Chapter overview	195
	17.2	Introduction to the rule in *Rylands v Fletcher*	195
	17.3	Parties to the claim	196
	17.4	Elements of the claim	196
		17.4.1 Dangerous thing	196
		17.4.2 Non-natural use of land	197
		17.4.3 Strict liability	197
		17.4.4 Damage	197
	17.5	Nuisance, negligence, and *Rylands v Fletcher* – which claim to bring?	198
		Chapter 17 revision points	199
18	**Public nuisance**		**201**
	18.1	Chapter overview	201
	18.2	The nature of public nuisance	201
	18.3	Definition	202
	18.4	Who can sue in public nuisance?	202
		18.3.1 Attorney General	202
		18.4.2 Individuals	202

Chapter 18 revision points — 203

Multiple choice questions for Part 10 — 204

Part 11: Protections for reputation and private information — 207

19 Defamation — 209
- 19.1 Chapter overview — 209
- 19.2 Introduction — 209
- 19.3 Defamatory statement — 210
- 19.4 Statement referring to the claimant — 210
- 19.5 Publication of a defamatory statement — 210
- 19.6 Defences to defamation — 211
  - 19.6.1 Truth — 211
  - 19.6.2 Honest opinion — 211
  - 19.6.3 Publication on a matter of public interest — 212
  - 19.6.4 Privilege — 212
  - 19.6.5 Limitation — 213
- 19.7 Libel and slander – damage in defamation claims — 214
- 19.8 Remedies for defamation — 215
  - 19.8.1 Damages — 215
  - 19.8.2 Injunction — 215
- Chapter 19 revision points — 216

20 Misuse of private information — 217
- 20.1 Chapter overview — 217
- 20.2 Introduction — 217
- 20.3 Elements of the tort — 218
  - 20.3.1 Reasonable expectation of privacy — 218
  - 20.3.2 Balancing freedom of expression — 218
- 20.4 Remedies for misuse of private information — 219
  - 20.4.1 Damages — 219
  - 20.4.2 Injunction — 219
- Chapter 20 revision points — 220

Multiple choice questions for Part 11 — 221

Part 12: Client case analysis in tort — 223

21 Client case analysis skills in tort — 225
- 21.1 Chapter overview — 225
- 21.2 Client case analysis — 225
  - 21.2.1 Identify the relevant tort — 225
  - 21.2.2 Identify the parties to the claim — 226
  - 21.2.3 Establish the elements of the claim — 226

21.3	Litigation risk		226
21.4	Assessing the evidence		227
	21.4.1	Lay witnesses	227
	21.4.2	Expert evidence	227
21.5	Advising and settlement		228
	21.5.1	What remedy?	228
	21.5.2	How much?	229
21.6	Decided cases – precedents in practice		229
	21.6.1	Principles drawn from litigated cases – piecemeal development	230
	21.6.2	Issues in litigated cases – chosen by the parties	230
	21.6.3	Limiting the issues – trial on preliminary issue only	231
	21.6.4	Using decided cases as a tool in client case analysis	231
	Chapter 21 revision points		232
22	**Key cases in tort law**		**233**
22.1	Chapter overview		233
22.2	Application of client case analysis skills to decided cases		233
22.3	Trespass		234
	22.3.1	Trespass to land	234
	22.3.2	Trespass to the person	235
22.4	Negligence		236
	22.4.1	Duty of care	236
	22.4.2	Breach of duty	240
	22.4.3	Causation of damage	244
	22.4.4	Remoteness of damage	246
22.5	Defences		248
22.6	Economic loss		249
	22.6.1	Negligent statements	249
	22.6.2	Acquisition of a defective product	249
22.7	Psychiatric harm		251
	22.7.1	Primary victims	251
	22.7.2	Secondary victims	252
22.8	Remedies		254
22.9	Employers' liability		255
22.10	Vicarious liability		257
22.11	Occupiers' liability		258
	22.11.1	Lawful visitors	258
	22.11.2	Trespassers	260
22.12	Product liability		262
22.13	Nuisance		263
22.14	Defamation		265

22.15	Misuse of private information	267
	Chapter 22 revision points	269
23	**Problem questions**	**271**
23.1	Chapter overview	271
23.2	Problem questions	271
24	**Answers to multiple choice questions**	**281**
24.1	Chapter overview	281
24.2	Part 2 – Trespass to land and to the person	282
24.3	Part 3 – Negligence	283
24.4	Part 4 – General defences	288
24.5	Part 5 – Negligence: limited duty situations	291
24.6	Part 6 – Remedies in tort	293
24.7	Part 7 – Employers' liability and vicarious liability	294
24.8	Part 8 – Occupiers' liability	296
24.9	Part 9 – Product liability	299
24.10	Part 10 – Nuisance	302
24.11	Part 11 – Protections for reputation and private information	305

Index 307

Table of cases

A v National Blood Authority [2001] 3 All ER 289 (QBD) **172n11**

Abouzaid v Mothercare (UK) Ltd [2000] All ER (D) 2436 (CA), [2001] CLY 920 (CA) **167n1, 262–263**

Alcock v Chief Constable of South Yorkshire [1992] 1 AC 310 (HL) **101n3, 102n5, 252–254**

Ali v Channel 5 Broadcasting Ltd [2019] EWCA Civ 677, [2019] All ER (D) 128 (Apr) **219n2, 268**

Attorney General v PYA Quarries Ltd (No.1) [1957] 2 QB 169 (CA) **202n2**

Austin v Commissioner of Police for the Metropolis [2007] EWCA Civ 989, [2008] 1 All ER 564 **35n6**

Bailey v Ministry of Defence [2008] EWCA Civ 883, [2009] 1 WLR 1052 **60n6**

Baker v Willoughby [1970] AC 467 (HL) **67n20**

Bamford v Turnley (1862) 3 B & S 66 **183n6**

Barber v Somerset CC [2004] UKHL 13, [2004] 2 All ER 385 **128n2**

Barker v Corus (UK) Plc [2006] UKHL 20, [2006] 2 AC 572 **61n7, 246**

Barnett v Chelsea & Kensington Hospital Management Committee [1969] 1 QB 428 (QB) **56n1, 244–245**

Bell v Tavistock and Portman NHS Foundation Trust [2020] EWHC 3274 (Admin), [2020] All ER (D) 30 (Dec) **31n3**

Blyth v Birmingham Waterworks Co (1856) 11 Ex 781 **47n1**

Bocardo SA v Star Energy UK Onshore Ltd [2010] UKSC 35, [2011] 1 AC 380 **23n4**

Bolam v Friern Hospital Management Committee [1957] 2 All ER 118 (QB) **50n6, 242–243**

Bolton v Stone [1951] AC 850 (HL) **48n3, 240–241**

Bonnard v Perryman [1891] 2 Ch 269 (CA) **215n17**

Bonnington Castings Ltd v Wardlaw [1956] AC 613 (HL) **59n4, 245–246**

Bourhill v Young [1943] AC 92 (HL) **44n4**

Byrne v Deane [1937] 1 KB 818 (CA) **265–267**

Cambridge Water Co Ltd v Eastern Counties Leather Plc [1994] 2 AC 264 (HL) **188n10, 198n6, 265**

Campbell v Mirror Group Newspapers Ltd [2004] UKHL 22, [2004] 2 All ER 995 **267–268**

Caparo Industries Plc v Dickman and Others [1990] 2 AC 605 (HL) **41n1, 94n3, 237–240**

Castle v St Augustine's Links Ltd (1922) 38 TLR 615 **203n4**

Chaudhry v Prabhakar [1989] 1 WLR 29 (CA) **95n4**

Clough v First Choice Holidays and Flights Ltd [2006] EWCA Civ 15, [2006] PIQR P22 **59n5, 246**

Corby Group Litigation v Corby DC

[2009] EWHC 1944 (TCC), [2010] Env LR D2 **201n1**
Coventry v Lawrence [2014] UKSC 13, [2014] AC 822 **183n1, 187n7, 191n13, 263–265**
Cox v Ministry of Justice [2016] UKSC 10, [2016] AC 660 **136n2–3**
Cream Holdings Ltd v Banerjee [2004] UKHL 44, [2005] 1 AC 253 **220n3**
Cross v Kirkby [2000] CLY 5110 **35n7**

Donoghue v Stevenson [1932] AC 562 (HL) **41n1, 236–237**

F v West Berkshire HA [1990] 2 AC 1 (HL) **31n2**
Fairchild v Glenhaven Funeral Services Ltd [2002] UKHL 22, [2003] 1 AC 32 **61n7, 246**
Fearn v Tate Gallery Board of Trustees [2020] EWCA Civ 104, [2020] 2 WLR 1081 **265**
Foster v Warblington UDC [1906] 1 KB 648 (CA) **181n4**
Froom v Butcher [1976] 1 QB 286 (CA) **78n1, 248–249**

Gee v DePuy International Ltd [2018] EWHC 1208 (QB), [2018] Med LR 347 **263**
Glasgow Corporation v Muir [1943] AC 448 (HL) **47n2**
Gore v Stannard [2012] EWCA Civ 1248, [2014] QB 1 **197n3**
Greene v Associated Newspapers Ltd [2004] EWCA Civ 1462, [2005] QB 972 **215n17**

Haley v London Electricity Board [1965] AC 778 (HL) **45n5**
Hartman v South Essex Mental Health and Community Care NHS Trust [2005] EWCA Civ 6, [2005] ICR 782 **128n2**

Hatton v Sutherland [2002] EWCA Civ 76, [2002] 2 All ER 1 **128n2**
Hedley Byrne & Co Ltd v Heller & Partners Ltd [1964] AC 465 (HL) **94n3, 249**
Henderson v Dorset Healthcare University NHS Foundation Trust [2020] UKSC 43, [2020] 3 WLR 1124. **83n19–20**
Hicks and Others v Chief Constable of the South Yorkshire Police [1992] 2 All ER 65 (HL) **118n11, 254–255**
Hotson v East Berkshire HA [1987] AC 750 (HL) **57n2**
Hughes v Lord Advocate [1963] AC 837 (HL Scotland) **66n18**
Hunter v Canary Wharf Ltd [1997] AC 655 (HL) **180n2, 265**

International Energy Group Ltd v Zurich Insurance Plc UK [2015] UKSC 33, [2016] AC 509 **61n7, 246**
Iqbal v London Transport Executive (1973) 16 KIR 329 **138n5**

James-Bowen v Commissioner of Police of the Metropolis [2018] UKSC 40, [2018] 4 All ER 1007 **240**
Jobling v Associated Dairies [1982] AC 794 (HL) **67n20**

Kelsen v Imperial Tobacco Co [1957] 2 QB 334 (QBD) **23n3**
Knightley v Johns [1982] 1 All ER 851 (CA) **62n11**

Lachaux v Independent Print Ltd [2019] UKSC 27, [2020] AC 612 **210n3, 215n16, 267**
Latimer v AEC Ltd [1953] AC 643 (HL) **49n4**
League Against Cruel Sports Ltd v Scott [1986] QB 240 (QB) **24n6**
Leakey v National Trust [1980] QB 485 (CA) **182n5, 188n9**

Lemmon v Webb [1895] AC 1 (HL) **24n5, 192n14, 234**
Limpus v London General Omnibus Co (1862) 158 ER 993 **138n6**

Marc Rich & Co AG v Bishop Rock Marine Co Ltd (The Nicholas H) [1996] AC 211 (HL) **45n6**
McGhee v National Coal Board [1972] 3 All ER 1008 (HL) **61n7, 246**
McKew v Holland & Hannen & Cubitts (Scotland) Ltd [1969] 3 All ER 1621(HL Scotland) **64n14**
McLoughlin v O'Brian [1983] 1 AC 410 (HL) **101n4, 254**
McPhail v Persons Unknown [1973] Ch 447 (CA) **23n1**
Mohamud v Wm Morrison Supermarkets Plc [2016] UKSC 11, [2016] AC 677 **139n7, 258**
Montgomery v Lanarkshire Health Board [2015] UKSC 11, [2015] AC 1430 **50n6, 243n3**
Muirhead v Industrial Tank Specialities Ltd and Others [1986] QB 507 (CA) **92n1, 249–251**
Murphy v Brentwood DC [1991] 1 AC 398 (HL) **92n1, 250**

Nettleship v Weston [1971] 2 QB 691 (CA) **50n5, 241–242**
Network Rail Infrastructure Ltd v Conarken Group Ltd [2010] EWHC 1852 **24n6**

Overseas Tankship (UK) Ltd v The Miller Steamship Co Pty and Another (The Wagon Mound), (No.2) [1967] 1 AC 617 (PC) **247**
Overseas Tankship (UK) Ltd v Morts Dock & Engineering Co (The Wagon Mound), (No.1) [1961] AC 388 (PC) **65n16, 246–247**

Page v Smith [1996] AC 155 (HL) **100n2, 251–252**
Page v Smith (No.2) [1996] 1 WLR 855 **252**
Paris v Stepney BC [1951] AC 367 (HL) **48n3**
Patel v Mirza [2016] UKSC 42, [2017] AC 467 **83n19**
Peires v Bickerton's Aerodromes Ltd [2016] EWHC 560 (Ch) **189n11**
Pitts v Hunt [1991] 1 QB 24 (CA) **83n17**
PJS v News Group Newspapers Ltd [2016] UKSC 26, [2016] AC 1081 **220n3**
Playboy Club London Ltd v Banca Nazionale del Lavoro SpA [2018] UKSC 43, [2019] 2 All ER 478 **249**

R (on the application of Jalloh (formerly Jollah)) v Secretary of State for the Home Department [2020] UKSC 4, [2020] 3 All ER 449 **33n4**
Ready Mixed Concrete (South East) Ltd v Minister of Pensions and National Insurance [1968] 2 QB 497 (QBD) **135n1**
Revill v Newberry [1996] QB 567 (CA) **161n6**
Richard v BBC [2018] EWHC 1837, [2019] 2 All ER 105 **219n2, 268**
Robinson v Chief Constable of West Yorkshire [2018] UKSC 4, [2018] AC 736 **43n2, 239**
Robson and Another v Hallett [1967] 2 QB 939, [1967] 2 All ER 407 **25n7**
Robinson v Post Office [1974] 2 All ER 737 (CA) **66n17**
Rylands v Fletcher (1868) LR 3 HL 330 (HL) **195–199**

St Helen's Smelting Company v Tipping (1865) 11 HLC 642 **188n8**
Scott v London & St Katherine Docks Co [1861–73] All ER Rep 248 **52n7**

Sedleigh-Denfield v O'Callaghan [1940] AC 880 (HL) **183n6**

Spartan Steel & Alloys Ltd v Martin & Co (Contractors) Ltd [1973] QB 27 (CA) **93n2, 251**

Stansbie v Troman [1948] 2 KB 48 (CA) **63n13**

Stoffel and Co v Grondona [2020] UKSC 42, [2020] 3 WLR 1156 **83n19**

Sturges v Bridgman (1879) 11 Ch D 852 (CA) **187n7, 190n12**

Tinseltime Limited v Roberts [2011] EWHC 1199 (TCC), [2011] CLY 2272 **180n3**

Tomlinson v Congleton BC [2003] UKHL 47, [2004] 1 AC 46 **159n2, 260–261**

Transco Plc v Stockport MBC [2003] UKHL 61, [2004] 2 AC 1 **196n2, 197n4–5**

Various Claimants v Barclays Bank Plc [2020] UKSC 13, [2020] 2 WLR 960 **136n2 and n4, 258**

Various Claimants v Wm Morrison Supermarkets Plc [2020] UKSC 12, [2020] 2 WLR 941 **139n7, 257–258**

Walker v Commissioner of Police of the Metropolis [2014] EWCA Civ 897, [2015] 1 WLR 312 **29n1, 235–236**

Walker v Northumberland CC [1995] 1 All ER 737 (QBD) **128n2**

Wheat v E Lacon & Co Ltd [1966] AC 552 (HL) **150n3, 258–260**

Wilsher v Essex AHA [1988] AC 1074 (HL) **58n3, 246**

Wilson v Pringle [1987] QB 237 (CA) **31n2**

Wilsons & Clyde Coal Co Ltd v English [1938] AC 57 (HL) **127n1, 129n4, 255–256**

YAH v Medway NHS Foundation Trust [2018] EWHC 2964, [2019] 1 WLR 1413 **99n1**

Zeromska-Smith v United Lincolnshire Hospitals NHS Trust [2019] EWHC 980, [2019] All ER (D) 92 (Apr) **99n1**

Table of statutes

Civil Liability Act 2018 **113n4**
Civil Liability (Contribution) Act 1978 **62n10**
Compensation Act 2006 **61n7, 246**
Consumer Protection Act 1987 **170–173, 262–263**
Consumer Rights Act 2015 **81n10–11 and n14, 154n5, 155n7**
Contracts (Rights of Third Parties) Act 1999 **168n2**
Damages Act 1996 **115n7**
Data Protection Act 1998 **257**
Defamation Act 1996 **213n10**
Defamation Act 2013 **210n2, 211n4 and n7–8, 212n9, 213n10–11, 214–215, 267**
Employer's Liability (Defective Equipment) Act 1969 **128n3, 129n5**
Enterprise and Regulatory Reform Act 2013 **130n6**
Fatal Accidents Act 1976 **118n12–13, 119n14, 255**

Health and Safety at Work etc. Act 1974 **130n6**
Human Rights Act 1998 **121, 216, 220**
Law Reform (Contributory Negligence) Act 1945 **79n2, 248–249**
Law Reform (Miscellaneous Provisions) Act 1934 **116n9, 117n10, 255**
Law Reform (Personal Injuries) Act 1948 **116n8**
Limitation Act 1980 **80n6–7, 213, 214n13**
Mental Capacity Act 2005 **34n5**
Occupiers' Liability Act 1957 **148–155, 259**
Occupiers' Liability Act 1984 **157–162, 261**
Police Act 1996 **236n2**
Road Traffic Act 1988 **81n9, 82n16**
Unfair Contract Terms Act 1977 **81n10–13, 154n5, 155n6**

Introduction

This book provides a clear, concise explanation of key principles of tort law. Its focus is on those areas which fall within the assessment specification for the **Solicitors Qualifying Examination Part 1 Functioning Legal Knowledge** ('SQE1').[1]

In so doing, it also covers the areas of tort law central to most undergraduate tort law modules (and, for this purpose, it also includes coverage of defamation and misuse of private information).

The style of the book reflects the SQE1 assessment specification:

- The SQE1 assessment requires knowledge and understanding of fundamental legal principles and the ability to apply them.
- Candidates are not required to recall specific case names or statutory provisions (except where they are normally used in practice to describe a legal principle).
- Candidates will be tested on the current law and will not be tested on the historical development of the law.

In order to reflect these requirements, the book explains the current key principles of tort law in a clear, easy-to-follow style. Principles are introduced and illustrated by reference to realistic factual examples. References to key cases and statutes are provided, but discussion of case law is reserved to the final section of the book.

This approach enables the book to provide a fluent narrative account of key principles which is clear and accessible, making it easier for the reader to understand the principles, remember them, and apply them in an assessment.

The final section of the book then introduces key case law, following a structured format which enables the reader to examine the application of key principles of tort law in the context of decided cases.

---

1 See: SQE1 Functioning Legal Knowledge Assessment Specification, updated 14 October 2020, published by the Solicitors Regulation Authority, available via www.sqe.sra.org.uk/exam-arrangements/assessment-information/sqe1-assessment-specification

DOI: 10.4324/9781003133698-1

Solicitors Qualifying Examination – SQE1

This book covers the areas of tort law in the **SQE1** assessment specification:

- Negligence
- Remedies for personal injury and death
- Defences
- Employers' liability
- Vicarious liability
- Occupiers' liability
- Product liability
- Nuisance.

It also covers **trespass**, since this is recognised as essential background for understanding the areas of tort law covered by the SQE1 assessment specification.

In addition, the book covers **defamation and misuse of private information**. The assessment specification for SQE1 does not include defamation and misuse of private information. However, they are included in this book because they often form part of undergraduate tort modules.

Key features to assist learning

Revision points: Each chapter concludes with a concise list of key revision points.

Multiple choice questions: The SQE1 assessment uses multiple choice questions to test understanding of key principles. Multiple choice questions, following the SQE format, are provided at the end of each section of the book (with answers at the end of the book).

A further set of review multiple choice questions and answers is provided at www.routledge.com/cw/sqe.

Client case analysis skills: This book sets consideration of key principles of tort law in the context of client case analysis skills. The ability to take a clear, concise, structured approach to analysing the facts of a client's case, and applying relevant principles of tort law, is an essential skill for those sitting the SQE. It also provides an efficient approach to answering problem questions in undergraduate exams. This skill is introduced at the beginning of the book so that clear case analysis structures can be kept in mind as readers go on to develop their understanding of key principles. The final part of the book then develops those skills further by presenting key decided cases within a structured framework, incorporating focused questions, to enable readers to undertake a clear, structured analysis of the legal principles arising in each case.

Problem questions: Problem questions are provided to enable readers to test their understanding and their client case analysis skills. Answers are available at www.routledge.com/cw/sqe.

The law is stated as at 3 January 2021.

PART 1
Introduction to claims and remedies in tort

1 Harms, remedies, and client case analysis

1.1 Chapter overview

This chapter provides an introductory overview of claims in tort. It begins with a broad overview of the range of harms covered by tort law – for example, personal injury, damage to property, interference with land, and interference with reputation. It then introduces the remedies that tort law can provide for those harms, such as damages and injunctions.

Then the chapter introduces the skill of client case analysis – that is, the use of a clear structured framework to analyse the client's claim to determine the appropriate tort to provide a remedy for the harm suffered. It begins with identifying the relevant tort by reference to the type of harm suffered. It then looks at identifying the parties to the claim and establishing the elements of the claim.

1.2 Introduction to the range of torts

Claimants in tort seek remedies for harm suffered. For example, a client injured in a road accident seeks damages; a person whose neighbour keeps them awake with loud music may want to force them to stop. So, the claimant needs to understand which tort would be appropriate to provide a remedy for the type of harm suffered (and the defendant needs to understand their potential liability).

The following table sets out some of the common types of harm, the torts that might be applicable, and the possible remedies.

As you look at the table, you should notice that there are overlaps. Some types of harm could have a remedy in more than one tort. In cases where more than one tort may be applicable on the facts, the claimant is likely to include all of them in their claim (though they will only be compensated once for the same harm).

Do remember that this is just an introductory overview. Each of the torts mentioned will be explained in more detail in the following chapters. Also, the remedies mentioned here are explained further in the following section of this chapter, as well as in later chapters.

DOI: 10.4324/9781003133698-3

So, do not worry about the details of each tort here. Our aim is simply to show how different types of harm should lead to consideration of different torts.

Harms, torts, and remedies

Type of harm suffered	Torts to consider	Possible remedies
Personal injury – caused carelessly	**Negligence** **Occupiers' liability** (if caused by the state of the premises)	Damages
Damage to property – caused carelessly	**Negligence** **Occupiers' liability** (if caused by the state of the premises)[1]	Damages
Personal injury – even if caused without carelessness[2]	Product liability under the *Consumer Protection Act 1987* – where caused by a defect in a product	Damages
Damage to property – even if caused without carelessness[3]	Product liability under the *Consumer Protection Act 1987* – where caused by a defect in a product. Subject to exceptions for some types of property	Damages
Interference with the claimant's bodily integrity (use of force, fear of force, imprisonment)	**Trespass to the person**	Damages
Direct interference with the claimant's possession of land	**Trespass to land**	Damages Injunction Declaration

Harms, remedies, and client case analysis

Type of harm suffered	Torts to consider	Possible remedies
Interference with the claimant's use and enjoyment of land This may include interference by things such as noise, smoke, and smells. Damage of this kind is called 'intangible' damage because it does not make a physical impact. ('Intangible' means 'cannot be touched'.)	**Nuisance**	Damages Injunction
Interference with reputation	**Defamation**	Damages Injunction
Disclosure of private information	**Misuse of private information**	Damages Injunction

[1] An occupier's liability to a trespasser does not extend to damage to the trespasser's property. See Chapter 14.
[2] There is nothing to prevent the **Consumer Protection Act 1987** ('CPA') from also applying to carelessly caused harm. So, if damage is caused by a defect in a product, and carelessness *can* be established, there is nothing to prevent a claimant from relying *both* on a claim in negligence *and* under the CPA. However, where carelessness *cannot* be established, then *only* the CPA is applicable.
[3] See note 2 above.

You probably noticed that the table does not include a separate heading for employers' liability. This is because employers' liability is part of the tort of negligence. It does have a separate chapter in this book because it has some special principles; but you should remember that it is still a claim in negligence.

Similarly, you may have come across claims described as 'medical negligence' or 'professional negligence'. Again, these are just specific applications of the general principles of the tort of negligence.

Also, the table does not mention vicarious liability. This is because vicarious liability is not a type of tort. It is a principle under which one person (usually an employer) can become liable for torts committed by another (usually an employee). Again, this is explained much more fully later (see Chapter 12).

1.3 Introduction to remedies in tort

As we began to see in the previous section, for a lawyer in legal practice, tort law is all about remedies. Clients consult a lawyer either because they have suffered harm and are seeking a remedy or because they are facing a claim made against them by someone who alleges that they have caused harm. The person who has suffered harm (the claimant) wants to obtain a remedy against the person who caused it (the defendant).[1]

The table below gives an overview of the remedies that tort law can provide. Do remember that this is just an introduction to remedies, and each of the remedies mentioned in the table will be explained more fully in later chapters.

Remedies in tort

Remedy	What is it?	What is its effect?	Example
Damages	A payment of money from the defendant to the claimant	To compensate the claimant for the harm suffered (so far as money can do so).[1]	A claimant is injured in a road accident and their car is damaged. An award of damages will result in a payment of money to the claimant to compensate them for: the pain and suffering caused by the injury, loss of earnings and medical expenses, etc, and the cost of the damage to their car.

---

1 Very often, a defendant will have a policy of insurance under which their insurer will pay any damages the defendant is ordered to pay to the claimant. In such a case, the insurer will deal with the claim on the defendant's behalf. So, it will be the insurer who consults lawyers and conducts the litigation or negotiations with a view to settlement. However, the proceedings are conducted in the defendant's name. So, when cases are reported, they show the name of the defendant, not the name of the defendant's insurer.

Remedy	What is it?	What is its effect?	Example
Injunction	An order of the court directing the defendant to do something or refrain from doing something. An injunction is a discretionary remedy. The court will decide, in the exercise of its discretion, whether or not to grant an injunction in the circumstances of the claimant's case.	An injunction can prohibit the defendant from carrying out activities that amount to a tort (a prohibitory injunction). An injunction could also require the defendant to take specified positive action (a mandatory injunction)[2]	A defendant plays loud music until late every evening, so committing the tort of nuisance. An injunction could be granted to prevent the defendant playing music after 9.00 pm on weekdays. A defendant has built a wall which interferes with the claimant's established right to have access to light through a window, so committing the tort of nuisance. An injunction could be granted to require the defendant to demolish the wall.
Declaration	An order of the court which declares the rights of the parties	A declaration states the existing rights of the parties. (The court is **not** exercising a **discretion** to change the rights of the parties. A declaration simply states the parties' existing rights.)	A claimant and defendant are in dispute over the location of the boundary between their land. The claimant alleges that the defendant has built a wall which sits on land belonging to the claimant, so committing the tort of trespass. The court may make a declaration specifying the correct location of the boundary.

[1] This refers to compensatory damages. Other forms of damages do exist, but our focus will be on compensatory damages as these are most important in practice.
[2] In general, it is less common for a mandatory injunction to be granted.

The table summarises the range of remedies in tort, but some remedies are not applicable to all torts. For example, an injunction is not available as a remedy for the tort of negligence. Again, this is explained more fully as we deal with each tort and its remedies.

Did you notice that the range of remedies is quite limited? In practice, clients often want to obtain remedies that tort law cannot provide. For example, clients often say that what they really want is to force someone to admit that they were at fault, or to obtain an apology. They sometimes want to find out exactly what happened and ensure that it does not happen to other victims. However, these are not outcomes the court has power to order. Sometimes, they may come about indirectly, as a result of litigation in tort cases. However, a large proportion of claims in tort are concluded by a negotiated settlement between the parties. This can achieve a payment of damages for the claimant, but claimants are sometimes frustrated that the defendant is not forced to admit what happened and who was at fault. So, when advising a client on remedies, it is important to bear in mind that their initial expectations may not always match the remedies that are actually available in tort.

To summarise so far:

- A claimant who seeks a remedy in tort must prove that the defendant has committed a tort against them.
- The claimant needs to identify the relevant tort, appropriate to provide a remedy for the harm suffered.
- Then the claimant needs to prove that the facts of their claim satisfy all the elements of the relevant tort. The terminology used to describe this is to say that the claimant has a **cause of action** against the defendant. So, for example, where the defendant has built a wall on land belonging to the claimant, we would say that the claimant has a cause of action in the tort of trespass.

The next section, on client case analysis, will examine this process in more detail.

1.4 Client case analysis in tort

1.4.1 Identifying the relevant tort

As we have just seen, a typical claim in tort begins with a victim who seeks a remedy for some kind of damage or interference suffered. The claimant's legal adviser needs to identify the relevant tort to provide a remedy. So, a key skill is the ability to determine which tort is relevant and applicable to a given set of facts.

When a client describes a series of events, how does the legal adviser draw upon their knowledge of tort law to identify the torts arising from the facts? A good way to begin is by focusing on the type of damage or interference for which the claimant seeks a remedy.[2]

So, for example, if the claimant complains about an interference with their land the legal adviser would consider claims in trespass or nuisance.[3] If the interference was direct and intentional (for example, building a wall on the claimant's land), trespass is likely to be the most relevant tort. If the interference was indirect (for example, regularly creating harmful smoke over the claimant's land), the tort of nuisance would be more relevant.

If the claimant complains of damage inflicted upon them by the defendant's carelessness, the legal adviser is likely to begin by considering a claim in negligence.

Of course, the claimant's damage might have a remedy in more than one tort. For example, physical damage caused to land by a defendant's carelessness could, in some circumstances, fall within both nuisance and the tort of negligence.

Identifying the type of damage or interference suffered may help rule out some torts at the outset. For example, the tort of negligence usually requires the claimant to have suffered some tangible damage.[4] So, if the claimant complains of intangible interference with their land by bad smells or smoke, negligence would not be the relevant tort to provide a remedy. Similarly, a claimant who suffers only anxiety and distress as a result of the defendant's carelessness would not have a remedy in the tort of negligence.

In some cases, the claimant seeks a remedy for interference with their rights, rather than for particular damage suffered. So, for example, a claimant momentarily detained unlawfully by a police officer may not suffer any tangible damage but may still have a claim in the tort of trespass, for false imprisonment.

Focusing on the type of damage suffered can also help identify when a claim falls outside the scope of tort law altogether. For example, if the claimant seeks damages for a loss of profit following the defendant's failure to perform an agreed bargain, the claim would be in contract, not tort.

---

2   See Section 1.2 for an overview of different types of harm in tort.
3   See Section 1.2 for an overview of these torts.
4   'Tangible' damage means something that has a physical impact – for example, personal injury – whereas 'intangible' damage is something which does not make a physical impact, such as noise. ('Intangible' means 'cannot be touched'.). Where a claimant suffers *only* a loss of money, this is intangible damage; but there are special rules for this 'pure economic loss' which mean that it is sometimes recoverable in the tort of negligence. Pure economic loss in negligence is explained in Chapter 8.

So, focusing on the damage or interference for which the claimant seeks a remedy can be a useful way to identify the relevant torts arising from the facts of the claim.

Remember that, as a matter of terminology, when the facts show that the claimant would have the right to pursue a claim against the defendant, we refer to this as the claimant's **cause of action**.

1.4.2 Identifying the parties to the claim

A claim in tort arises because one party (the claimant) complains of damage or interference caused by another party (the defendant).

A legal adviser instructed to pursue a remedy in tort must first identify the relevant claimant. Look at this problem scenario:

> A mother takes her child to a supermarket. The child picks up a bottle of bleach. The bottle has a broken cap which allows bleach to spill out and burn the child. In a claim for the injuries caused to the child, who should be the claimant?

The claimant should be the person who suffered the damage complained of – so, in this example, the child who was injured. Since the child is too young to make a claim himself, an adult (known as a litigation friend) could act for him. When advising in this situation, it would be a mistake to identify the child's mother as claimant, since she has not suffered any damage.

The legal adviser must also identify the correct defendant(s). Continue with the above problem:

> Evidence shows that the bottle of bleach was safe when manufactured but was damaged when it reached the supermarket. An employee of the supermarket carelessly damaged the cap when unpacking the bleach but failed to notice when putting it on display. Who should be the defendant to the child's claim?

The legal adviser will consider who is responsible for the damage caused to the child. The supermarket employee appears to have been careless, so could be a defendant. However, it is unlikely that the individual employee would have insurance against such claims. So, the legal adviser would also consider a claim against the supermarket. Under the principle of vicarious liability (explained more fully in Chapter 12) the supermarket may be responsible for the tort of its employee, so could also be a defendant.

Before pursuing a claim, a legal adviser must be careful to ensure that there is a claimant who has suffered harm. For example:

> Residents complain that a youth has been seen driving his car at speed along a residential street. The incident only happened once, and no one was injured. The youth has clearly been careless, but there appears to be no one who has suffered the harm necessary to found a claim in negligence (and no basis for a claim in nuisance).

The adviser must also ensure that there is an identifiable defendant. For example:

> A landowner finds a leaking container of toxic chemicals dumped on his land. He suspects that it came from the premises of a neighbouring company. However, no individual employee can be identified as responsible, and the company has ceased to trade and no longer exists. Although the landowner's damage could have a remedy in tort, there is no identifiable defendant against whom the claim can be pursued.

So, a legal adviser should always analyse the facts to identify not only what claims in tort might arise but also the correct claimant and defendant.

A common error in assessments is to fail to consider and identify the correct parties to the claim – for example, identifying a parent as claimant when a child is injured, or assuming that a claim can be pursued without noting that there is no identifiable defendant.

1.4.3 Establishing the elements of the claim

The burden is on the claimant to prove each element of the claim on the balance of probabilities.

So, having identified the parties to the claim and the relevant tort (or in some cases more than one tort), the legal adviser must check that the claimant can establish each element of the claim. For example, in a claim in the tort of negligence: did the defendant owe the claimant a duty of care; was that duty breached; did the breach cause damage?[5] They will also consider any relevant defences. This analysis involves both fact and law.

On the facts, the claimant must produce evidence to support each element of the claim. The defendant may simply present a different version of the facts from that alleged by the claimant.

---

5   Each of these elements of a claim in the tort of negligence is explained more fully in later chapters.

For example, a key element in a negligence claim is breach of duty: the claimant must prove that the defendant fell below a reasonable standard of care. So, in a road traffic accident, a claimant pedestrian may produce witness evidence to show that the defendant driver carelessly exceeded the speed limit. The driver may counter this with evidence showing that he was driving carefully, and the pedestrian suddenly stepped out into the road.

In particular, the claimant must produce evidence to substantiate the damage they have suffered. So, for example, a claim for personal injury would be supported by a medical report.

On the law, the defendant may argue that, as a matter of law, the claimant's version of events, even if true, is not sufficient to establish a claim. For example, in a negligence claim, a defendant may argue that, as a matter of law, they did not owe any duty of care to the claimant. In a claim in the tort of nuisance, the defendant may argue that the claimant did not have the interest in land necessary to found a claim.

Overall, both parties must examine the evidence on the facts, and the arguments on the law, to assess their chances of success in making or defending the claim.

1.4.4 Client case analysis as the foundation for litigation

It is important to appreciate the link between the 'academic' analysis of claims in tort and the practicalities of civil litigation. An analysis of the substantive law of tort applicable to the facts of the claim is an essential foundation to litigation.

Pursuing litigation in tort is expensive. Both parties will incur legal costs: the fees paid to their lawyers and money spent (disbursements) on expert witness fees, etc.[6] In very broad terms, the further the litigation progresses, the greater the costs incurred.

Often the parties will seek to minimise costs by reaching a negotiated settlement. The defendant may agree to pay compensation to the claimant. Alternatively, a claimant who is persuaded by the defendant's case may agree to discontinue the claim. An agreed settlement in the early stages of a claim could avoid the need to commence court proceedings.[7]

Alternatively, a settlement could be reached during proceedings, thus bringing them to an end. So, even where proceedings are commenced, parties may adopt

---

6 It is important to distinguish these costs, of pursuing the claim, from the damages sought as a remedy for the harm suffered by the defendant.
7 As noted in Section 1.3 on remedies, clients are sometimes frustrated that a negotiated settlement can only result in the payment of compensation, not in an admission of liability. However, a claimant who refuses to accept a negotiated settlement, but fails to be awarded more money at trial, is likely to be penalised financially by being ordered to pay costs.

an approach to litigation in which they both pursue negotiations with a view to settlement and at the same time continue to prepare for a contested trial.

Thus, in conducting litigation parties must always have a clear understanding of the strengths of their claim or defence and their likely prospects of success. A clear analysis of the substantive law of tort, as applied to the factual evidence, forms the basis for this assessment.

1.4.5 Further development of client case analysis skills

You should keep the structure for client case analysis in mind as you read the following chapters, where you will focus on the elements and principles of each of the torts covered.

In the final part of this book (Part 12) you will have the opportunity to further develop your client case analysis skills in the context of decided cases that established or applied the key principles of tort law.

Chapter 1 revision points

- Consider the type of harm suffered: what tort(s) may provide a remedy?
- Identify the relevant claimant: who has suffered harm?
- Identify the relevant defendant: who is responsible for the claimant's harm?
- Apply the elements of the tort to the facts: can the claimant establish a *cause of action*?
- Assess the strengths and weaknesses of the claim: how likely is the claim to succeed?

PART 2

Trespass to land and to the person

# 2

Trespass to land

2.1 Chapter overview

Chapters 2 and 3 introduce the torts of trespass to land and trespass to the person. To put trespass in context, this chapter begins with an overview of some issues which are relevant to both trespass to land and trespass to the person – for example, the nature of trespass as actionable per se.

This chapter then outlines the elements of a claim in trespass to land: an unlawful interference with the claimant's possession of land. It explains the meaning of possession, and the definition of land. It then notes the nature of the interference as direct and caused by actions which are (usually) intentional. Finally, it outlines defences to trespass to land and the remedies for a successful claim.

2.2 Overview of trespass

In this section we look at some issues which are relevant to both trespass to land and trespass to the person.

Trespass is an intentional tort, so understanding it will provide a useful contrast with the tort of negligence. It will enable us to see the difference between liability based on intentional conduct which interferes with rights and is actionable per se (trespass) and liability based on conduct which falls below a reasonable standard of care and requires proof of damage (negligence).

In addition, it is important to understand trespass because of its interaction with other areas of tort law. For example, vicarious liability claims (in which a claimant seeks to hold an employer responsible for the tort of their employee) often involve the torts of assault and battery, committed by the employee. Trespass to land interacts with the tort of nuisance and the principles of occupiers' liability.

2.2.1 Trespass actionable per se

Trespass to land and to the person are actionable per se. This means that they are actionable without proof that damage has been suffered. This is because the trespass torts protect the claimant's rights (rights in land and rights to bodily

DOI: 10.4324/9781003133698-5

integrity). So, if the relevant right is infringed, an action arises, even if the claimant has not suffered any damage or harm beyond infringement of the right itself.

2.3 Introduction to trespass to land

Look at these problem scenarios. In each one, identify the interference with rights in land and think about the remedy that might be sought.

> A local authority owns a car park. A group of travellers has taken up occupation of the car park with caravans and has been there for a number of months. The local authority now wishes to force the travellers to leave the car park so that it is available for use by motorists.
>
> A music festival is being held in a privately owned country park. A teenager, who was unable to obtain a ticket, enters the site secretly and without permission.
>
> A mining company occupies a site under a licence (permission) from the owner and is beginning a new mining operation there. The site is in a picturesque rural area. Large groups of environmental protestors regularly gather on the site to try to halt the work. The company would like to obtain an injunction prohibiting them from entering the site.
>
> A dispute has arisen between neighbours. A householder recently erected a new garden building, intending to place it on his own land, close to the boundary between the properties. His neighbour claims that the building sits partly on his side of the boundary so that it is on land owned by him.

All of the above examples could fall within the scope of trespass to land.

2.4 Definition and elements

- Trespass is an unlawful interference with the claimant's possession of land.

2.4.1 Possession

To bring an action in trespass the claimant must have exclusive possession of the land concerned. A person has possession of land if they occupy it or exercise control over it. Possession is exclusive where it excludes anyone else from taking possession.

An obvious example of exclusive possession, sufficient for an action in trespass, is that of an owner occupier. So, from our examples above, the neighbour has exclusive possession of his garden.

A person may also have exclusive possession under a licence (permission) granted by the owner (e.g., the mining company in our example).

What happens if a person takes possession of land without permission so that they have exclusive possession of it simply as a matter of fact (de facto possession)? In a case like this, the person in exclusive possession (often referred to as a squatter) can bring an action in trespass against anyone interfering with their possession, except for the true owner of the land.

Look again at the example of the local authority car park. The local authority, as owner of the car park, was in exclusive possession of it by controlling its use for parking. However, travellers have taken occupation of the car park and have been there for some months. So, it appears that the local authority has lost possession of the land.[1] Where the actions of a trespasser amount to taking possession of the land from the owner, so dispossessing them, the owner can bring an action to recover possession of the land[2] (see further 'remedies' below). (Strictly speaking this is an action distinct from trespass, but closely related to it.)

2.4.2 Land

Land includes the surface of the land and buildings, and other structures on the land and things growing on the land.

It also includes airspace above the land.[3] However, this only extends up to such height as is necessary for the ordinary use of the land. So, for example, it would be a trespass for the operator of a crane on a building site to swing the arm of the crane in the airspace over neighbouring land without permission.

Land also includes the substrata beneath the surface.[4] So, for example, a person could commit trespass by digging a tunnel under land in the possession of someone else without authority.

2.4.3 Interference

For a claim in trespass the interference with the claimant's possession must be **direct**. Examples of direct interference include:

- entering the land (as in our example of the boy entering the festival site without a ticket, and protestors entering a mining site);
- placing something on the land (such as our example of a building constructed on land belonging to a neighbour);
- removing part of the land (for example cutting down a tree).

---

1 A trespasser entering land and taking up occupation does not immediately dispossess the true owner and gain possession (see **McPhail v Persons Unknown** [1973] Ch. 447 (CA)), but in our example the trespassers have been in occupation for a number of months.
2 There are some limited circumstances in which it is no longer possible to recover possession after a lapse of time – but the details are beyond the scope of this book.
3 See, for example, **Kelsen v Imperial Tobacco Co** [1957] 2 QB 334 (QBD).
4 See, for example, **Bocardo SA v Star Energy UK Onshore Ltd** [2010] UKSC 35, [2011] 1 AC 380.

The requirement for the interference to be direct distinguishes trespass from the tort of nuisance. Nuisance provides a remedy for indirect interferences. So, for example, placing a building on someone else's land is trespass; but allowing guttering to spill water onto neighbouring land would be actionable in nuisance because it is indirect. Similarly, planting a tree on someone else's land would be trespass; but planting a tree on your own land whose branches gradually grow over the boundary and overshadow the claimant's land would be nuisance.[5]

Having established that for a claim in trespass the interference must be direct, we now need to consider the nature of the defendant's actions in causing the interference.

Look back at the problem scenarios considered in Section 2.3. In all of them the defendant's actions constituting a trespass were intentional. Protestors intended to enter the mining company's land; the teenager intended to enter the land where the festival was being held.

What about the example in which a mistake as to land ownership was made (a building accidentally placed on land belonging to a neighbour)? Even in this case the defendant's actions (constructing the building) were intentional. Another example would be where someone mistakenly believes that they are walking on a public right of way. If, in fact, they have no right to walk on the land they are committing trespass. Their actions, in walking on the path, are intentional.

So, trespass generally involves **intentional** interference with possession of land. The intention relates to an intention to do the acts complained of, not an intention to commit trespass by deliberately infringing the claimant's rights.

In a very small number of cases the courts have extended this a little further to grant remedies in trespass where the entry onto land was not deliberate – for example, where the defendant failed to prevent hunting dogs from chasing their prey onto the claimant's land.[6]

---

5   For an example of the interaction between trespass and nuisance see **Lemmon v Webb** [1895] AC 1 (HL) covered in Chapter 22.
6   See: **League Against Cruel Sports Ltd v Scott** [1986] QB 240 (QB). In this case the remedy sought was an injunction to prevent future trespasses, a remedy not available had the claim been pleaded in negligence. See also: **Network Rail Infrastructure Ltd v Conarken Group Ltd** [2010] EWHC 1852 (which proceeded to the Court of Appeal on further issues affecting quantum of recoverable damages: [2011] EWCA Civ 644).

2.5 Defences to trespass to land

Trespass to land is an **unlawful** interference with possession of land. So, if the defendant had a lawful justification for entering the land, no trespass is committed. The lawful justifications recognised by the law form the basis for the defences to trespass, each of which we now consider.

2.5.1 Licence (permission)

A person does not commit trespass if they have permission to enter the land. So, in our examples, a mining company would commit trespass if they entered land and began mining without permission; but it is not a trespass if they have a licence (permission) from the owner to do this.

In some circumstances permission to enter land may be implied. For example, a person entering onto land to communicate with the occupier is likely to have implied permission to do so (unless the occupier has indicated otherwise).[7] This implied permission explains why, for example, people entering onto land to deliver post or goods do not commit trespass.

2.5.2 Necessity

A person has a defence to trespass if they enter land where it is reasonably necessary to do so to prevent harm to people or property.

2.5.3 Other lawful justification

In some circumstances statute confers rights of entry onto land, so authorising what would otherwise be a trespass (for example, statutory rights which permit suppliers of gas or electricity to enter land under certain conditions to disconnect the supply). The statutory powers of entry exercised by the police are a further example.

Another important example of lawful justification is entry onto land pursuant to a right of way. For example, a person lawfully walking on a public footpath does not commit a trespass.

2.6 Remedies for trespass to land

2.6.1 Declaration

In our above example of neighbours disputing the position of a boundary, the claimant wants the court to determine the true position of the boundary between the properties and to find that construction of the new building amounted to a

---

7   *Robson and Another v Hallett* [1967] 2 QB 939, [1967] 2 All ER 407.

trespass. In circumstances like these the remedy sought is a declaration. This remedy shows us how the tort of trespass to land is used to adjudicate disputes over ownership of land.

2.6.2 Injunction

In the context of trespass to land, an injunction is an order of the court directing the defendant not to trespass on the claimant's land. So, in our examples above, an injunction could order the removal of the building from the neighbour's land; an injunction could order the protestors not to enter the mining site.[8]

2.6.3 Damages

We have already noted that trespass to land is actionable per se – that is, without proof of damage.

In cases where the trespass has not caused the claimant to suffer any actual damage, the claimant is still entitled to be compensated for the interference with their rights in the land. For example:

> The defendant constructing houses on a building site swings the arm of a crane over the claimant's land without permission. The damages awarded for this trespass could reflect the cost the defendant would have had to pay to the claimant to obtain such permission.

Where the claimant has suffered actual damage as a result of the trespass, damages are awarded to compensate for the harm suffered. For example, where there is physical damage to the land, damages may reflect the reduction in value of the land.

In trespass, damage is recoverable provided that it is a direct consequence of the defendant's act.[9]

2.6.4 Order for possession of land

Trespass is based on an interference with possession of land. Where the actions of the trespasser amount to taking possession of the land from the owner, so dispossessing them, the owner can bring an action to recover possession of the land.[10]

This is based on the fact that the claimant did have possession of the land and has been dispossessed by the defendant; so the order for possession orders the defendant to leave the land, thus returning possession to the claimant.

---

8 Injunctions are considered further in Chapter 10 (Remedies) and Chapter 16 (Private nuisance).
9 This is different from the principles for tort of negligence (covered in Chapter 6, under remoteness of damage). In negligence, not only must the harm be a consequence of the defendant's act, but also it must be reasonably foreseeable.
10 See the example above of a local authority seeking to recover possession of a car park occupied by travellers.

Strictly speaking, an action to recover possession of land is an action in its own right closely related to trespass. However, it is convenient to discuss it here, alongside remedies for trespass.

Chapter 2 revision points

Trespass to land

- An unlawful interference with the claimant's possession of land
- Interference is direct and (usually) intentional
- Actionable per se

3

Trespass to the person

3.1 Chapter overview

Before reading this chapter you may find it useful to refer to the overview of trespass at the beginning of Chapter 2, noting in particular the principle that trespass is actionable per se, which is explained there.

This chapter sets out the three individual torts which together make up trespass to the person:

- Battery
- Assault
- False imprisonment.

Then it sets out the defences to trespass to the person, which are applicable to all three forms of the tort.

3.2 Introduction

Trespass to the person protects rights to bodily integrity.[1] We will see that this is further broken down into interference by physical contact, the threat of such contact, and interference with freedom of movement. Look at these problem scenarios. In each one, identify how these rights have been interfered with:

> A march is planned for a city centre. It is feared that the march may become violent and a ban is issued against the march. Despite this, large numbers of people take part in the march. Many of them are arrested for breach of the ban and detained. It later transpires that the ban was invalid, so there were no lawful grounds for the arrests and detentions.

> A farmer who is out shooting rabbits is angry when he sees a group of walkers trespassing on his land. In an attempt to frighten them off, he aims his gun towards

---

1 For an example of this protection of rights see *Walker v Commissioner of Police of the Metropolis* [2014] EWCA Civ 897, [2015] 1 WLR 312 covered in Chapter 22.

DOI: 10.4324/9781003133698-6

them, firing above their heads. The walkers say that they had lost their way and would have left the land peacefully if the farmer had asked them to do so.

A teacher is employed to care for children residing at a school. Whilst carrying out his duties the teacher has contact with the children which amounts to sexual abuse. The children later pursue claims against the employer of the teacher.

Each of these situations could fall within the scope of trespass to the person.

Notice in particular the case of the teacher committing the tort of trespass during the course of his employment. The tort is committed by an employee, but the claimant is likely to want to pursue a claim against the employer (who is more likely to be insured). So, an understanding of trespass to the person can be important in analysing some of the claims you will encounter when studying vicarious liability (which is covered in Chapter 12).

3.3 Battery

- Battery is defined as the intentional infliction of unlawful force.

Force in this context means any unwanted physical contact with the claimant. For example, touching someone to attract their attention or taking them by the arm could satisfy the requirement of force. In our examples above, the teacher abusing children in his care commits battery.

The physical contact must be direct but may take various forms. For example, it would be battery to throw something which hits the claimant or to push a ladder so that the claimant falls off it.

The requirement of intention means only that the defendant must have intended to make physical contact. There is no requirement that the defendant intended to cause harm.

As we have noted, trespass is actionable per se (without proof of damage).

So, taken together, without more, these elements of the tort of battery could mean that almost any physical contact might amount to a battery. However, to constitute battery the force must also be unlawful.

Force (physical contact) is not unlawful if the claimant has consented to it. For example:

A hairdresser cutting your hair would commit trespass where it not for the fact that you consent to it.

Players making physical contact during sport rely on the fact that individuals who voluntarily take part impliedly consent to the physical contact which is a normal part of the game.

These are examples of physical contact to which the claimant has specifically consented, either expressly or impliedly by their conduct.

However, in everyday life, physical contact occurs between individuals very frequently. For example, you may tap someone on the shoulder, push into them as you board a train, or squeeze past them in a shop. These are examples of intentional physical contact. However, they are unlikely to give rise to a claim in battery because case law shows that battery does not extend to physical contacts which are generally acceptable in the ordinary conduct of everyday life.[2]

Another instance in which consent is important is medical treatment. Applying the elements of battery above, you should be able to see that medical treatment administered to an individual would amount to battery unless they consent to it. (In the case of children too young to give consent, consent can be given on their behalf by their parents.[3]) So, medical treatment given with consent does not amount to battery. However, what if the claimant refuses their consent?

Consider the following problem scenario:

> A woman is admitted to hospital. She is an adult and has full mental capacity. Doctors recommend a particular medical treatment, but the woman refuses her consent to it. The doctors advise her that refusal of the treatment will endanger her health, but she continues to refuse.

How does the law deal with this? Can the doctors force the woman to undergo medical treatment?

The answer is that an adult who has full mental capacity is entitled to refuse medical treatment. This is so even if the refusal endangers their health. In these circumstances a doctor does not have the power to compel the patient to undergo treatment, and treatment administered without consent would be a battery.

---

2 The issue was discussed in: *F v West Berkshire HA* [1990] 2 AC 1 (HL). See also: *Wilson v Pringle* [1987] QB 237 (CA).
3 Children under the age of 16 can consent to medical treatment if they have the necessary understanding; and, if they do not, parents can consent on their behalf. For discussion and guidance on the capacity of a child to consent to medical treatment see: *Bell v Tavistock and Portman NHS Foundation Trust* [2020] EWHC 3274 (Admin), [2020] All ER (D) 30 (Dec).

(Administration of medical treatment to persons who lack mental capacity is considered in Section 3.6, under defences to trespass.)

So, we can see from the above that battery is able to protect the individual's rights to bodily integrity. For example, a police officer who takes hold of a person without their consent in order to question them must do this pursuant to some lawful authority; otherwise the contact will amount to a battery. Damages could be awarded to reflect this infringement of rights, even though no actual physical harm was caused.

This means that the tort of battery, along with false imprisonment considered below, has an important role to play in the protection of personal freedoms.

3.4 Assault

- An assault is an act which causes the claimant reasonably to apprehend the immediate infliction of unlawful force.

So, an assault is committed when the defendant's actions cause the claimant to fear a battery.

The defendant's threat must be one of immediate force. So, it would not be an assault merely to use threatening words towards the claimant if it were clear that the defendant had no immediate intention of carrying out the threat.

Similarly, an assault requires that the defendant has the capacity to carry out the threat of force. Consider this problem scenario:

> Protestors gather outside an industrial site. They are on strike and wish to persuade other workers not to enter the site to work. A group of workers who are not on strike are taken into the site by bus. As the bus passes through the crowd of protestors they shout insults and threats at the workers inside the bus, who fear for their safety. Could the workers bring a claim for assault?

In this situation, there could not be a successful claim for assault because the protestors, unable to reach the workers inside the bus, did not have the capacity to carry out an immediate battery.

Of course, this does not mean that a battery must occur. The tort of assault can be committed even though the threatened battery is not carried out. Look back at the problem scenario in which a farmer shot his gun over the heads of trespassers on his land. He did not inflict any force upon them, so there was no battery. However, his actions could amount to an assault because he caused them to apprehend the immediate infliction of unlawful force.

3.5 False imprisonment

- False imprisonment is the unlawful restriction of the claimant's freedom to move from a particular place.

To amount to a false imprisonment the claimant's freedom of movement must be completely restricted. For example, the claimant wishes to walk in a protest march along a road, but the police have erected a road block. The claimant cannot walk where he wishes but is free to walk back the way he came. This would not amount to false imprisonment.

Compare the situation where police impose a cordon confining a group of demonstrators to a defined area which they are not permitted to leave. Unless the police act with lawful authority (as considered below under defences) this is likely to amount to false imprisonment.

The restriction on the claimant's freedom of movement might be imposed by force, or by the threat of force (e.g., where the claimant is locked in a room so that he cannot leave, or where the door is not locked but a guard stands outside to prevent his leaving). However, the tort of false imprisonment is wider than this. The constraint on the claimant's freedom of movement need not be imposed by force. It is sufficient that the claimant is subject to compulsion.[4] For example, a false imprisonment may occur where a claimant is simply told (without lawful authority) that he is under arrest.

For a successful claim in false imprisonment, the defendant's conduct must be intentional. However, the defendant only needs to intend to restrict the claimant's freedom of movement. The defendant need not intend to infringe the claimant's rights. So, the defendant need not know that the restriction is unlawful.

For example:

> A government official orders a person to be detained, believing that he has lawful authority to do so. It later transpires that the powers under which he purported to act were invalid, so there was no lawful authority for the detention. In these circumstances, a claim for false imprisonment could arise.

As with the other torts which make up trespass to the person, false imprisonment is actionable per se (without proof of damage). So, for example, provided that the claimant is subject to compulsion and there is a complete restriction on his freedom of movement, a claim in false imprisonment may arise even if the duration of the restriction is only short or temporary.

---

4 See, for example, *R (on the application of Jalloh (formerly Jollah)) v Secretary of State for the Home Department* [2020] UKSC 4, [2020] 3 All ER 449.

So, the tort of false imprisonment has an important role to play in protecting an individual's rights.

3.6 Defences to trespass to the person

Trespass to the person is an **unlawful** interference with the claimant's rights to bodily integrity. So, if the defendant had a lawful justification for the interference, no trespass is committed. The lawful justifications recognised by the law form the basis for the defences to trespass to the person, each of which we now consider.

3.6.1 Consent

We saw above, in our discussion of the elements of battery, that the claimant's consent to the defendant's actions provides a defence to trespass.

One important application of the rules of consent was in the context of medical treatment. We saw that consent prevents medical treatment from being a battery, but that an adult with full mental capacity has the right to refuse consent.

The question of what happens where an individual lacks capacity to consent is considered below under the defence of necessity.

3.6.2 Necessity

A defendant may have a defence to trespass to the person where their actions were necessary either for protection of the claimant themselves or for the protection of others.

Protection of the claimant

One example of protection of the claimant where necessity may be applicable is the provision of medical treatment.

What is the position if the patient lacks the capacity to consent to medical treatment?

This could arise in a situation where the patient is temporarily unable to consent, for example where they are unconscious after an accident. It could also arise in the case of patients who have a permanent mental incapacity.

In cases of this kind statute provides a defence to battery which applies where the person administering the treatment reasonably believes that the patient lacks capacity to consent and that the treatment will be in their best interests.[5]

---

5 See: **Mental Capacity Act 2005** ('MCA'). The MCA only applies to treatment administered to adults and to minors over the age of 16. So, where a child is under the age of 16 and consent cannot be obtained, the court may be asked to authorise the treatment on grounds of necessity.

Protection of others

The defence of necessity can also be relied on where action is taken to protect the public.

For example, this defence has been relied on in cases involving large-scale public protests, where police restrained demonstrators in ways which would have amounted to false imprisonment. The police were able to rely on the defence of necessity because the actions were necessary to prevent an imminent breach of the peace.[6]

3.6.3 Self-defence

A defendant who takes action to protect themselves may rely on the defence of self-defence.[7] This defence applies where:

- The defendant has an honest and reasonable belief that they face imminent attack by the claimant, and
- The force used in self-defence is reasonable and proportionate to the threat.

For example:

> A motorist is unlocking his car in a car park when a teenager approaches him and asks for money. When the man refuses, the teenager becomes angry and throws a punch at the motorist. Fearing that the teenager is about to strike him again, the man jumps into his car, starts the engine, and drives at speed into the teenager, causing him a serious injury. The motorist is unlikely to be able to rely on the defence of self-defence because the force he used was disproportionate to the threat from the teenager.

This defence may also apply to actions taken in defence of property. However, the defendant's actions must be reasonable and proportionate to the threat. Look again at the problem scenario in which a farmer committed assault by shooting his gun over the heads of walkers trespassing on his land. The farmer is not likely to have a defence here because the force used was not reasonable and proportionate.

3.6.4 Lawful arrest

A person who carries out a lawful arrest has a defence to an action in trespass.

In the absence of this defence, the physical contact involved in an arrest would amount to battery, and the restraint on liberty would amount to false imprisonment.

---

6   See: ***Austin v Commissioner of Police for the Metropolis*** [2007] EWCA Civ 989, [2008] 1 All ER 564 (appealed to the House of Lords on other grounds: [2009] UKHL 5, [2009] 3 All ER 455).
7   See, for example, ***Cross v Kirkby*** [2000] CLY 5110.

Similarly, a lawfully imposed period of imprisonment does not give rise to a claim in trespass. However, an action for trespass will lie where a period of detention is imposed unlawfully.

Hence, an action in trespass can be used to challenge the actions of public bodies where arrest or detention is not lawfully justified.

3.7 Remedies for trespass to the person

The usual remedy for trespass to the person is an award of damages. We have already noted that trespass to the person is actionable per se – that is, without proof of damage. In cases where the trespass has not caused the claimant to suffer any actual damage, the claimant is still entitled to be compensated for the interference with their rights. For example, a brief unlawful detention can still give rise to an award of damages to recognise the infringement of the claimant's rights.

Where the claimant has suffered actual damage as a result of the trespass, damages are awarded to compensate for the harm suffered. For example, damages could be awarded for a battery inflicting personal injury on the claimant.

Chapter 3 revision points

Trespass to the person

- Battery – the intentional infliction of unlawful force
- Assault – an act which causes the claimant reasonably to apprehend the immediate infliction unlawful force
- False imprisonment – the unlawful restriction of the claimant's freedom to move from a particular place
- Actionable per se

Multiple choice questions for Part 2

1. Recently, a developer purchased a plot of land and erected a fence around the boundary. However, his neighbour objected, claiming that the fence was in the wrong place. Enquiries revealed that the developer had made a mistake and the new fence did stand on the neighbour's land, enclosing a small area of uncultivated waste land belonging to the neighbour. The neighbour wants the fence removed but the developer is reluctant to do so.

   Which one of the following best explains the advice that should be given to the parties?

   A. The developer has not committed the tort of trespass to land because he did not intend to erect the fence on his neighbour's land.
   B. The developer has committed the tort of trespass to land, and the neighbour may seek either an award of damages or an injunction requiring removal of the fence, but not both.
   C. The developer has committed the tort of trespass to land, and the neighbour is entitled as of right to demand both damages and an injunction requiring the removal of the fence.
   D. The developer has not committed the tort of trespass to land because the land in question was uncultivated waste land, so the neighbour has not suffered any loss.
   E. The developer has committed the tort of trespass to land, and the neighbour could make a claim for damages and also request the court to exercise its discretion to grant an injunction requiring the removal of the fence.

2. As a customer entered a nightclub the doorman grabbed hold of him and then detained him in an office for five minutes without his consent, in order to check that he was suitably dressed to enter the club. He was then released, unharmed but very angry. He has sought compensation from the club. The club accepts responsibility for the doorman's actions but wishes to know whether the doorman's actions amounted to a tort against the customer.

Which one of the following best explains the position?

A. The actions of the doorman did not amount to a tort because the customer was only detained very briefly.
B. The actions of the doorman amounted to the tort of false imprisonment only.
C. The actions of the doorman amounted to the tort of battery only.
D. The actions of the doorman amounted to the torts of both battery and false imprisonment.
E. The actions of the doorman did not amount to a tort because the customer was not harmed.

PART 3

Negligence

4 Negligence: duty of care

4.1 Chapter overview

This chapter begins with an overview of the tort of negligence, setting out the elements a claimant must establish for a successful claim: duty of care; breach of duty; and causation of damage.

It then explains the principles for the first of those elements: duty of care. It explains that there is a range of established duty situations, contrasting this with novel duty situations in which a duty of care has not been previously established. It then outlines the factors to be considered by the court when deciding whether or not a duty of care is owed in a novel duty situation.

4.2 The tort of negligence – overview

A claim in the tort of negligence requires the claimant to establish that:

- The defendant owed the claimant a duty of care.
- The defendant breached that duty by falling below a reasonable standard of care.
- The defendant's breach of duty caused the harm the claimant suffered, and the harm was not too remote a consequence of the breach.

The defendant may seek to defend the claim either by showing that one of these elements has not been made out or by establishing a specific defence to the claim. Each of these aspects is described in more detail in the following chapters.

In this chapter we outline the first of those elements, duty of care. The claimant must show that the defendant owed them a duty of care. If it is found that no duty of care was owed, then the claim will fail. In other words, a defendant may have acted carelessly and caused damage to the claimant; but if no duty of care is owed, there will not be a successful claim.

The existence of a duty of care depends on the relationship between the claimant and the defendant.[1] There is a wide range of relationships which are recognised as

---

1 For key cases establishing the broad principles of duty of care (further developed in later cases) see ***Donoghue v Stevenson*** [1932] AC 562 (HL) and ***Caparo Industries Plc v Dickman and Others*** [1990] 2 AC 605 (HL) covered in Chapter 22.

DOI: 10.4324/9781003133698-8

giving rise to a duty of care. These are referred to as established duty situations. New situations may arise in which there are no previous decisions to establish whether or not a duty of care is owed. These are referred to as novel duty situations.

4.3 Established duty situations

- An established duty situation is one in which previous case law clearly established that a duty of care is owed by the defendant to the claimant.

Some common examples of established duties are the duties owed by:

- Drivers to other road users (such as other drivers, passengers, and pedestrians)
- Parents to their children
- Teacher to pupil
- Doctor to patient (and hospital to patient)
- Solicitor to client
- Employer to employee (and employees to fellow employees).

4.3.1 Situations in which case law establishes that no duty is owed

Case law has also established a number of situations in which a duty of care is *not* owed. The first example of this is in the case of omissions.

Omissions to act

Where damage is suffered as a result of an omission to act, the general rule is that no duty of care arises. So, for example, a bystander who takes no action to stop a chid running into a busy road does not owe the child a duty of care.

However, a duty of care can arise where the particular relationship between claimant and defendant creates a special responsibility. For example, a parent who took no action to stop their child running into a busy road would owe a duty of care to the child. The same would apply to the relationship of teacher and pupil.

Similarly, a defendant may owe a duty of care where the claimant is harmed by the actions of a party with whom the defendant has a relationship of control. For example, a teacher who fails to prevent a young child running into a busy road could owe a duty to a motorist injured when swerving to avoid the child.

The general principle that no duty of care arises in respect of an omission to act has particular application in the case of rescue situations. First, it means that, in general, there is no duty to intervene to carry out a rescue (as we saw in the case of a bystander who does not intervene to prevent a child running into the road). Second, the courts have therefore held that where a person does choose to intervene to carry out a rescue, they do not have a positive duty to make sure that the rescue is carried out successfully. Their only duty is to take reasonable care not to make the situation worse than it would have been had they not intervened. For example:

> A fire brigade is called to a burning house. They do not have a duty to save the house from the fire. However, they do have a duty not to make the situation worse. So, if they negligently order water sprinklers to be turned off, they may be liable.

Other non-duty situations

There are also other situations in which case law has established that a duty of care is *not* owed.

For example, the police do not generally owe a duty of care to individuals who suffer damage as a result of a failure to investigate crime or apprehend offenders.[2]

On the other hand, it is clearly established that the police *do* owe a duty of care to individuals who suffer damage as a result of ordinary operational activities. For example, the driver of a police vehicle owes a duty of care to road users.

The police may also owe a duty of care where they have assumed a responsibility to a particular individual. For example, a duty of care was owed where police were aware that an individual prisoner was at particular risk of suicide but failed to take precautions to protect him.

A further instance in which case law shows that a duty of care may not be owed is in the limited duty situations of pure economic loss and psychiatric harm (see further Part 5 – *Negligence: limited duty situations*).

4.3.2 Summary

In summary, on established duties, we have seen that there is a wide range of situations in which a duty of care clearly *is* owed, and a number of instances (based on the type of act or the nature of the harm) where a duty of care clearly is **not** owed.

So, as a broad principle, it is possible to begin from the starting point that:

- A duty of care is likely to arise whenever the defendant has engaged in a *positive act* which has caused foreseeable *physical damage* to the claimant.[3]

---

2 See discussion in **Robinson v Chief Constable of West Yorkshire** [2018] UKSC 4, [2018] AC 736. In **Robinson**, the Supreme Court explained the principle – that the police do not generally owe a duty of care to individuals who suffer damage as result of a failure to investigate crime or apprehend offenders – as an application of the ordinary rule that, in general, no liability arises from an omission to act. Three out of the five judges preferred to explain the position on police duties of care as an application of the rules on omissions rather than a matter of policy.
3 This broad established duty is drawn from the principles in **Donoghue v Stevenson** [1932] AC 562 (HL) as developed in subsequent cases.

This is in contrast to situations in which the defendant is guilty of an *omission* to act, or where the nature of the harm is *purely economic* or *purely psychiatric*. In these cases, special and more complex rules apply.

Having noted the range of cases in which an established duty of care arises, and those in which it is established that no duty is owed, we are left with a residual category of cases in which the issue of duty of care has not previously been decided. These are novel duty situations, considered in the following section.

4.4 Novel duty situations

- A novel duty situation is one in which previous case law does not clearly establish whether a duty of care is owed.

In a novel duty situation, the court must determine whether or not a duty of care should be imposed on the defendant. Case law has held that the courts should only develop new duties of care incrementally and by analogy with existing duty situations. In other words, if the novel situation is similar to ones in which a duty of care is already established, the court is more likely to find that a duty is owed. Within this context, the court applies the following factors to determine whether or not a duty of care is owed in a novel situation:

- Foreseeability
- Proximity
- Fair, just and reasonable.

To understand how these factors are applied it can be useful to look at previous cases in which the court was required to decide the issue of duty of care in a novel situation. However, remember that once the issue of duty of care has been decided in a particular situation, it is no longer novel.

4.4.1 Foreseeability

The issue of foreseeability refers to the fact that the claimant must be a reasonably foreseeable victim of the defendant's negligence. For example:

> A motorist carelessly causes an accident. A passer-by, who is unrelated to anyone involved in the accident, witnesses the aftermath, and suffers an injury caused by shock. Case law[4] suggests that the motorist would not owe a duty of care to the passer-by because she was not a foreseeable victim of his negligence.

The principles for duty of care where an injury is caused by shock are now well established (see Chapter 9). So, this example would no longer be a novel duty situation. However, it illustrates the denial of a duty of care on grounds of lack of foreseeability.

4 *Bourhill v Young* [1943] AC 92 (HL)

In this context, foreseeability is more than just asking: did the defendant's actions create a foreseeable risk that someone would be harmed? It is about establishing that the defendant's actions created a foreseeable risk of harm to this particular claimant. For example:

> An electricity company opens an excavation in the street. A blind person encounters it and is injured. A sighted person would have seen the excavation, but the precautions taken were not adequate to protect a blind person.

Case law[5] suggests that the issue of whether a duty of care would be owed to the blind person would depend on whether the presence of the blind person in the vicinity of the excavation could reasonably have been foreseen. That is, whether they were a foreseeable victim.

4.4.2 Proximity

The issue of proximity refers to the closeness of the relationship between the claimant and the defendant. If the relationship between the claimant and the defendant is not sufficiently close, then no duty of care will be owed. For example:

> Carelessly spoken words may cause harm to a wide range of people; but only those with a sufficiently close relationship to the speaker are likely to be owed a duty of care.

The principles of duty of care for negligent statements are now well established (see Chapter 8), so this is no longer a novel duty situation. However, the example illustrates the denial of a duty on grounds of lack of proximity.

4.4.3 Fair, just and reasonable

This factor requires the court to consider whether or not it would be fair, just and reasonable to impose a duty of care on the defendant, and enables the court to take policy considerations into account. For example:

> The defendant, a not-for-profit body whose aim is to promote safety at sea, certifies a ship as seaworthy. The ship later sinks and the claimant, whose cargo was on the ship, suffers a loss. Case law suggests that the defendant would not owe a duty of care to the claimant cargo owner because imposing a duty could hinder the purpose of ensuring safety at sea for the common good.[6]

---

5 *Haley v London Electricity Board* [1965] AC 778 (HL).
6 See *Marc Rich & Co AG v Bishop Rock Marine Co Ltd (The Nicholas H)* [1996] AC 211 (HL) (where the factors considered also included the contractual structures and insurance arrangements covering cargo owners).

This example illustrates the denial of a duty of care on grounds that policy factors render it not fair, just and reasonable to impose a duty of care on the defendant in the circumstances.

4.4.4 Summary

Overall, a novel duty situation is one in which the question of duty of care has not been determined by previous case law. Once the courts have determined the duty of care issue in a particular situation, it ceases to be novel and it is no longer necessary to decide the duty issue afresh.

So, when advising, it would be a mistake to apply the novel duty factors of foreseeability, proximity and fair, just and reasonable in an already established duty situation. (A common error in assessments is to apply the factors of foreseeability, proximity, and fair, just and reasonable to every duty of care question – even where, on the facts, a clearly established duty arises.)

Chapter 4 revision points

Elements of negligence:

- Duty of care
- Breach of duty
- Causation of damage
- Defences

Duty of care:

- Established duty situations (e.g., drivers to road users)
- Novel duty situations
    - Developed incrementally and by analogy with existing duty situations
    - Factors: foreseeability, proximity, fair, just and reasonable

5 Negligence: breach of duty

5.1 Chapter overview

Before reading this chapter you may find it helpful to refer to the overview of the elements of the tort of negligence at the beginning of Chapter 4. Always keep in mind the structure of a claim in negligence:

- Duty of care
- Breach of duty
- Causation of damage
- Defences.

As this structure shows, once it has been established that the defendant owed the claimant a duty of care, the claimant must then prove that the defendant was in breach of that duty. This chapter explains the test for breach of duty: did the defendant fall below a reasonable standard of care?

5.2 The standard of reasonable care

- To establish breach of duty the claimant must prove that the defendant fell below a reasonable standard of care.

The standard of reasonable care means that the defendant must meet the standard of care to be expected of a reasonable person in the defendant's position.[1]

5.2.1 Reasonable person – objective standard

- The standard of reasonable care is objective and impersonal.[2] It does not depend on the personal characteristics of the individual defendant.

---

1 *Blyth v Birmingham Waterworks Co* (1856) 11 Ex 781.
2 *Glasgow Corporation v Muir* [1943] AC 448 (HL).

So, a defendant who did their best to take care but nevertheless failed to meet the standard to be expected of a reasonable person would be in breach of duty. For example:

> The defendant stores a large amount of hay. He is not aware that when hay gets damp it may heat up and burst into flames. The hay does burst into flames and the claimant suffers damage as a result of the ensuing fire. Provided the claimant can prove that a reasonable person would have appreciated the risk and taken precautions against it, the defendant will be in breach of duty, despite his own lack of appreciation of the risk.

In order to decide whether a defendant did fall below a reasonable standard of care two questions are considered:

- What was the level of risk created by the defendant's actions?
- What precautions should the defendant have taken against that risk?

5.2.2 Level of risk

Assessing the level of risk created by the defendant's action involves two issues:

- How likely was it that the defendant's actions could cause some harm?
- If some harm did occur, how serious was the harm likely to be?

The higher the risk of the defendant's actions causing harm, and the more serious the potential harm, the greater the precautions the defendant could be expected to take.[3]

Look at these problem scenarios:

> The defendant is the operator of a sports ground. A cricket ball is hit out of the ground and strikes the claimant. The claimant alleges that the defendant should have installed a higher fence. Evidence from previous games shows that it is rare for balls to be hit out of the ground. In deciding whether the defendant should have installed a higher fence, the court will consider the low level of risk, and may decide that the defendant *did not* fall below a reasonable standard of care.

> The defendant employs the claimant to work on vehicle maintenance. The defendant knows that the claimant is blind in one eye but fails to provide safety goggles. Whilst working without goggles the claimant is blinded in his other eye by a metal fragment. Given that the claimant was exposed to a risk of very serious harm (blindness), the court is likely to decide that the defendant *did* fall below a reasonable standard of care in not providing goggles.

---

3   See, for example, **Bolton v Stone** [1951] AC 850 (HL) covered in Chapter 22, and **Paris v Stepney BC** [1951] AC 367 (HL) on which the following examples are based.

5.2.3 Reasonable precautions

Once it is established that the defendant's actions carried a risk of harm, the court considers what precautions a reasonable person would have taken against that risk.

The defendant only has to do what is reasonable. The defendant's duty is not to avoid harm at all costs. For example, driving a car carries a risk of causing harm. A defendant is not expected to avoid any risk by not driving the car. However, the defendant is expected to take the reasonable precautions of driving within the speed limit, keeping a proper look-out, etc.

This means that the **cost and practicability** of precautions are factors to be taken into account.[4] For example:

> A sudden flood causes a factory floor to become slippery. The owner takes precautions to deal with the slippery floor, but decides not to close the factory because this would be costly and impracticable. An employee slips and is injured. Despite the fact that the risk of injury could have been prevented entirely by closing the factory, the court may conclude that the defendant *did not* fall below a reasonable standard of care.

It is also relevant to consider the **social utility** of the defendant's conduct. For example:

> A defendant undertaking an emergency rescue of persons in immediate danger might be justified in omitting some safety precautions which would be appropriate in a non-emergency situation.

However, the precautions still have to be balanced against the degree of risk. For example:

> A fire service might be justified in allowing a fire engine to set off without first strapping down loose equipment. However, it might not be justifiable for the fire engine to drive through a red traffic light, in busy traffic, without stopping.

5.3 Under-skilled defendants

We have already said that the standard of reasonable care is objective and impersonal. This means that:

- When a defendant undertakes a task, they must meet the standard of care appropriate for that task.

---

[4] See, for example, ***Latimer v AEC Ltd*** [1953] AC 643 (HL) on which the following example is based.

This is the case even if they personally lack the necessary skills to meet that standard.[5] For example:

> A learner driver who takes on the task of driving a car must exercise the same level of care and skill as a reasonable qualified driver.

> Similarly, a newly qualified doctor must meet the same level of care and skill as a qualified doctor undertaking the same task.

5.4 Defendants exercising special skills

A defendant may hold themselves out as possessing a special level of skill by exercising a particular profession – for example, the profession of doctor or lawyer. When a breach of duty is alleged, such defendants are not judged against the level of care and skill of the ordinary reasonable lay person. Instead:

- Defendants exercising special skills are judged against the standard of an ordinary reasonable person exercising that special skill.

For example, a doctor must meet the level of care and skill of a reasonable doctor.

This also applies where a person claims to have a special skill which they do not in fact possess. For example, a person who is not a qualified lawyer but holds themselves out as such must meet the same level of care and skill as a qualified lawyer.

If the defendant is to be judged by the standards of the profession, what happens when there is a difference of opinion within the profession as to the correct practice? For example, what if some doctors approve of a particular treatment but others do not?

The general rule is that a defendant will not be in breach of duty if they have acted in accordance with a responsible body of professional opinion – even if there are other members of the profession who would take a different view.[6]

However, without more, this would allow professions to set their own standards of care. Therefore, case law has held that that the court remains the final judge of

---

5   See, for example, **Nettleship v Weston** [1971] 2 QB 691 (CA) covered in Chapter 22.
6   **Bolam v Friern Hospital Management Committee** [1957] 2 All ER 118 (QB) covered in Chapter 22. However, a doctor who fails to disclose the risks of medical treatment to their patient cannot rely on the fact that other doctors would have done the same. This is because case law has recognised the importance of the patient's self-determination and has held that, where the patient is an adult of sound mind, the doctor is under a duty to take reasonable care to make the patient aware of any material risks in the treatment which is recommended and of any reasonable alternatives. See **Montgomery v Lanarkshire Health Board** [2015] UKSC 11, [2015] AC 1430.

whether the defendant did exercise reasonable care. So, a court could still decide that a particular practice was negligent even if there was a body of professional opinion in support of it – though this is likely to be rare.

5.5 Child defendants

A child may be a defendant to a claim in negligence.

- In determining whether a child failed to exercise reasonable care, they are judged against the standard of care to be expected of a reasonable child of the same age.

There is no minimum age for a child defendant. However, given the level of care which can reasonably be expected of young children, it is likely to be difficult to establish that a very young child was in breach of duty.

Also, a child is often unlikely to have the resources to meet any successful claim against them, and may not be covered by insurance. So, claims against children may be difficult in practice.

Finally, it is important to note that a parent is not responsible for the negligence of their child. So, where an injury is caused by the carelessness of a child, the child's breach of duty does not give rise to a claim against their parents. (However, the parent could, depending on the facts, be in breach of their own duty of care to exercise reasonable supervision of their child.)

5.6 Proving breach of duty

- The burden of proving breach of duty is on the claimant.

Breach must be proved on the **balance of probabilities** – i.e., it is more likely than not that the defendant fell below a reasonable standard of care.

So far, our discussion has focused on the principles applied by the courts to determine whether or not, on a given set of facts, the defendant's conduct fell below the required standard of care. However, in a large proportion of contested cases, the parties do not accept that there is one given set of facts. Instead, they are in dispute as to what exactly happened. For example:

> In a road accident the claimant may assert that the defendant drove into their path, whilst the defendant asserts that the claimant was driving too fast.

In a case like this, each party will normally produce witness evidence to support their version of events.

So, the usual way for the claimant to discharge the burden of proving breach of duty is to produce evidence from witnesses of fact to establish what happened. The claimant relies on this evidence to demonstrate how the defendant failed to exercise reasonable care.

5.6.1 Res ipsa loquitur

However, what happens if an accident occurs but there are no witnesses who saw what happened? The claimant can establish that they suffered an injury, caused by the defendant, but cannot show precisely how it happened and so cannot demonstrate how the defendant fell below a reasonable standard of care.

In a situation like this the claimant may be able to argue that the available facts simply speak for themselves.[7] For example:

> The claimant was walking past a warehouse owned and operated by the defendant. A heavy load fell from an upstairs window and injured the claimant. The claimant did not see why the load fell, and there were no witnesses who saw it. The claimant may argue that the defendant must have been negligent because they were in control of the warehouse and the load could not have fallen without a lack of reasonable care on their part.

In a case like this, the claimant is relying on the evidential rule: **res ipsa loquitur**, which means **'the thing speaks for itself'**. In order for this rule to apply, the following conditions must be met:

- The accident would not have happened without a lack of reasonable care
- The thing which caused the accident must have been under the exclusive control of the defendant, and
- There must be a lack of evidence to explain how the accident occurred.

If the rule does apply, it can assist the claimant in proving breach of duty. However, it is open to the defendant to rebut this by adducing evidence to show how the accident could have happened without any lack of reasonable care on their part.

It is important to remember that this rule only applies in cases where there is a complete lack of evidence to explain how the accident occurred. In most cases there *is* some evidence of what happened, and in such cases the rule cannot be used to avoid the need for the claimant to establish that what happened amounted to a lack of reasonable care by the defendant.

---

7 See, for example, ***Scott v London & St Katherine Docks Co*** [1861–73] All ER Rep 248, on which the following example is based.

Chapter 5 revision points

Breach of duty
- Did the defendant fall below a reasonable standard of care?
- The standard is objective and impersonal
- The standard of care to be expected of the ordinary reasonable person in the position of the defendant

What is a reasonable standard of care?
- Level of risk
  - How likely was the harm to occur?
  - How serious was the harm likely to be?
- Reasonable precautions
  - What precautions ought the defendant to have taken in response to the risk?

6 Negligence: causation of damage and remoteness

6.1 Chapter overview

Before reading this chapter you may find it helpful to refer to the overview of the elements of the tort of negligence at the beginning of Chapter 4. Always keep in mind the structure of a claim in negligence:

- Duty of care
- Breach of duty
- Causation of damage
- Defences.

As this structure shows, once it has been established that the defendant owed the claimant a duty of care, and was in breach of that duty, the claimant must then prove that the defendant's breach was the cause of the claimant's harm. This chapter explains the principles for establishing causation of damage.

It first explains factual causation, beginning with the 'but for' test used to determine whether the defendant's breach of duty was a cause of the claimant's harm. It then proceeds to the more complex principles applied where there are multiple causes of the claimant's harm.

It next explains new intervening acts which may break the chain of causation between the defendant's negligence and the claimant's harm.

Finally, it covers the principles of remoteness of damage, applied where the claimant's damage – although caused by the defendant's negligence – is too far removed from it to attract an award of compensation.

6.2 Introduction to causation

A claimant brings an action in the tort of negligence because they have suffered damage. In order to obtain a payment of compensation for that damage the claimant must link the harm they have suffered with the actions of the defendant.

The first stage in making this link is to show that the defendant owed the claimant a duty of care. The second stage is to show that the defendant breached that duty

DOI: 10.4324/9781003133698-10

by falling below a reasonable standard of care. The claimant must then complete the third stage: they must show that the damage they suffered was caused by the defendant's breach of duty.

So, the legal principles on causation of damage have developed in order to answer a practical question based on money: was the harm suffered by the claimant sufficiently linked to the negligence of the defendant, so that the defendant (or their insurer) is obliged to pay compensation to the claimant?

The principles on causation of damage encompass three broad issues:

- Can the claimant show that, as a matter of fact, the defendant's breach caused the claimant's damage? (factual causation)
- Did any further act or event intervene between the defendant's breach and the claimant's damage? (intervening acts)
- Can the claimant show that their damage was not too remote a consequence of the defendant's breach? (remoteness of damage).

To explain the first of these, factual causation, we begin with the 'but for' test. Then, we move on to the alternative and more complex principles that apply where there are multiple causes of the claimant's damage.

6.3 The 'but for' test for causation

The basic test to establish causation of damage is the 'but for' test:

- Can it be said that 'but for' the defendant's breach the claimant would not have suffered harm?

Often this test is straightforward to apply. For example:

> The claimant is driving her car carefully along a road. The defendant, driving carelessly, pulls out in front of the claimant's car and a collision occurs. The claimant can show that 'but for' the defendant's breach the accident would not have occurred, and the claimant would not have suffered personal injury and damage to her car.

Sometimes, however, the claimant is able to show that the defendant was in breach of duty but is *not* able to show that 'but for' that breach the claimant would not have suffered damage. In other words, the claimant would have suffered the damage in any event.[1] For example:

---

1   See ***Barnett v Chelsea & Kensington Hospital Management Committee*** [1969] 1 QB 428 (QB) covered in Chapter 22, on which the following example is based.

> The claimant drinks a cup of tea containing a poisonous substance. The claimant begins to feel ill and attends a hospital. The doctor on duty negligently fails to examine the claimant, and sends him away. The claimant later dies. However, the medical evidence shows that he would have died in any event, even if the doctor had examined him. So, it cannot be said that 'but for' the doctor's breach of duty the claimant would not have suffered the harm. The causal link between the doctor's breach and the claimant's harm is not established, and the doctor is not liable to pay compensation.

In a situation like this, the defendant has been negligent; but their negligence is not the cause of the claimant's harm, so the defendant (or their insurer) is not required to compensate the claimant.

The two examples above assume that the facts show clearly that the defendant's breach was, or was not, the cause of the claimant's harm. However, often the parties do not agree, and, where the parties dispute the issue of causation, the burden of proof is on the claimant. The standard of proof is **on the balance of probabilities**.

The defendant asserts that, although they were in breach of duty, the claimant would have suffered the same harm in any event. The claimant must counter this by proving that *on the balance of probabilities* they would not have suffered the harm had it not been for the defendant's breach. Where the claimant cannot meet this standard of proof, the claim will fail.[2] For example:

> The claimant fell from a tree and injured his hip. The hospital where he was treated was negligent in that diagnosis and treatment were delayed. The claimant suffered a permanent disability. The defendant hospital asserted that the claimant would have suffered the same disability as result of the fall even had the medical treatment not been negligent. The claimant could not prove, *on the balance of probabilities*, that he would not have suffered the disability had it not been for the defendant's negligence. So, the claim failed.

In cases like this the claimant often *can* prove that there was a *chance* he might not have suffered the harm had the defendant not been negligent. However, this does not satisfy the burden of proving causation *on the balance of probabilities*. For example, the claimant who fell from a tree was able to prove that, with the correct medical treatment, he had a 25 per cent chance of making a full recovery without any disability. However, this meant that there was a 75 per cent chance he would have suffered the disability in any event. So, causation was not established *on the balance of probabilities*.

---

2   See, for example, **Hotson v East Berkshire HA** [1987] AC 750 (HL) on which the following example is based.

Sometimes, a claimant has suffered an injury for which there are several possible **alternative causes**.[3] For example:

> A premature baby was negligently treated in hospital. The baby subsequently suffered blindness. The facts show that the negligent treatment was capable of resulting in blindness. However, the baby also suffered from four other medical conditions, unrelated to the negligent treatment, each of which was capable of resulting in blindness. The baby seeks compensation for the blindness from the negligent hospital.

Given that there are several possible alternative causes of the blindness, the baby's claim depends on proving *on the balance of probabilities* that the blindness was caused by the hospital's negligence, rather than one of the four alternative possible causes. If that burden of proof cannot be satisfied, the claim will fail.

This example assumes that a claimant's damage has only *one* cause, so that, where there are several possible alternatives, the claimant must prove which *one* was *the* cause of his damage.

However, it is also possible for a claimant's damage to have more than one cause. For example:

> A pedestrian is crossing the road. He is struck by a car (A) and thrown into the path of another car (B), which also strikes him. In this instance it is likely that both A and B have together caused the injury suffered by the pedestrian.

On facts like these we would say that, rather than *one* out of many alternative possible causes, the claimant's damage results from **multiple causes** which have combined together to cause the harm. Where the claimant's injury does have multiple causes in this way, different principles apply to establishing causation (see Section 6.4).

Of course, it may not always be easy to determine how the facts of a particular claim should be interpreted. Is it one of **alternative causes**, requiring the claimant to prove which *one* caused his injury? Alternatively, is it one of **multiple causes** combined together? The parties are likely to disagree; and, if they cannot reach a negotiated settlement, the correct interpretation will be for the court to decide.

6.4 Multiple causes

What then are the principles of causation which apply where multiple causes combine together to cause the claimant's damage?

---

3   See, for example, ***Wilsher v Essex AHA*** [1988] AC 1074 (HL) on which the following example is based.

6.4.1 Material contribution to harm

Look at these problem scenarios:

> A factory worker contracts lung disease after being exposed to toxic dust by his employer. There are multiple sources of dust in the factory, and the employer is only in breach of duty in relation to one of those sources.
>
> A worker is employed by employer A for five years. He is subsequently employed by employer B for ten years. Both employers negligently exposed him to excessive levels of noise. He now suffers from noise-induced deafness.

In each case, the claimant has suffered one injury (lung disease or deafness) caused by multiple causes combining together.

Those causes may impact on the claimant at the same time (as with the multiple exposures to dust) or one after another (as with the periods of employment). In either case, they combine together to produce one injury.

Also, there may be more than one defendant, each guilty of negligence (as with the claimant moving between several employers), or there may be just one defendant whose breach has combined with innocent causes (as with the employer whose breach in exposing the claimant to one source of dust combined with other non-negligent exposures).

In cases like this, given that the defendant's negligence has combined with other causes to harm the claimant, it is not possible for the claimant to prove that 'but for' the defendant's negligence the claimant would not have been harmed at all.

Therefore, in cases of this kind the courts have relaxed the rules of causation:

- The claimant can establish causation provided that he can show that the defendant's negligence made at least a *material contribution to the claimant's harm*.[4]

Consider again the example of the worker subjected to multiple exposures to dust, only one of which was a breach of the employer's duty. The claimant could not prove that 'but for' his employer's breach he would not have suffered lung disease. However, he could prove that his employer's breach had made at least a material contribution to the lung disease. This was held to be sufficient to establish causation.[5]

---

4 See **Bonnington Castings Ltd v Wardlaw** [1956] AC 613 (HL) covered in Chapter 22, on which the following example of the worker subjected to multiple exposures to dust is based.
5 Note, however, that for the material contribution principle to apply, the case must be one in which the claimant's injury does have multiple causes. In an ordinary case, where there is just one specific act of negligence, the principle cannot be used to assist the claimant to discharge the burden of proving causation. See **Clough v First Choice Holidays and Flights Ltd** [2006] EWCA Civ 15, [2006] PIQR P22.

Assuming that the claimant can establish causation by proving that the defendant made a material contribution, a further question then arises: what proportion of the claimant's harm must the defendant pay for? The principles developed to answer this question are as follows.

- If the claimant has suffered one single **indivisible injury**, then the defendant must pay damages for the whole of it.

An example of an indivisible injury would be a broken leg. If two drivers both drive negligently so that their actions combine together to cause the claimant to suffer a broken leg, each is liable to the claimant for the full extent of his injury. Of course, the claimant can only recover his total damages once. Also, each defendant may claim a contribution from the other (see further below).

This applies even where there is only one 'guilty' defendant, whose negligence has combined with an 'innocent' cause.[6] For example:

> A hospital patient suffers brain damage. The evidence shows that this was caused partly by the claimant's weakened state of health (an innocent cause) and partly by the hospital's negligence. On the facts the brain damage is shown to be an indivisible injury.

Since the defendant hospital made a material contribution to the claimant's indivisible injury, it is liable for the whole of the brain damage suffered. (In this situation, there is no other defendant from whom the defendant could claim a contribution.)

- If the injury suffered by the claimant is **divisible**, then the defendant is only liable to pay for the proportion of damage caused by their breach.

An example of a divisible injury would be industrial deafness – because the degree of deafness becomes worse the longer the claimant is exposed to noise. Where two employers have exposed the claimant to periods of excessive noise, each pays for the proportion of the claimant's deafness they caused.

In this situation, the claimant would need to sue both employers in order to be compensated in full. (Also, since each defendant only pays for the harm they caused, there is no scope for them to claim a contribution from the other.)

6.4.2 Material increase in the risk of harm

Finally, we note a very limited class of cases in which the courts have relaxed the rules of causation even further. Look at this scenario:

---

6   See, for example, *Bailey v Ministry of Defence* [2008] EWCA Civ 883, [2009] 1 WLR 1052, on which the following example is based.

The claimant has contracted mesothelioma (a lung disease). He *can* prove that mesothelioma is caused by exposure to asbestos. He *can* prove that the defendant's negligence has exposed him to asbestos. However, he has also been exposed to other sources of asbestos. There is scientific uncertainty about mesothelioma which makes it scientifically impossible to determine which of the exposures to asbestos caused the claimant to contract the disease.

In cases of this kind, the claimant cannot prove that 'but for' the defendant's negligence he would not have contracted the disease. He cannot even prove that the defendant's negligence made at least a material contribution to the disease.

Therefore, in cases of this kind the courts have relaxed the rules of causation:

- The claimant can establish causation provided he can show that the defendant's negligence *materially increased the risk of harm* to the claimant.[7]

This is a very limited class of cases, of which mesothelioma is the main example. Lung cancer caused by exposure to asbestos has also been accepted as falling into this class.[8] In cases of this kind there is one disease-causing agent (e.g., asbestos), but the claimant has been exposed to several sources.

The 'material increase in risk' exception depends upon scientific uncertainty which makes it impossible to determine which exposure has caused the claimant's harm. This is not the same as a lack of evidence. The claimant who has contracted the disease must produce evidence to prove both that the disease is caused by exposure to the substance in question (e.g., asbestos) and that the defendant's negligence has exposed him to that substance. If the claimant cannot prove those facts, the claim will fail.

The final question to consider is: where a defendant is liable on the basis that they materially increased the risk of harm to the claimant, how much of the claimant's harm must the defendant pay for?

The courts have answered this by holding that a defendant is only liable to pay damages proportionate to the extent of the risk they caused. So, where a number of potential defendants exposed the claimant to risk, the claimant would need to sue all of them to recover his losses in full. (This has been reversed by statute in the specific case of mesothelioma so that, in those cases, each defendant is liable for the whole of the damage.[9])

---

7 ***McGhee v National Coal Board*** [1972] 3 All ER 1008 (HL); ***Fairchild v Glenhaven Funeral Services Ltd*** [2002] UKHL 22, [2003] 1 AC 32; ***Barker v Corus (UK) Plc*** [2006] UKHL 20, [2006] 2 AC 572, and ***Compensation Act 2006*** s.3; ***International Energy Group Ltd v Zurich Insurance Plc UK*** [2015] UKSC 33, [2016] AC 509.
8 There is no fixed, definitive list of diseases falling within the material increase in risk principle. However, its scope is very limited.
9 ***Compensation Act 2006*** s.3.

6.5 Contribution between tortfeasors

We have seen that it is possible for two or more defendants to be liable to the claimant in respect of the *same* **damage**. Where this happens, the claimant can recover the full award of damages from any of the liable defendants.

As between the defendant's themselves, statute[10] provides for each to recover a **contribution** from the others. The contribution is to be assessed as:

- Such amount as the court thinks just and equitable having regard to the extent of each defendant's responsibility for the damage.

So, as we noted above, this will apply where two or more defendants have contributed to causing a single *indivisible* injury. In this case the defendants are all liable in respect of the *same* damage.

This is to be contrasted with the situation in which two or more defendants have contributed to causing a *divisible* injury. Here, each defendant is only liable for the *proportion* of damage they caused. They are **not** all liable in respect of the *same* damage, and there is no scope for contribution between defendants.

6.6 Intervening acts

We have seen that, in order to be compensated for damage, the claimant must prove that it was caused by the defendant. What happens where a defendant is negligent, but a further act intervenes between the defendant's negligence and the harm ultimately suffered by the claimant?[11] For example:

> The defendant's negligence causes a road accident. A police officer arrives and directs the traffic in such a way as to cause a collision in which the claimant is injured.

In a case like this, is the defendant responsible for the claimant's damage? Clearly, it is possible to say that 'but for' the defendant's negligence the claimant's damage would not have occurred. In the above example: 'but for' the defendant's negligence the original accident would not have happened, so the police officer would not have been directing the traffic and the second collision would not have occurred. Despite this basic causal link, the defendant is likely to argue that they are not responsible for the damage suffered by the claimant after the intervention of the new act. The defendant's negligence is just a background cause of the claimant's damage.

---

10 *Civil Liability (Contribution) Act 1978*.
11 See, for example, ***Knightley v Johns*** [1982] 1 All ER 851 (CA), on which the following example is broadly based.

Recognising this argument, the court may find that the new intervening act **broke the chain of causation** between the defendant's negligence and the claimant's harm.[12] In that case, the defendant is not liable for the claimant's harm. (Of course, the claimant might have an action against the person who intervened.) So, when will a new act be sufficient to break the chain of causation?

6.6.1 Acts of a third party

Whilst it is not possible to state a definitive test for when the actions of a third party will break the chain of causation, an important factor is the extent to which the third party's actions were foreseeable. Although not a conclusive test, we can say that:

- The actions of a third party which were foreseeable as a result of the defendant's negligence are less likely to break the chain of causation.
- Actions of a third party which were not foreseeable are more likely to break the chain of causation.

In the above example: it was not reasonably foreseeable that the police would direct the traffic in such a way as to cause a further accident. So, the chain of causation was broken.

Where the third party acts **instinctively**, in response to the danger created by the defendant's negligence, the chain of causation is less likely to be broken – because their act is a foreseeable result of the defendant's negligence. For example:

> A motorist carelessly drives on the wrong side of the road towards an oncoming bus. The bus driver swerves to avoid a collision, and injures a passenger on the bus. The actions of the bus driver are not likely to break the chain of causation. The motorist is liable to the passenger.

On the other hand, **intentional wrongdoing** by a third party is more likely to break the chain of causation because their actions are less likely to be a reasonably foreseeable result of the defendant's negligence.[13]

What happens where the actions of the third party were **negligent**? The mere fact that the actions of the third party were negligent does not mean that they will necessarily break the chain of causation. For example:

> A claimant injured by the defendant's negligence may receive medical treatment, which is carried out negligently, causing further injury.

---

12 A new intervening act is sometimes referred to by the Latin: *novus actus interveniens*.
13 For an example, where the chain of causation was *not* broken by the intentional actions of a thief because the theft was a reasonably foreseeable result of the defendant's negligence, see: **Stansbie v Troman** [1948] 2 KB 48 (CA).

This is unlikely to break the chain of causation because it is reasonably foreseeable that an injured person will need medical treatment, with some risk that such treatment might be negligent.

However, if the medical treatment is so negligent as to be a completely inappropriate response to the injury, it may break the chain of causation because then it is not a reasonably foreseeable result of the defendant's negligence.

So, the more unreasonable the actions of the third party, the less they are foreseeable, and the more likely they are to break the chain of causation.

6.6.2 Acts of the claimant

Sometimes, the claimant's own actions may amount to a new intervening act breaking the chain of causation. In broad terms:

- The claimant's own actions will only break the chain of causation if they were **unreasonable**.[14]

For example:

> The claimant suffered a leg injury caused by the defendant's negligence. As a result, the leg was weak and likely to give way. Knowing this, the claimant chose to descend steep stairs without using the handrail. His leg gave way and he fell, suffering a further injury. The claimant's own actions broke the chain of causation so that, although the defendant was liable for the initial leg injury, they were not liable for the injury suffered in the subsequent fall.

Where the claimant's own actions break the chain of causation, the claimant will not be compensated for the injury which follows. This can be harsh, and it may be more appropriate, depending on the facts, for the court to apply the partial defence of contributory negligence.[15] This would allow the claimant's damages to be reduced to reflect his fault, rather than causing the claim to fail entirely.

6.7 Remoteness of damage

Should a negligent defendant be responsible for all resulting damage, no matter how extensive or unusual it might be?

In answer, the law recognises that, even where it can be said that 'but for' the defendant's negligence the damage would not have occurred, there should be some limits on the extent of recoverable damage.

---

14 See, for example, **McKew v Holland & Hannen & Cubitts (Scotland) Ltd** [1969] 3 All ER 1621(HL Scotland), on which the following example is based.
15 For the defence of contributory negligence see further Chapter 7.

6.7.1 Reasonable foreseeability

The extent of the defendant's liability in negligence is limited by the principle that:

- Damage is not recoverable if it was not a **reasonably foreseeable consequence** of the defendant's negligence.

Damage which is not reasonably foreseeable is said to be **too remote**.[16] For example:

> The defendant negligently spilled oil onto the waters of a harbour. The oil came into contact with the claimant's nearby premises where they were welding, causing sparks. They were assured that the sparks could not ignite the oil, so they continued. However, the oil did ignite, and the fire destroyed the claimant's property. The defendant was held not liable because it was not reasonably foreseeable that the oil could catch fire.

There are exceptions to the principle that damage which is not reasonably foreseeable is too remote and not recoverable. They are covered in the following paragraphs.

6.7.2 The 'egg shell skull' rule

The so-called **'egg shell skull'** rule is the first exception to the requirement for damage to be reasonably foreseeable. To illustrate this, consider the situation in which a claimant suffers from a pre-existing vulnerability, so that when they are injured by the defendant's negligence the damage is more extensive than it would otherwise have been. For example:

> The defendant's negligence causes the claimant to suffer a fall. The claimant suffers from a disease of the bones which makes them more brittle than usual. As a result, the claimant suffers a fracture, whereas had it not been for the disease, he would only have suffered minor bruising.

In a situation like this, although the **type** of harm suffered was reasonably foreseeable, the full **extent** of the claimant's damage is not. As an exception to the principle that damage which is not reasonably foreseeable is too remote, the courts have held that:

- Provided the **type** of harm was foreseeable, the defendant is liable for the full extent of the claimant's damage, even though the **extent** of the damage was not foreseeable.

---

16 See ***Overseas Tankship (UK) Ltd v Morts Dock & Engineering Co (The Wagon Mound), (No.1)*** [1961] AC 388 (PC) covered in Chapter 22, on which the following example is based.

This is expressed by saying that the defendant must take his victim as he finds them.[17] As noted above, this is often referred to as the 'egg shell skull' rule.

The principle also applies in other situations where the claimant's particular characteristics make his loss more extensive than usual. For example, a highly paid claimant is not prevented from recovering a loss of earnings caused by the defendant, even though the amount of the loss was higher than might reasonably have been foreseen.

6.7.3 The 'similar in type' rule

In a further exception to the requirement for damage to be reasonably foreseeable, the courts have held that only the broad **type** of damage suffered by the claimant needs to be reasonably foreseeable:

- It is not necessary for the precise **way** in which the damage was inflicted to be foreseeable.[18]

For example:

> Employees had negligently left paraffin lamps unattended next to an open manhole. A child, attracted to the open manhole, suffered burns when one of the lamps was knocked or dropped into the manhole and exploded. Despite the fact that this chain of events was not reasonably foreseeable, the defendant was held liable for the child's damage. This was on the basis that the broad type of damage suffered by the child was reasonably foreseeable, even if the precise way in which it was caused was not.

So, provided the damage is **similar in type** to that which was foreseeable, it will not be too remote.

6.8 Causation and quantifying damages

As noted above, a defendant only has to pay damages for the harm they caused. One aspect of this is: what happens where the claimant (or their property) was already suffering from some **previous** injury, damage, or disease **prior** to being damaged or injured by the defendant?[19] For example:

> The claimant owns a vintage motor car. It is damaged in an accident caused by the first defendant. The car is then further damaged in the same place in a later accident caused by the second defendant.

---

17 For an example see ***Robinson v Post Office*** [1974] 2 All ER 737 (CA).
18 See ***Hughes v Lord Advocate*** [1963] AC 837 (HL Scotland), on which the following example is based.
19 The points covered here are often important in practice. A defendant (or their insurer) may try to reduce the amount of damages they have to pay by proving that the claimant already suffered from a pre-existing medical condition, so that the defendant's negligence has only made their condition worse to a limited extent.

The claimant has a pre-existing medical condition which renders her likely to suffer from back pain. In an accident at work, caused by the negligence of her employer, she suffers a back injury. Medical evidence shows that she was likely to have suffered from back pain at some time in the future in any event, even without the injury caused by her employer's negligence.

In each case, the defendant responsible for the *later* damage or injury needs to know how much of the claimant's damage they must pay for. The principles here are as follows.

- Where one negligent act causing damage or injury is later followed by a **second negligent act** causing further damage or injury, the **second tortfeasor** is only responsible to the extent that they made the original injury or damage **worse**.

So, in the example of the damaged car, the **second** defendant is only liable to the extent that the second accident made the damage worse. (This means that, to recover in full, the claimant would need to sue both tortfeasors.)[20]

Where an injured claimant suffers from a **pre-existing vulnerability**, we have already seen that the **'egg shell skull'** rule applies. This means that the defendant must take their victim as they find them. The application of the 'egg shell skull rule' means that:

- Where the claimant's injuries are made worse by a **pre-existing vulnerability**, the defendant is liable for the **full extent** of the claimant's damage.

However, this is subject to the qualification that the claimant's damages are likely to be **reduced** to some extent to reflect the likelihood that they would have suffered some symptoms from the pre-existing condition, at some time in the future, in any event.

---

20 The position is more complicated where the defendant *first* injures the claimant and a *subsequent* event then causes further injury. If you wish to read further on this, you may wish to look at: ***Baker v Willoughby*** [1970] AC 467 (HL) and ***Jobling v Associated Dairies*** [1982] AC 794 (HL). The two cases are difficult to reconcile with each other.

Chapter 6 revision points

Causation and remoteness of damage

- The 'but for' test – can it be said that 'but for the defendant's breach of duty the claimant would not have suffered harm?
- Multiple causes:
  - Material contribution
  - Material increase in risk
- Contribution between tortfeasors – two or more persons liable to the claimant in respect of the same damage
- Intervening acts – did a new act (or event) intervene between the defendant's breach of duty and the claimant's damage, so breaking the chain of causation?
- Remoteness of damage – was the harm suffered by the claimant a reasonably foreseeable consequence of the defendant's breach of duty?
  - Exceptions: 'egg shell skull' rule and 'similar in type' rule

Multiple choice questions for Part 3

1. A motorist drove his car carelessly in excess of the speed limit. As a result, he collided with a pedestrian, who was carefully crossing the road, and caused him serious injury.

Which one of the following best explains the liability of the motorist to the pedestrian?

A. He is liable because his driving was the cause of the injury suffered by the pedestrian.
B. He is liable because it would be fair, just and reasonable to find that he owed a duty of care to the pedestrian.
C. He is liable because he owed the pedestrian an established duty of care.
D. He is liable because he failed to exercise reasonable care, so breaching the duty of care owed to the pedestrian and his breach caused the injury to the pedestrian.
E. He is liable provided that he foresaw that driving too fast created a risk of injury to the pedestrian.

2. The driver of a taxi was driving carefully along a road, within the speed limit, when a lorry pulled into his path suddenly and without warning. The taxi collided with the lorry, and the passenger in the taxi was injured.

Which one of the following best explains the liability of the taxi driver if a claim is brought against him by his passenger?

A. He is not liable because, in the circumstances, it would not be fair, just and reasonable to impose a duty of care on him.
B. He is liable because, by failing to avoid injury to his passenger, he breached his duty of care owed to the passenger.
C. He is not liable because the passenger could pursue a claim against the lorry driver.
D. He is liable because driver to passenger is an established duty situation.
E. He is not liable because he did not fall below the standard of care to be expected of a reasonable taxi driver.

3. A school teacher in charge of pupils aged five sent them outside to play in the playground. She left them unattended for ten minutes whilst she checked her emails. One of the pupils left the playground and ran into the road. A passing motorist had to swerve to avoid hitting the child. This resulted in his car hitting a tree and he was injured. The motorist pursued a claim against the teacher in respect of his injuries.

Which one of the following best explains whether the teacher is liable to the motorist?

A. The teacher is not liable because she was guilty of an omission to act and no duty of care is owed in respect of omissions.
B. The teacher is liable because teacher to pupil is an established duty of care, which she breached by leaving the pupils unsupervised.
C. The teacher is not liable because the actions of the motorist broke the chain of causation.
D. The teacher is liable because her failure to supervise was a breach of the duty of care she owed to the motorist.
E. The teacher is liable because she was negligent in checking her emails instead of supervising the children.

4. A newly qualified chemistry teacher asked pupils to undertake an experiment heating chemicals. Her inexperience led her to omit to tell the pupils to wear safety glasses. A pupil carefully conducting the experiment suffered an eye injury when the chemicals exploded.

Which one of the following best explains the likely outcome of a claim by the pupil against the teacher?

A. The teacher is not liable because the accident was caused by her inexperience, not by her carelessness.
B. The teacher is not liable because her failure to require safety glasses was an omission to act in respect of which no duty of care is owed.
C. The teacher is liable because she failed to meet the standard of care expected of a reasonable chemistry teacher, so breaching the duty of care she owed to the pupil.
D. The teacher is liable because a teacher owes an established duty of care to their pupils.
E. The teacher is not liable because it would not be fair, just and reasonable to impose liability for an accident caused by her inexperience.

Multiple choice questions for Part 3

5. A patient arrived at a hospital, unconscious and requiring urgent medical treatment. A doctor administered a drug which saved the patient's life but had unpleasant permanent side effects. Once recovered, the patient consulted a different hospital, where he was told of an alternative treatment without any side effects. The medical literature shows that both treatments are supported by a substantial body of opinion. The patient sought advice on a potential claim against the doctor but was told that it was unlikely to succeed.

Which one of the following best explains why the claim is unlikely to succeed?

A. The doctor was not in breach of her duty of care because she did what was best in her professional opinion.
B. The doctor was not in breach of her duty of care because she acted in accordance with a responsible body of professional opinion.
C. The doctor was not in breach of her duty of care because she saved the patient's life.
D. The doctor was not in breach of her duty of care because she reached the standard of care to be expected of the ordinary reasonable lay person.
E. The doctor was not in breach of her duty of care because she did the best that her own level of skill and experience allowed.

6. An employer provided a staff car park outside its factory. During the months November to March the car park sometimes became slippery with ice. So, the employer ensured that grit was put down during those months. Last September the car park unexpectedly, and unusually, became slippery with ice. An employee, hurrying to work because she was late, slipped and broke her wrist.

Which one of the following best explains whether the employer will be liable to the employee for her injury?

A. The employer will be liable because it was exercising control over the car park.
B. The employer will be liable because employer to employee is an established duty situation.
C. The employer will be liable because it has breached the duty of care owed to its employees.
D. The employer will not be liable because the employee was guilty of contributory negligence.
E. The employer will not be liable because it did not fall below a reasonable standard of care given that the risk of ice was very low at the time.

7. A woman fell and damaged her eye. Her doctor diagnosed bruising, and prescribed cream to reduce the swelling. After three days she was still experiencing pain. So, she attended hospital, where it was found that the injury was severe and would cause blindness in that eye. Expert evidence shows that a competent careful doctor should have diagnosed the injury immediately, but that earlier treatment would not have prevented the blindness. The woman wishes to claim damages from her doctor for the blindness, and seeks advice on her prospects of making a successful claim.

Which one of the following best explains the advice that should be given to the woman?

A. The claim is likely to succeed because the doctor owed the woman an established duty of care.
B. The claim is not likely to succeed because the doctor is not in breach of duty.
C. The claim is not likely to succeed because it cannot be said that 'but for' the doctor's negligence the woman would not have fallen and injured her eye.
D. The claim is likely to succeed because the evidence shows that a competent doctor should have diagnosed the injury immediately.
E. The claim is not likely to succeed because the evidence shows that earlier treatment would not have prevented the blindness.

8. A passenger in a taxi was injured when it was involved in a collision with a bus. She suffered serious injuries. The evidence shows that the accident was caused by the negligence of both the taxi driver and the bus driver. It also confirms that the passenger, who was properly wearing a seatbelt, was not in any way responsible for the accident or her injuries.

Which one of the following best explains the liability of the drivers to the passenger?

A. The passenger can make a successful claim against both drivers by relying on the provisions of the ***Civil Liability (Contribution) Act 1978***.
B. The passenger can make a successful claim against both drivers by showing that each of them made a material contribution to the harm she suffered.
C. The passenger cannot make a successful claim against either driver because in neither case can she show that 'but for' their negligence she would not have been injured.
D. The passenger can make a successful claim against one of the drivers but not both, since she cannot claim that they are both liable for the same damage.
E. The passenger can make a successful claim against both drivers by relying on the provisions of the ***Law Reform (Contributory Negligence) Act 1945***.

9. A heating engineer working at a block of flats carelessly damaged the heating system serving several flats. Their residents were forced to move out temporarily. In their absence, the landlord employed a decorator to redecorate the flats. However, the decorator carelessly misunderstood his instructions and emptied the flats, disposing of the residents' possessions. The residents wish to claim against the heating engineer.

Which one of the following best explains whether that claim is likely to succeed?

A. The claim is likely to succeed because the heating engineer was in breach of his duty to the building owner.
B. The claim is unlikely to succeed because it cannot be said that 'but for' the heating engineer's negligence the residents' possessions would not have been destroyed.
C. The claim is unlikely to succeed because the actions of the decorator were not reasonably foreseeable as a result of the heating engineer's negligence.
D. The claim is likely to succeed because the heating engineer's carelessness in causing damage to the heating system led to the residents having to vacate their flats.
E. The claim is unlikely to succeed because the residents should sue the decorator instead.

10. An employer required its staff to use a strong chemical to clean machinery. In breach of its duty of care to employees, the employer failed to issue protective gloves. As a result, staff got the chemical on their hands. Most of them suffered a mild rash which cleared up after a few days. However, one employee suffered an unusually severe reaction, resulting in lasting injury to his hands. The employee seeks compensation from the employer for his injury.

Which one of the following best explains the likely outcome of the employee's claim?

A. The employer will not be liable to compensate the employee for the full effects of his injury because, but for his unusually severe reaction, he would not have suffered the injury.
B. The employer will be liable to compensate the employee for the full effects of his injury, despite the fact that the extent of his injury was not reasonably foreseeable.
C. The employer will not be liable to compensate the employee at all because it would not be fair, just and reasonable to impose a duty of care in respect of an unusually severe reaction.
D. The employer will be liable to compensate the employee, but only to the extent of the mild rash that everyone else suffered, because the employer did not foresee the full extent of the injury as a consequence of its breach of duty.
E. The employer will be liable to compensate the employee, but only to the extent of the mild rash that everyone else suffered, because no reasonable employer could have foreseen his unusually severe reaction.

PART 4
General defences

7 General defences

7.1 Chapter overview

This chapter outlines a number of general defences. They are 'general' defences because they can apply (depending on the circumstances) to all torts, not just to the tort of negligence. However, it is useful to consider them here, following on from the chapters on the elements of negligence, because the final stage in a negligence claim would be to consider defences.

The chapter begins with the defence of contributory negligence. This is an important defence in practice since, in a large proportion of defended claims in negligence, the defendant is likely to allege that the claimant failed to take reasonable care for their own safety in some way.

It next considers the defence of limitation, which restricts the time available to a claimant to commence an action. Then it looks at the principles governing when a defendant can effectively exclude their liability. Finally, it outlines the defences of voluntary assumption of risk and illegality.

7.2 Introduction: analysing defences in negligence claims

Although the defences outlined in this chapter apply to other torts as well as negligence, it is useful to have a reminder of how defences fit into the analysis of a negligence claim. Always keep in mind the structure for analysis of a claim in negligence:

- Duty of care
- Breach of duty
- Causation of damage
- Defences.

For a successful claim in the tort of negligence the claimant must establish that the defendant owed them a duty of care, that such duty was breached, and that the breach caused the claimant's damage. When analysing a claim in negligence, it is important to begin by considering whether or not the claimant can establish those elements. If the claimant *cannot* establish all of those elements, then the claim will fail, and the issue of defences to the claim will not arise.

However, even if all of those elements are established, the defendant may then be able to rely on a defence to the claim. The defendant bears the **burden** of proving his defence on the balance of probabilities.

7.3 Contributory negligence

The defence of contributory negligence arises where:

- The claimant has failed to take reasonable care for their own safety, and
- The claimant's lack of care has contributed to causing the harm they suffer.[1]

7.3.1 Claimant's lack of care for their own safety

To rely on the defence of contributory negligence, the defendant must show that the claimant failed to take reasonable care for their own safety. For example:

> A claimant trips over a defective pavement and is injured. The defendant, responsible for the condition of the pavement, may argue that the claimant failed to take reasonable care to look where they were walking.

The standard of care expected of the claimant is that of a reasonable person in the claimant's position.

7.3.2 Contributing to the harm suffered

The defence of contributory negligence only arises where the claimant's lack of care contributed to the harm suffered. For example:

> A motorcyclist who fails to wear a crash helmet and suffers a head injury is likely to be found contributorily negligent. On the other hand, if the motorcyclist suffered a broken collar bone, unrelated to his failure to wear a helmet, then the defence would not apply.

The claimant's negligence need *not* have contributed to causing the accident. For example:

> A passenger in a car is injured in an accident caused by the defendant's negligence. The passenger is not wearing a seatbelt, and this causes their injuries to be more serious than they would otherwise have been. The claimant's failure to wear a seatbelt did not contribute to causing the accident, but the defence of contributory negligence will still apply.

---

1 For an example illustrating the points here see ***Froom v Butcher*** [1976] 1 QB 286 (CA) covered in Chapter 22.

7.3.3 Reduction in damages

Contributory negligence is not a complete defence. It does not defeat the claim entirely. Instead, the effect of the defence is to reduce the amount of damages the claimant recovers.

Statute provides that the claimant's damages are to be reduced to such extent as the court thinks just and equitable having regard to the claimant's share in responsibility for the damage.[2] So, in each case the court will consider the facts and decide upon a percentage reduction in damages.

For example, damages may be reduced by 25 per cent for a claimant who fails to wear a seatbelt and would not have suffered any injury had they done so.

7.3.4 Children

There is no fixed age below which the defence does not apply. So, contributory negligence can apply to a child claimant. However, children are expected to meet a lower standard of care for their own safety than adults. Where the claimant is very young, it may not be possible to establish a lack of reasonable care at all.

Also, it is important to note that contributory negligence only applies where the ***claimant themselves*** failed to take reasonable care.[3] For example:

> A very young child suffers burns by approaching a fire the defendant has left unattended. The court is satisfied that the child is too young to appreciate the risk. The child's mother failed to properly supervise the child. The defence of contributory negligence would *not* apply to the child's claim.

(Given that the mother's failure to supervise has contributed to causing the harm suffered by the child, the mother might be in breach of her own duty of care owed to the child.[4] In that case, both the mother and the defendant would be liable to the child, and the defendant could seek a **contribution** from the mother towards the damages awarded to the child.)[5]

7.4 Limitation of actions

When an accident occurs, the claimant is unlikely to be in a position to bring a claim in tort immediately. They will need to seek legal advice, gather evidence, and

---

2   *Law Reform (Contributory Negligence) Act 1945*.
3   It is a common error in assessments to confuse contributory negligence (which applies where the claimant's own lack of care has contributed to the harm they suffer) with contribution between tortfeasors (which may apply where someone else has contributed to the claimant's harm).
4   Parent to child is an established duty situation – see Chapter 4.
5   On contribution between tortfeasors see Chapter 6.

communicate with the potential defendant. Indeed, the rules of civil procedure, which govern the conduct of the parties to litigation, oblige the parties to exchange information before proceedings are commenced.

However, statute does provide for a period of time within which court proceedings must be commenced.[6] If the claimant does not commence proceedings within that period, the claim is statute barred and the defendant can rely on this as a compete defence to the claim.

- For proceedings in the tort of negligence, other than claims for personal injury, the statutory limitation period is six years.

This period begins to run from the date the claimant first suffers damage caused by the defendant's tort.[7]

- In claims for personal injury, the limitation period is three years.

This period begins to run either from the date of the injury[8] or from the claimant's date of knowledge if that is later. The 'date of knowledge' means the date when the claimant first knew that the injury was significant, the cause of the injury, and the identity of the defendant.

In a personal injury claim the court has discretion to extend the limitation period if it considers it equitable to allow the action to proceed.

Finally, where the claimant is a child under 18, the period for bringing an action is six years (or three years for personal injury) from the date they reach 18.

7.5 Exclusion of liability

It is common to see notices (or contractual terms) which state that no liability is accepted for loss or damage suffered. When considering the effect of such exclusions, there are two stages. First is whether or not the notice (or term) properly came to the attention of the claimant and covered the damage caused. Second is whether or not the notice (or term) is subject to any statutory controls limiting its effectiveness.

7.5.1 Effective notice

Before a defendant can rely on an exclusion notice (or term), the defendant must first show:

---

6   ***Limitation Act 1980***.
7   The limitation period runs from the time the claimant's cause of action accrued. In negligence, damage is an essential element of the claim, so the cause of action accrues when damage is suffered. The ***Limitation Act 1980*** contains provisions dealing with extension of the limitation period in cases of latent damage.
8   Since that is when the cause of action accrues.

- For a non-contractual exclusion notice – that reasonable steps were taken to bring it to the claimant's attention.
- For a contractual term – that the clause was effectively incorporated as a term of the contract between the claimant and the defendant.

If these requirements are not satisfied, the notice (or term) will *not* be effective, and the defendant will not be able to rely on it as a defence to the claim.

Also, the **wording** of the exclusion notice (or term) must cover the kind of damage suffered by the claimant. For example: a water park excludes liability for damage to customers' clothing caused by water splashing. This would not be effective to exclude liability if a customer's clothing were damaged by some other means.

7.5.2 Statutory controls

Even if these requirements are satisfied, there are statutory provisions that limit the effectiveness of such exclusion notices (or terms).

The first of these is in relation to:

- **Motor vehicles** – statute prevents the driver of a motor vehicle from excluding liability to passengers.[9]

Second, statutory controls apply when:

- The defendant acts **in the course of a business**.[10]

They depend on the type of loss suffered and the status of the parties.

- **Death or personal injury** caused by negligence – liability cannot be excluded where the defendant acts in the course of a business.[11]
- **Other loss and damage:**
  - Where both claimant and defendant act in the course of business, liability for negligence can only be excluded if the notice (or term) satisfies the requirement of reasonableness.[12] This means that the notice (or term) must be fair and reasonable in the circumstances.[13]
  - Where the defendant acts in the course of a business but the claimant acts as a consumer (a person not in business), an unfair notice (or term) is not binding on the consumer. A notice (or term) is unfair if, contrary to the requirement of good faith, it causes a significant imbalance in the parties' rights and obligations to the detriment of the consumer.[14]

---

9 *Road Traffic Act 1988* s.149.
10 See: *Consumer Rights Act 2015* and *Unfair Contract Terms Act 1977*. Where the defendant does *not* act in the course of a business these controls do not apply. So, the defendant is free to exclude liability (subject always to the requirements explained in Section 7.5.1, 'Effective notice').
11 *Consumer Rights Act 2015* s.65 and *Unfair Contract Terms Act 1977* s.2(1).
12 *Unfair Contract Terms Act 1977* s.2(2).
13 *Unfair Contract Terms Act 1977* s.11.
14 *Consumer Rights Act 2015* s.62.

7.6 Voluntary assumption of risk

- It is a complete defence to a claim in negligence to show that the claimant voluntarily accepted the risk of being harmed by the defendant's negligence.[15]

For example:

> Two workmen agree to carry out a dangerous task involving explosives. They both agree to disregard safety precautions in order to get the job done more quickly. An explosion ensues and one of them is injured. His claim might be met with a successful defence of voluntary assumption of risk (depending on the precise circumstances).

For the defence to apply:

- The claimant must know of the risk of harm, its nature and extent, and
- The claimant must voluntarily consent to such risk.

The mere fact that the claimant is aware of the risk is not sufficient. The claimant must agree to take the risk, and must make a free and voluntary choice. (For example, in the case of the two workmen above, if one of the men was the foreman in charge of the operation and the injured man worked under his direction, the injured man's agreement is unlikely to amount to a free choice giving rise to the defence.)

The claimant's agreement may be express, or it may be implied from the claimant's conduct.

The driver of a motor vehicle in a road traffic accident is prevented by statute from relying on this defence against their passengers.[16]

7.6.1 Distinguished from consent

It is important to distinguish between the defence of voluntary assumption of risk and the defence of **consent**. Voluntary assumption of risk applies to the tort of negligence – the claimant consents to the risk of the defendant's negligence.

In contrast, the defence of **consent** is applicable in the case of intentional torts, such as trespass. In this defence, the claimant consents to something which would otherwise be a tort. For example:

> Where a patient consents to undergo medical treatment, the doctor does not commit the tort of battery.

---

15 This defence is sometimes referred to by the Latin: *volenti non fit injuria*.
16 **Road Traffic Act 1988** s.149.

Where a landowner gives permission to use a footpath, a hiker does not commit the tort of trespass to land.

7.7 Illegality

A defendant whose tort has injured the claimant may have a defence where the claimant was engaged in an illegal activity.[17] For example:

> Two teenage boys ride together on a motorbike. The driver of the bike deliberately drives in a fast and dangerous way and the passenger encourages him to do so, knowing that the driver is intoxicated and does not have a licence or insurance. The motorbike is involved in a crash caused by the negligence of the driver, and the passenger is seriously injured. The passenger's claim against the driver is likely to be met with a successful defence of illegality.

The defence of illegality is a rule of public policy, that:

- A person cannot recover compensation for loss they have suffered as a result of their own illegal actions.[18]

The defence applies when the circumstances of the claim are such that it would be damaging to the integrity of the law to allow the claimant to recover compensation. So, when considering whether or not the defence of illegality should apply on the facts of a particular case, the court must take into account a range of policy considerations to decide whether or not the claimant should be denied compensation. The court must consider: the purpose of the legal rule the claimant broke; any other relevant policy considerations; and whether denying the claim would be a proportionate response to the claimant's illegal conduct.[19]

The defence of illegality is justified on public policy grounds that it would be offensive and unfair for a claimant to be compensated for the consequences of his own illegal conduct. This means that, for the defence to apply, the claimant's illegal conduct must have been sufficiently serious. For example:[20]

> An NHS trust negligently fails to take action to treat the claimant who is suffering from mental illness. As a result, she stabs and kills her mother and is

---

17 See, for example, **Pitts v Hunt** [1991] 1 QB 24 (CA), on which the following example is based.
18 This is sometimes referred to by the Latin maxim: *ex turpi causa non oritur actio*.
19 See further: **Patel v Mirza** [2016] UKSC 42, [2017] AC 467 applied in **Henderson v Dorset Healthcare University NHS Foundation Trust** [2020] UKSC 43, [2020] 3 WLR 1124 and **Stoffel and Co v Grondona** [2020] UKSC 42, [2020] 3 WLR 1156.
20 This example is based on **Henderson v Dorset Healthcare University NHS Foundation Trust** [2020] UKSC 43, [2020] 3 WLR 1124.

convicted of a crime. In these circumstances the defence of illegality would apply to prevent the claimant from recovering compensation for the adverse consequences she suffered as a result of her illegal actions.

In contrast, if the claimant's illegal conduct is only minor or is just an incidental part of the background to the defendant's tort, then the defence of illegality will not apply. So, for example:

> The fact that a claimant car driver was exceeding the speed limit when involved in a collision caused by the defendant's negligence would not mean that his claim was barred by the defence of illegality. Similarly, the fact that the claimant's car was illegally parked when it was damaged by the defendant's negligence will not allow the defendant to rely on the defence of illegality. (Though, in both of these examples, the partial defence of contributory negligence might apply.)

Chapter 7 revision points

General defences

Ask first: Can the claimant establish all the elements of the claim? Then consider defences.

- Contributory negligence:
  - Claimant failed to take reasonable care for their own safety
  - Claimant's lack of care contributed to the harm suffered
  - Does not defeat claim entirely
  - Results in a reduction in damages
- Limitation of actions:
  - Statute imposes periods of time within which action must be commenced
- Exclusion of liability:
  - Effective notice
  - Statutory controls
- Voluntary assumption of risk:
  - Claimant knows of the risk of harm, its nature and extent, *and*
  - Voluntarily consents to such risk
- Illegality:
  - Public policy considerations
  - Offensive and unfair for claimant to be compensated for the consequences of their own illegal conduct

Multiple choice questions for Part 4

1. A warehouse employee often engaged in the dangerous practice of taking a lift on the front of an automated driverless truck instead of walking the length of the warehouse. Recently, he was seriously injured when a truck on which he was riding malfunctioned and crashed into a shelving unit. The employer accepts that it was in breach of its duty of care to the employee because it knew of the dangerous practice but did nothing to prevent it. However, it asserts that the employee is responsible for riding on the truck. The employee is now pursuing a claim for damages against the employer.

   Which one of the following best explains the effect of the employee's own behaviour on his claim?

   A. The employee's behaviour means that, although the employer is liable, his damages are likely to be reduced.
   B. The employee's behaviour has no effect on his claim because he did not foresee that it could cause him to be injured.
   C. The employee's behaviour means that the employer has no liability to him because he failed to take reasonable care for his own safety.
   D. The employee's behaviour will have no effect on his claim because it did not contribute to causing the accident to happen.
   E. The employee's behaviour means that the employer has no liability to him because he voluntarily accepted the risk of an accident by riding on the truck.

2. At a country fair a professional riding instructor was offering free horse rides to promote her business. A woman accepted a free ride. She was shown a notice which read:

This ride is provided free of charge. Therefore, no liability is accepted for any injury, loss, or damage, whether caused by negligence or otherwise.

The woman suffered a serious head injury when she fell from the horse during the ride. The instructor accepts that this was caused by her negligence in failing to ensure that the woman wore a riding helmet. The riding instructor now seeks advice on her liability to the woman.

Which one of the following best explains the advice that should be given to the riding instructor?

A. The instructor is not liable for the woman's injury. She can rely on the notice because it clearly excludes her liability and was brought to the woman's attention.
B. The instructor is liable for the woman's injury. She cannot rely on the exclusion notice because the lesson was to promote her business.
C. The instructor is not liable for the woman's injury. She can rely on the exclusion notice because she provided the ride for free.
D. The instructor is liable for the woman's injury. She cannot rely on the exclusion notice because liability for personal injury can never be excluded in any circumstances.
E. The instructor is not liable for the woman's injury because, by not wearing a helmet, the woman is guilty of contributory negligence.

3. A youth and his friend travelled in the friend's van. Clearly displayed on the dashboard was the following notice:

No liability accepted for injury to passengers, whether caused by negligence or otherwise.

They travelled to a house and, whilst the friend remained in the driving seat, the youth stole some ladders. As the youth was strapping the ladders to the van, the police arrived. The friend drove off and the youth was thrown from the van, suffering a serious injury. One year later, the youth issued proceedings against the friend to recover damages for his injuries. At the trial, four years later, the court found the friend not liable.

Which one of the following best explains why the friend was not liable?

A. The friend was not liable because the defence of illegality applied.
B. The friend was not liable because the defence of voluntary assumption of risk applied.
C. The friend was not liable because the defence of contributory negligence applied.
D. The friend was not liable because the defence of limitation applied.
E. The friend was not liable because the defence of exclusion of liability applied.

4. A railway museum had a working steam train, maintained by an engineer who worked as an unpaid volunteer. Another volunteer was responsible for cleaning the exterior of the train, and was advised to wear overalls because of the risk of damage to his clothing. One day, he forgot his overalls but decided to work anyway. As he did so, a valve broke, releasing hot steam which burnt his hands. Expert evidence shows that the accident was caused by the negligence of the engineer.

In a claim by the injured man against the engineer, which one of the following best states the likely outcome?

A. The engineer is not liable. The defence of voluntary assumption of risk applies because the injured man volunteered to work on the train.
B. The engineer is not liable. The defence of voluntary assumption of risk applies because, by not wearing overalls, the injured man voluntarily consented to the risk of harm.
C. The engineer is liable. He was in breach of a duty of care owed to the injured man, the breach caused the injury, and no relevant defences apply.
D. The engineer is liable. He was in breach of a duty of care owed to the injured man and the breach caused the injury. However, the partial defence of contributory negligence may apply to reduce the damages awarded.
E. The engineer is not liable. The engineer did not owe any duty of care to the injured man because the engineer was an unpaid volunteer.

PART 5
Negligence: limited duty situations

8 Negligence: limited duty situations – economic loss

8.1 Chapter overview

Previous chapters have outlined the structure for a claim in the tort of negligence:

- Duty of care
- Breach of duty
- Causation of damage
- Defences.

The first element a claimant must establish is that the defendant owed them a duty of care. This and the following chapter examine two particular types of loss where the courts have imposed limits on the circumstances in which a duty of care may be owed:

- Loss which is purely economic (as compared, for example, to damage to property)
- Pure psychiatric harm (as compared, for example to physical injury).

It is important to remember that if no duty of care is owed by the defendant to the claimant, there will be no remedy. A defendant may have behaved carelessly, causing harm to the claimant; but if no duty of care was owed, the claimant will be uncompensated.

So, the principles on duty of care for pure economic loss and psychiatric harm place limits on the types of harm for which compensation may be recovered in tort.

Pure economic loss is dealt with in this chapter, and psychiatric harm in Chapter 9.

8.2 Distinguishing pure economic loss from consequential economic loss

To understand pure economic loss, it is first necessary to distinguish it from economic loss, which is simply ***consequential*** on physical damage or injury. When a defendant's negligence causes personal injury or damage to property, there are usually financial consequences. For example:

> The defendant is a bus driver. He fails to exercise reasonable care and skill in driving the bus, and he collides with the claimant's car. The claimant is injured,

and as a result she is off work and suffers a loss of wages. Her car is damaged, and she has to pay for repairs.

Here, the victim has suffered physical damage with *consequential* economic loss. In this situation, there are no special rules for duty of care. We can simply say that the defendant bus driver owes an established duty of care to the claimant, which covers the physical injury to her, the physical damage to her property, and the *consequential* economic loss flowing from such damage.

In contrast, there are special rules for duty of care in relation to other forms of economic loss – which we call 'pure' economic loss to distinguish them.

Pure economic loss covers the following:

- Damage to a defective product acquired by the claimant
- Damage to property which does not belong to the claimant
- Financial loss which is not caused by damage to property (e.g., financial loss caused by a negligent statement).

When we discuss each of these kinds of pure economic loss, we will see that the rules are often a matter of policy – with the result that the classification of certain kinds of loss as 'purely economic' may not always appear logical.

8.3 Damage to a defective product acquired by the claimant

Consider this scenario:

> A businessman purchases an industrial refrigerator from a retail supplier. Unfortunately, the refrigerator suffers from a manufacturing defect. It breaks down and fails to work. The businessman is unable to pursue a claim in contract against the supplier because the supplier has gone out of business. He has no contract directly with the manufacturer.

If the businessman could prove that the defect was caused by the manufacturer's failure to exercise reasonable care and skill, could he pursue a claim against the manufacturer in the tort of negligence to recover the purchase or repair costs of the defective refrigerator? The answer is that he could *not* pursue such a claim.

■ In the tort of negligence, no duty of care is owed in respect of damage to a defective product acquired by the claimant.[1]

To allow such claims would undermine the law of contract.

---

1 See, for example, ***Muirhead v Industrial Tank Specialities Ltd and Others*** [1986] QB 507 (CA) covered in Chapter 22; also, ***Murphy v Brentwood DC*** [1991] 1 AC 398 (HL).

However, where the manufacturer's negligence results in damage caused *by* a defective product to *other property* owned by the claimant, a duty of care can be owed in respect of that damage.

In the above example, suppose that the businessman, unaware of the defect in the refrigerator, had filled it with expensive cuts of meat to be sold in the course of his business, and that the meat was damaged when the refrigerator unexpectedly broke down. The manufacturer would owe the businessman a duty of care in respect of the damage to the meat, covering both the cost of the meat and the profit he had expected to make on selling it.

8.4 Damage to property which does not belong to the claimant

When property is damaged, the owner is likely to incur the costs of repair or replacement. However, damage to property may also cause financial loss to *other people*, who are *not* the owners. For example:

> A company contracts with the owner of a ship for the transport of goods. Shortly before the ship is due to leave port, it is destroyed by the negligence of the defendant. The owner of the ship gives the company a full refund of the transport costs. However, the company loses the profit it expected to make.

Of course, the defendant does owe a duty of care to the ship *owner*, in respect of the financial costs of replacing the ship – but can the company which contacted for transport on the ship also recover its financial losses from the defendant? The answer is that it could **not** recover those losses.

- In the tort of negligence, no duty of care is owed in respect of financial loss caused by damage to property which does not belong to the claimant.[2]

8.5 Financial loss which is not caused by damage to property (statements/services)

In some cases, there is no property damage at all. Instead, the only loss caused is financial loss. This is the case where the claimant relies on a negligent statement made by the defendant. Compare these examples:

> A small investor reads a magazine article in which a financial adviser suggests that diamonds are a good investment. The investor puts all her savings into purchasing diamonds. She loses all of her investment when the price of dia-

---

2 ***Spartan Steel & Alloys Ltd v Martin & Co (Contractors) Ltd*** [1973] QB 27 (CA). Note that a person in possession of goods (e.g. a hirer) is treated as an owner for this purpose.

monds falls suddenly. It transpires that the financial adviser failed to exercise reasonable care in making the recommendations. Can the small investor recover her lost money from the financial adviser?

A customer wishing to acquire an expensive diamond ring on credit authorises her bank to provide the seller with a credit reference. The bank provides a favourable reference. In reliance on this, the seller allows the customer to purchase the ring on credit, with the price to be paid by instalments. Subsequently, the customer defaults on payment and disappears. It transpires that the credit reference was inaccurate because the bank had failed to exercise reasonable care in checking the customer's assets. Could the seller recover the unpaid price of the ring from the bank?

In these situations, the answer depends on the nature of the relationship between the parties.

Just as with other forms of pure economic loss, the general rule is that no duty of care is owed. However, in the case of negligent statements, there is a limited exception to this, which depends on the nature of the relationship between the person making the negligent statement and the person relying on it.

- A defendant who makes a negligent statement causing pure economic loss may owe a duty of care where there is a **special relationship** between the parties involving: an **assumption of responsibility** by the defendant and **reasonable reliance** by the claimant.

So, case law[3] suggests that a duty of care is likely to arise where:

- The adviser knows the purpose for which the advice is required.
- The adviser knows that his advice will be communicated to the advisee, either individually or as a member of an identifiable class, in order to be used for that purpose.
- The adviser knows that the advisee is likely to rely on the advice without making further independent enquiries.
- It is reasonable for the advisee to rely on the advice.
- The advisee does rely on the advice and suffers loss.

So, in our original examples above, the financial adviser writing in a magazine for the public in general is not likely to owe a duty of care to the individual investor. In contrast, the bank providing a credit reference direct to a seller, knowing that it will be relied on, may owe a duty of care.

---

3   This section summarises the principles to be drawn from the case law. See further: ***Hedley Byrne & Co Ltd v Heller & Partners Ltd*** [1964] AC 465 (HL); ***Caparo Industries Plc v Dickman and Others*** [1990] 2 AC 605 (HL) applied in ***Playboy Club London Ltd v Banca Nazionale del Lavoro SpA*** [2018] UKSC 43, [2019] 2 All ER 478.

The requirements for an assumption of responsibility and reasonable reliance mean that it is normally unlikely that a duty of care will arise in relation to advice given on a purely social occasion.[4]

So far we have focused on negligent statements; but case law has expanded the principles in this area to cover services which are provided negligently, causing pure economic loss. For example:

> A solicitor who provides the service of drafting a will for a testator may owe a duty of care to a beneficiary who suffers financial loss when the will is drafted negligently.

In a case of this kind, it was the testator who relied on the solicitor, not the beneficiary, but the duty of care has been extended to cover this situation.

8.6 Breach of duty and causation of damage

In this chapter we have considered when a duty of care will be owed in respect of pure economic loss. However, it is important to remember that establishing a duty of care is only the first element necessary for a successful claim. The claimant must also show that the duty of care was breached, and that such breach caused the damage they suffered.

Chapter 8 revision points

Limited duty situation – economic loss

- Distinguish pure economic loss and consequential economic loss
- Damage to a defective product acquired by the claimant
  - Pure economic loss
  - No duty of care owed
  - Not recoverable
- Financial loss caused by damage to property which does not belong to the claimant
  - Pure economic loss
  - No duty of care owed
  - Not recoverable

---

4 See: *Chaudhry v Prabhakar* [1989] 1 WLR 29 (CA) where, on the particular facts, a duty was owed.

- Financial loss which is not caused by damage to property (statements/services)
  - Pure economic loss
  - No duty of care owed *unless* special relationship involving assumption of responsibility and reasonable reliance
- After duty of care – complete analysis by considering:
  - Breach of duty
  - Causation of damage
  - Defences

9 Negligence: limited duty situations – psychiatric harm

9.1 Chapter overview

Before reading this chapter you may find it helpful to refer to the chapter overview of Chapter 8, which introduced the concept of limited duty situations.

This chapter focuses on duty of care in cases of psychiatric harm. That is, cases in which the defendant's negligence does not cause any direct physical impact on the claimant but exposes the claimant to a shock which causes them to suffer a psychiatric illness or a shock-induced physical illness or injury.

It explains the key distinction between primary and secondary victims:

- Primary victims are those in the area of danger created by the defendant's negligence.
- Secondary victims are those not in the area of danger.

It explains the duty of care owed to primary victims. It then shows how secondary victims are only owed a duty of care if they are able to satisfy a restrictive set of conditions.

9.2 Distinguishing pure psychiatric harm from consequential psychiatric harm

Look at this problem scenario:

> The defendant is a bus driver. He fails to exercise reasonable care and skill in driving the bus, and he crashes the bus into a low bridge.
>
> The first victim, a passenger on the bus, suffers a broken wrist. She also suffers recurring nightmares and a continuing phobia of travelling by bus.
>
> The second victim is also a passenger on the bus. She is pregnant. She is not injured by the impact of the crash, but she is so shocked that she suffers a miscarriage.

DOI: 10.4324/9781003133698-15

The third victim, a passenger on the bus, does not suffer any physical injury in the accident. However, the shock of the accident causes her to suffer from post-traumatic stress disorder ('PTSD').

The fourth victim is a mother waiting at a nearby bus stop to meet her daughter who is on the bus. She witnesses the accident and fears for her daughter's safety. The shock causes her to suffer a diagnosed depressive illness.

All of the victims have suffered some form of psychiatric harm.

The first victim has suffered a physical injury (broken wrist) with **consequential** psychiatric harm. In this situation, there are no special rules for duty of care. We can simply say that the bus driver owes an established duty to his passengers which covers both the physical injury and the *consequential* psychiatric harm which flows from it.

In contrast, the other victims in the example have suffered psychiatric harm caused by shock rather than by a physical impact. (The victim who had a miscarriage falls into this category because her condition was caused by shock rather than by a physical impact on her.) This is often referred to as **'pure' psychiatric harm**, and special rules apply to limit when a duty of care is owed.

9.3 Primary and secondary victims

In cases of pure psychiatric harm, the special rules for duty of care depend on the type of victim. So, we must first draw a distinction between victims who are themselves endangered (such as the passengers in our example, who were on the bus when it was involved in the accident) and victims who are not in danger themselves but fear for others (such as the mother in our example, who witnessed the accident in which her daughter was involved).

- Victims who are in the actual area of danger are described as primary victims.
- Those who are not in the actual area of danger are secondary victims.

9.4 Medically recognised condition and sudden shock

9.4.1 Medically recognised condition
For both primary and secondary victims, the first limitation on duty of care is that no duty of care is owed unless the harm amounts to:

- a recognised psychiatric illness, or
- a shock-induced physical condition.

In the example in Section 9.2, post-traumatic stress disorder would be an example of a recognised psychiatric illness, and the miscarriage would be an example of a shock-induced physical condition.

In contrast to this, imagine a situation in which a victim is not physically injured but suffers effects such as anxiety or distress or nightmares, not amounting to a medically recognised psychiatric illness. In these circumstances, no duty of care would be owed.

(We can compare this with the position of a person who does suffer a physical injury and also suffers *consequential* psychiatric harm – e.g., the victim in our example who suffered a broken wrist. The duty of care owed to victims of this kind does extend to effects such as distress, anxiety, and nightmares, even though they may not amount to a recognised psychiatric illness.)

9.4.2 Sudden shock

The very nature of pure psychiatric harm is such that it results from a shock suffered by the claimant (either the shock of being directly involved in the dangerous situation caused by the defendant or the shock of witnessing harm to others caused by the defendant).

However, cases have drawn a distinction between harm which is caused by a sudden shocking event and harm which is caused by exposure to shock over a longer period. For example, a mother suffers a sudden shock when she sees her child hit by a car. If the child's father later goes to the hospital and sits with the child over a period of days until the child dies, the father has not suffered a sudden shock.

In the case of secondary victims, the law is clear that no duty of care is owed unless the pure psychiatric harm is caused by a sudden shocking event. So, in our example, the father would not be owed a duty of care.

However, in the case of primary victims, more recent case law[1] suggests that the requirement for harm to be caused by a sudden shock does not always apply. For example, a mother goes into labour but suffers a stillbirth caused by the defendant's negligent medical treatment. The mother is classed as a primary victim. She may suffer pure psychiatric harm, not caused by any physical effects of the birth. It cannot be said that this psychiatric harm has been caused by a 'sudden' shock because it has been caused over a longer period – both during the birth and after the baby's death. Nevertheless, the mother is owed a duty of care in respect of her pure psychiatric harm.

---

1 See: ***YAH v Medway NHS Foundation Trust*** [2018] EWHC 2964, [2019] 1 WLR 1413 and ***Zeromska-Smith v United Lincolnshire Hospitals NHS Trust*** [2019] EWHC 980, [2019] All ER (D) 92 (Apr).

Bear these points in mind as we now look at the rules for duty of care in relation to primary and secondary victims.

9.5 Primary victims

Primary victims are those who were in the actual area of danger created by the defendant's negligence. They were at risk of physical injury but in fact 'escaped' such injury, suffering instead pure psychiatric harm. In our example, the passengers on the bus who suffered a miscarriage and PTSD were primary victims.

We have noted the limitation placed on duty of care owed to a primary victim: that the pure psychiatric harm they suffer must amount to a medically recognised psychiatric illness (such as PTSD) or a shock-induced physical condition (such as a miscarriage).

Subject to this:

- Primary victims are owed a duty of care provided they were placed at a foreseeable risk of physical injury.[2]

This can be justified on grounds that a defendant whose negligence places a person in danger of physical injury should owe them a duty of care, even if the victim in fact escapes physical injury and instead suffers pure psychiatric harm.

9.6 Secondary victims

Secondary victims are those who were not in the actual area of danger created by the defendant's negligence. They suffer pure psychiatric harm because they witness shocking events caused by the defendant's negligence. In our example in Section 9.2 the mother waiting at the bus stop was a secondary victim.

Remember that we have already identified two limitations placed on the duty of care owed to a secondary victim:

- The victim must suffer from a medically recognised psychiatric illness (or shock-induced physical condition).
- The harm must result from a sudden shocking event. No duty of care is owed in respect of psychiatric harm caused by witnessing events over a prolonged period. For example:

> A defendant causes a road accident seriously injuring a woman. In hospital she is critically ill; her condition deteriorates over a period of days, and she then dies. During this period, she is regularly visited by her

---

2 *Page v Smith* [1996] AC 155 (HL) covered in Chapter 22.

husband, who suffers a medically diagnosed psychiatric illness as a result. The defendant is not likely to owe any duty of care to the husband. So, the husband will not be compensated for the harm he has suffered.

However, these limitations are not sufficient by themselves. A single act of carelessness can create a very large class of secondary victims. A large number of people, who are not themselves placed at risk of physical injury, may witness a sudden shocking event, and suffer a medically recognised psychiatric illness. Therefore, further limits are imposed.

- Secondary victims are *not* owed a duty of care *unless* they *also* satisfy all of the following conditions:[3]
  - Reasonable foreseeability of psychiatric harm
  - Close ties of love and affection with the immediate victim
  - Proximity to the accident
  - Direct perception by sight or hearing.

We will consider each of these in turn.

9.6.1 Reasonable foreseeability of psychiatric harm

Secondary victims suffer psychiatric harm as a result of witnessing the consequences of the defendant's negligence. For a duty of care to be owed to them, they must show that it was reasonably foreseeable that a person of ordinary fortitude would suffer psychiatric harm as a result of witnessing such events.

9.6.2 Close ties of love and affection with the immediate victim

A duty of care is owed only to those secondary victims who have close ties of love and affection with the immediate victim of the defendant's negligence. In our original example, the mother witnessing an accident in which her daughter was involved would satisfy this requirement. A witness who did not know any of the persons involved in the accident would not satisfy this requirement.

It is usually presumed that close ties of love and affection exist between spouses and between parents and children. For other relationships, the claimant would usually need to prove that close ties of love and affection existed.

9.6.3 Proximity to the accident

For a duty of care to be owed to a secondary victim, they must have been in close proximity to the accident in both time and space. So, they must witness the event as it occurs or witness the immediate aftermath.[4] For example:

---

3   See **Alcock v Chief Constable of South Yorkshire** [1992] 1 AC 310 (HL) covered in Chapter 22.
4   On witnessing the immediate aftermath, see e.g., **McLoughlin v O'Brian** [1983] 1 AC 410 (HL), on which the following example is based.

A father and children were involved in a car accident. The mother did not witness the accident but rushed to the hospital, where she witnessed the suffering of her family as they were receiving emergency treatment. She witnessed the immediate aftermath, and this was sufficient for a duty of care to be owed to her in respect of the psychiatric harm she suffered.

9.6.4 Direct perception by sight or hearing

When an accident happens, its effects may be transmitted in many ways. Some people may see or hear it as it happens; but others may be told about it, see photographs of it, or read about it. However, not everyone who is affected is owed a duty of care.

A duty of care is only owed to those who themselves directly see or hear the accident or its immediate aftermath. (Obviously, this is closely linked to the requirement for proximity in time and space.)

Therefore, case law[5] has held that victims who suffered psychiatric harm as a result of seeing events live on television were not owed a duty of care. (However, it remains open to question whether a duty *might* be owed if simultaneous live pictures directly showed the suffering of identified, recognisable individuals.)

So, in summary, a secondary victim is only owed a duty of care if they satisfy all of the above conditions. This does mean that some secondary victims who suffer pure psychiatric harm by witnessing sudden shocking events may not be owed a duty of care, and so will not be compensated for their injury.

9.7 Rescuers

Where the defendant's negligence causes an accident to occur, there will often be rescuers who come to the scene to help the immediate victims. It is clearly established that such a defendant owes a duty of care to rescuers who suffer *physical injury*. However, what is the position where a rescuer suffers psychiatric harm without any physical impact?

The answer depends on whether the rescuer was a primary or secondary victim, as defined above. If the rescuer was in the area of danger, and so at risk of physical injury, they are a primary victim, and a duty of care is owed to them in respect of their psychiatric harm (provided that it amounts to a recognised psychiatric illness, as explained above).

However, if a rescuer is not in the area of danger, they are only a secondary victim. So, for a duty of care to be owed to them in respect of their psychiatric harm, they

---

5 *Alcock v Chief Constable of South Yorkshire* [1992] 1 AC 310 (HL).

would need to satisfy all of the conditions outlined above. It will very often be the case that rescuers do not have any relationship to the immediate victims of the accident. This means that they would not satisfy the requirement for close ties of love and affection, and, in that case, a duty of care would not be owed to them.

9.8 Breach of duty and causation of damage

In this chapter we have considered when a duty of care will be owed in respect of psychiatric harm caused without physical impact. However, it is important to remember that establishing a duty of care is only the first element necessary for a successful claim. The claimant must also show that the duty of care was breached, and that such breach caused the damage they suffered.

However, in practical terms, it is often admitted that a defendant failed to take reasonable care, and that this did cause psychiatric harm to the claimant. The argument about duty of care then determines whether or not the claimant will be compensated for the damage caused by the defendant's negligence.

Chapter 9 revision points

Limited duty situation – psychiatric harm

- Distinguish:
  - Consequential psychiatric harm: caused by physical injury to claimant – no special rules for duty of care
  - Pure psychiatric harm: caused without physical impact on the claimant
- Pure psychiatric harm: no duty unless claimant suffers medically recognised condition:
  - Recognised psychiatric illness, or
  - Shock-induced physical condition
- Primary victims: in the area of danger – owed a duty of care provided they were placed at a foreseeable risk of physical injury
- Secondary victims: not in the area of danger – no duty of care owed unless satisfy:
  - Sudden shock
  - Reasonable foreseeability of psychiatric harm
  - Close ties of love and affection with the immediate victim
  - Proximity to the accident
  - Direct perception by sight or hearing
- After duty of care – complete analysis by considering:
  - Breach of duty
  - Causation of damage
  - Defences

Multiple choice questions for Part 5

1. A supplier of alcoholic drinks accepted a large order from a new customer, subject to a favourable credit reference from the customer's bank. To protect customer privacy, rather than disclose to the bank its identity as a supplier of alcohol, the supplier used an agent to request the credit reference. The bank provided a favourable reference, and the goods were delivered. However, the customer failed to pay. He is now insolvent and has consumed the alcohol. Enquiries revealed that the bank did not exercise proper care in giving the favourable reference, and the supplier is considering a claim in negligence against the bank.

   Which one of the following best explains the liability of the bank to the supplier?
   A. The bank will be liable in negligence because the supplier relied on the reference provided.
   B. The bank will not be liable in negligence because a duty of care is never owed in respect of pure economic loss.
   C. The bank will not be liable in negligence because it was not aware of the identity of the supplier.
   D. The bank will be liable in negligence because it fell below a reasonable standard of care in providing an inaccurate reference.
   E. The bank will be liable in negligence because it undertook a responsibility towards the supplier by agreeing to provide the reference.

2. Alison worked in a pizza restaurant where the kitchen was open to customers' view. Her fiancé, Bernard, went to the restaurant and sat at a table near the kitchen. As Alison was working in the kitchen, the pizza oven suddenly exploded, sending flames across the kitchen. Alison was unhurt but very shaken. Bernard witnessed the incident from his table and was very afraid for Alison's safety. Another customer, Carol, sitting next to Bernard, also witnessed the shocking scenes. Alison, Bernard, and Carol have now been diagnosed with post-traumatic stress disorder (PTSD). An expert report shows that the oven exploded because the restaurant owner had negligently continued to use it knowing that it had not been properly maintained.

   Which one of the following correctly identifies who can/cannot make a successful claim against the restaurant owner?
   A. Only Alison can claim.
   B. Only Alison and Bernard can claim.
   C. Alison, Bernard, and Carol can all claim.
   D. None of them can claim.
   E. Only Alison cannot claim.

Summary overview of negligence

The preceding chapters have covered each of the elements of a claim in negligence:

- Duty of care
- Breach of duty
- Causation of damage
- Defences.

This section now gives an overview of the structure of a claim in negligence.

Before reading this overview you may wish to test your understanding by creating your own concise summary, using the headings above.

Overview of the tort of negligence

Duty of care

- Established duty situations
- Novel duty situations:
  - Foreseeability
  - Proximity
  - Fair, just and reasonable
- Limited duty situations: economic loss; psychiatric harm

Breach of duty

- Standard of care – objective and impersonal
  - The standard to be expected of the ordinary reasonable person in the position of the defendant
- Did the defendant fall below a reasonable standard of care?
  - What is reasonable? – Degree of risk/precautions in response to risk

Causation of damage

- Was defendant's breach in fact a cause of claimant's damage?
  - 'But for' defendant's breach, would claimant have suffered damage?
  - Multiple causes – Did defendant's breach make at least a material contribution to claimant's damage? (extended in limited cases to material increase in risk)
- Contribution between multiple tortfeasors – where injury is indivisible
- Intervening acts – Did a new act intervene between defendant's breach and claimant's damage, breaking the chain of causation?
- Remoteness of damage – Was claimant's damage a reasonably foreseeable consequence of defendant's breach?
  - Exceptions: 'egg shell skull' rule; 'similar in type' rule

Defences

- Contributory negligence:
  - Claimant failed to take reasonable care for their own safety
  - Claimant's lack of care contributed to the damage suffered
- Limitation of actions – time limits for commencing claims
- Exclusion of liability
  - Effective notice
  - Statutory controls
- Voluntary assumption of risk – Claimant voluntarily accepted the risk of being harmed by defendant's negligence
- Illegality – Public policy: offensive and unfair for the claimant to be compensated for the consequences of their own illegal conduct

PART 6
Remedies in tort

10 Remedies

10.1 Chapter overview

This chapter explains the remedies that may be available for a successful claim in tort.

It first introduces the remedy of damages. It then considers in more detail the damages awarded for personal injury to a living claimant.

This is followed by an explanation of damages awarded on death, covering:

- Damages awarded to the estate of a deceased person
- Damages awarded to dependants
- Bereavement damages.

Finally, the chapter outlines the remedy of injunction.

10.2 Introduction to damages

Clients bring claims in tort because they are seeking a remedy. Where the client's aim is to obtain financial compensation for harm suffered, the appropriate remedy is compensatory damages.

> ■ The aim of compensatory damages is to put the claimant into the position they would have been in had the tort not occurred (so far as money can do so).

They compensate the claimant for damage suffered, for example: personal injury, damage to property, or interference with land.

We have also noted some torts which are actionable without proof of damage (actionable per se), such as trespass to land. In these torts, damages compensate the claimant for the infringement of their right (as well as for any actual damage suffered).

The general principle is that damages are awarded in one lump sum.[1] Damages awarded as a lump sum cover all of the claimant's losses, including losses already incurred up to the date of trial (or settlement) and losses the claimant will suffer in the future. This means that the court, at the time of trial (or the parties, at the time of negotiating an agreed settlement), must assess the likely amount of such future loss – for example, a claimant's future loss of earnings where a personal injury has a lasting effect.

An important limitation on the amount of damages a claimant can recover is the principle of **mitigation of loss**. The claimant must take reasonable steps to mitigate (or reduce) the amount of loss they suffer.

So, for example, a claimant whose car is damaged may recover the costs of hiring a replacement. However, the model of car hired would need to be reasonably equivalent to the claimant's own damaged car. A claimant who incurred the extra expense of hiring a much more luxurious model would not have mitigated their losses, and so would not recover all of the costs. The principle of mitigation of loss also applies to damages for personal injury. For example, a claimant who is unable to continue with their pre-accident work would be expected to mitigate their loss by taking reasonable steps to find alternative employment.

It should also be remembered that recovery of damages is subject to the rules on remoteness of damage. So, in general, losses can only be recovered if they were reasonably foreseeable.[2]

10.2.1 Damage to property

Where the claimant's property has been damaged, the measure of damages is the reduction in value of the property. This is usually the cost of repairing it. Where the property has been destroyed, the measure of damages is the cost of replacing it. In both cases, damages also cover consequential loss. Consequential losses might cover, for example, the cost of hiring a replacement for the damaged property or, where the property was used for business purposes, loss of profits. For example:

> A claimant whose car is damaged in an accident caused by the negligence of the defendant may recover damages for: the cost of repairs to the car; the cost of storing the car pending repairs; and the cost of hiring a replacement car whilst repairs are carried out.

---

1 In some circumstances it is possible for a court awarding damages for personal injury to make an order for periodic payments or provisional damages.
2 A different rule for remoteness of damage applies to claims in trespass, where damage is recoverable provided it is a direct consequence of the defendant's act. See Chapter 2.

10.3 Damages for personal injury – living claimant

This section considers the damages awarded to a living claimant who has suffered personal injury.

10.3.1 Non-financial losses – pain, suffering, and loss of amenity

The court will award damages to cover the pain, suffering, and loss of amenity caused by the injury.[3] Loss of amenity covers the effects of the injury on the claimant's life – for example, where the claimant is no longer able to continue to play sport or pursue a hobby.

These damages are assessed by the court at the time the case is tried. They cover past pain etc. suffered up to trial and future pain etc. the claimant is expected to experience. Medical evidence will be presented to the court to provide details of the effects of the injury on the claimant.

Damages of this kind cannot be mathematically calculated. Instead, they are assessed by the court. In making this assessment the court will have regard to awards of damages in previously reported similar cases.[4]

Note that a claimant cannot recover damages for pain and suffering for any period where they are unconscious as they are unable to experience the pain. However, such a claimant can still recover damages for their loss of amenity during a period when they are unconscious because they still suffer this loss, even if they are unaware of it at the time.

10.3.2 Financial losses

Damages will also be awarded to cover the financial loss incurred by the claimant as a consequence of the injury.[5] These damages are awarded at the time of trial, and cover both past losses and expected future losses.

---

3 These non-financial losses are sometimes referred to as 'non-pecuniary loss'.
4 The parties and the court will refer to published guidelines that reflect the awards made in previous cases. See: Judicial College, *Guidelines for the Assessment of General Damages in Personal Injury Cases*, 15th edn, Oxford University Press, 2019. Note also that where the claim concerns a whiplash injury lasting less than two years suffered in a road traffic accident, the **Civil Liability Act 2018** provides for regulations to specify a fixed tariff of damages for pain, suffering, and loss of amenity.
5 These financial losses are sometimes referred to as 'pecuniary loss'.

Loss of earnings – past and future

Often the most substantial financial loss suffered by the claimant is loss of earnings. The calculation is based on the claimant's *net* loss – i.e., their salary after *deduction* of tax and national insurance (and any sick pay).[6]

The claimant's past loss of earnings, from the date of the injury to trial, can be precisely calculated as this is the amount of net earnings that the claimant has actually already lost.

Future loss of earnings is different. The court must assess the amount of earnings the claimant is expected to lose in the future. Since the future is not certain, the award for future loss of earnings is a matter for assessment by the court, rather than a pure mathematical calculation.

Having said that, the court's assessment will be *based* on a calculation prepared by the claimant to show the claimant's *expected* future loss. The calculation will be based on the claimant's annual loss (called the **multiplicand**). This will be multiplied by the period off work (called the **multiplier**).

The starting point for the claimant's annual loss is their current salary. However, where a claimant can provide evidence that they were likely to have achieved *promotion* to a higher salary, this can be taken into account. (Salary increases due to *inflation* are not taken into account here because inflation is considered as part of investing the lump sum; see below.)

The medical evidence will indicate how long the claimant is likely to be unable to work. This could be a limited period, after which the claimant is expected to return to work. Alternatively, if the injuries are such that the claimant can never return to work, it could be the remainder of the claimant's working life.

So, the starting point will be:

Claimant's net annual loss of earnings (multiplicand)	Multiplied by ×	Period for which unable to work (multiplier)

However, the sum of money resulting from such calculation is only a starting point, and it must then be adjusted.

---

6 Where the claimant has received social security benefits the defendant may be required to reimburse the state, with a consequential deduction of benefits from the claimant's damages. The recovery of social security benefits is administered by the Government Compensation Recovery Unit. Further details are beyond the scope of this book.

First, the court must take into account that the claimant will receive all of the compensation for loss of earnings together as a lump sum, rather than being paid their earnings periodically over a longer period. The claimant is assumed to invest the lump sum.

In normal circumstances, money which is invested earns sufficient interest so that, even taking into account inflation, it grows in value. So, to prevent the claimant from being better off, the court will reduce the lump sum to take account of such interest.

However, there are periods in which interest rates are so low compared to the rate of inflation that money invested falls in value in real terms. In these circumstances, the court needs to increase the amount of the lump sum to prevent the claimant from being worse off.

The assumed (positive or negative) rate of return on invested damages is specified by statutory instrument (modified from time to time).[7] In calculating the resulting adjustment to the lump sum, the court makes use of actuarial tables.

Second, the court must take into account the possibility that the claimant may not, in any event, have been able to continue in the same employment. This covers the possibility of events such as redundancy, illness, or accident (referred to as *the contingencies of life*). So, again, an adjustment is made to reduce the lump sum to reflect this.

In some cases, the claimant's injuries reduce the claimant's life expectancy. The claim for future loss of earnings will then include an amount for the wages the claimant would have been able to earn in the 'lost years' had they lived. However, calculating the claim in this way could lead to the claimant being overcompensated. A claimant who is alive spends part of their earnings on maintaining themselves. So, damages awarded to cover the 'lost years' in which the claimant is not expected to be alive are reduced by deducting a sum to cover the living expenses that the claimant would have spent on themselves during that period.

Other financial losses

A claimant is likely to incur other financial losses as a consequence of their injury – for example, medical expenses, extra travel costs, or costs for special equipment and home adaptations. Again, these may already have occurred prior to trial, or may be expected to occur in the future. The claimant will provide evidence of such losses and may recover them as part of the award of damages.

One example of financial loss that may be suffered as a result of personal injury is the cost of care, such as nursing care and help with household tasks, etc. A

---

[7] Made under the ***Damages Act 1996*** s.A1.

claimant can recover the reasonable costs of necessary care. Often, a claimant will pay for care services commercially. However, sometimes care may be provided by a relative or friend, free of charge. In this case, the claimant can still recover damages to reflect their need for care. It is important to note that the person providing the care does not themselves have a separate claim against the defendant for their losses in providing the care.

As noted above, the claimant must take steps to mitigate their loss, so expenses which were incurred unreasonably would not be recoverable. However, statutory provisions[8] apply to the costs of medical treatment: where the claimant pays for private medical treatment, the defendant cannot argue that they should have mitigated their loss by accepting treatment provided by the National Health Service (NHS).

10.3.3   Terminology – special and general damages

We have seen that past financial loss, incurred up to the date of trial, can be precisely calculated. In litigation these losses are referred to as **special damages**.

Other damages that cannot be precisely calculated and must be assessed by the court are referred to as **general damages**. We have seen that this covers damages for past and future pain, suffering, and loss of amenity and damages for future financial losses.

10.4   Damages on death

10.4.1   The effect of death on liability in tort

Suppose that a victim, A, has a cause of action in tort against B but, before a claim can be completed, B dies. What happens to A's claim in tort? Conversely, what happens if A dies before a claim can be completed? In these circumstances, the general rule established by statute is that the cause of action in tort survives.[9] If the tortfeasor dies, the cause of action survives against their estate. If the victim dies, it survives for the benefit of their estate. The victim may die because of the tortfeasor's tort or for some unrelated reason, but the rule is the same in both cases – the cause of action survives.

Now focus on what happens when a victim dies *as a result of* the defendant's tort. Look at this problem scenario:

> A car driver is seriously injured in a car crash caused by the negligence of a lorry driver. She is taken to hospital where she survives for one month, during

---

8   *Law Reform (Personal Injuries) Act 1948* s.2.
9   *Law Reform (Miscellaneous Provisions) Act 1934*. (As an exception to the general rule, a cause of action in defamation does not survive the death of either party.)

which time she is conscious and in pain. She then dies as a result of her injuries. Prior to her death, the deceased was employed as a lawyer. Her salary supported her husband and young children.

As we have just noted, the deceased lawyer's own claim against the lorry driver will survive for the benefit of her estate. In addition to this, further claims arise for her dependent relatives and for bereavement. So, in the sections below we will consider the following claims arising where the defendant's negligence causes death:

- The deceased victim's own cause of action surviving death
- Damages for loss of dependency
- Damages for bereavement.

10.4.2 Deceased victim's own cause of action surviving death

The damages to compensate for the deceased's personal injuries are assessed on the same principles as for a living claimant (with the exception of future loss of earnings – see below).

So, in our example, the deceased's estate should recover damages for her pain, suffering, and loss of amenity during the one month for which she survived. The estate should also recover any financial losses suffered during that period. This would include her loss of earnings for the period between the accident and her death.

However, damages awarded to the estate of a deceased victim differ from those of a living claimant in that statute[10] provides that there can be no claim for loss of income in the period after death. So, the estate cannot recover the deceased's future loss of earnings.

Returning to the example in Section 10.4.1, we can see that this would leave the deceased's husband and children without the financial support that she had been providing. However, they should recover this loss in their own separate claim for loss of dependency – see Section 10.4.3.

In addition, where the deceased's funeral was paid for out of their estate, damages can be awarded for those expenses.

It is important to note that no damages are awarded for death itself. So, if a victim is killed instantly – suffering no pain and incurring no property damage – they

---

10 *Law Reform (Miscellaneous Provisions) Act 1934*.

have not suffered any actionable damage, so there is no claim capable of surviving after their death.[11]

10.4.3 Damages for loss of dependency and for bereavement

Where a tort causes death, statute[12] creates a new cause of action for dependants, and for a very limited class of persons suffering bereavement.

These new claims can only arise if the deceased victim would have been able to pursue a successful claim themselves, had they survived. This means that the liability of the defendant towards the deceased victim must be established in the usual way.

Returning to our example in Section 10.4.1, any claim by the husband of the deceased lawyer for loss of dependency and bereavement would depend upon showing that she herself would have been able to pursue a successful claim in negligence against the lorry driver, had she not died.

Loss of dependency

Assuming then that a successful claim by the deceased could have been pursued, what is the content of the statutory claim for the benefit of dependants?

Statute provides a complete list of all categories of dependants eligible to make a claim.[13] These include those in the following relationships to the deceased:

- Wife, husband, or civil partner (including former wife, husband, or civil partner)
- Unmarried cohabitees living in the same household as the deceased immediately before death, provided they had been living as the wife, husband, or civil partner of the deceased for at least two years before death
- Parents and other ascendants (such as grandparents)
- Children and other descendants (such as grandchildren)
- Brothers, sisters, uncles, aunts, nephews, nieces, cousins.

The damages awarded are for loss of *financial* dependency. So, a person wishing to pursue a claim must show that they had a reasonable expectation of receiving a financial benefit from the deceased. For example, an adult child who received no financial support from the deceased would not have a claim.

A person who *is* financially dependent on the deceased but who does *not* fall into a category on the statutory list cannot make a claim. For example, an unmarried

---

11 For a case illustrating the limitations of the rules for awarding damages on death see **Hicks and Others v Chief Constable of the South Yorkshire Police** [1992] 2 All ER 65 (HL) covered in Chapter 22.
12 **Fatal Accidents Act 1976**.
13 **Fatal Accidents Act 1976** s.1(3).

cohabitee who is completely dependent on the deceased but has only lived with the deceased for one year would not have a valid claim.

So, to have a valid claim, a person must be *both* on the statutory list *and* financially dependent.

The claim for loss of financial dependency on the deceased is calculated by a method similar to that for loss of future earnings for a living claimant. The starting point is the deceased's net annual income – less the amount they would spend on themselves for their own living expenses.

This is then multiplied by the period of dependency. For example, a spouse might have expected support for the remainder of the deceased's working life. Children might expect support until the end of their education.

This calculation produces a lump sum which is the basis for the award. Where there are a number of dependants, one claim is made on behalf of them all. The court will assess the amount of their combined annual dependency and the resulting award will be shared between them.

In addition, if the dependants paid for the deceased's funeral, damages can be awarded for those expenses.

Bereavement

The class of people who can claim bereavement damages is very limited.[14] It covers only:

- The wife, husband, or civil partner of the deceased
- An unmarried cohabitee living in the same household as the deceased immediately before death, provided they had been living as the wife, husband, or civil partner of the deceased for at least two years before death
- Parents of a child under 18 (provided the child was never married or a civil partner).

It is important to note that a child cannot claim bereavement damages in respect of the death of a parent.

The award of bereavement damages is a fixed statutory sum, which is updated from time to time. It is currently £15,120.

Contributory negligence

We have seen that the rights to claim damages for loss of dependency and bereavement are both dependent on the validity of the deceased's own claim. This

---

14 See: ***Fatal Accidents Act 1976*** s.1A.

means that where the deceased was guilty of contributory negligence, the damages for loss of dependency and bereavement will be reduced proportionally.[15]

Benefits received on death

It may happen that a person claiming damages for loss of dependency or bereavement also receives a financial benefit they would not have received had it not been for the death. For example, they might receive a legacy under the deceased's will. The statute provides that such benefits are disregarded in assessing damages.

10.5 Injunctions

We have seen that compensatory damages provide a remedy for past torts (including their future consequences). So far, we have focused on single tortious events, such as a road accident causing personal injury. We have seen that, in such cases, the general rule is that damages are awarded in one lump sum to cover both past and anticipated future consequences of the tort which has occurred.

However, what happens when a defendant's tort continues? For example, a defendant builds a house that interferes with the claimant's right to light, so committing a continuing tort of nuisance. Similarly, what happens when the defendant's tort recurs? For example, the defendant repeatedly enters the claimant's land, so committing the recurring tort of trespass on each occasion.

In cases like this, each time a new cause of action arises the claimant has a new claim for damages. However, this is unlikely to be the remedy the claimant wants. The claimant does not want to wait until further harm occurs and then seek damages. The claimant wants a remedy which will stop the defendant from causing the harm. So, in cases like this the claimant is likely to seek the remedy of an injunction.

An injunction is an order of the court that directs the defendant to behave in a certain way. The most usual form of an injunction is one that orders the defendant not to do something (a prohibitory injunction). Less commonly, an injunction can also order the defendant to take some positive action to do something (a mandatory injunction).

Whereas compensatory damages look backwards, to compensate for torts which have already occurred, an injunction looks forwards to the future, to prevent tortious behaviour.

Note that an injunction is not available as a remedy for the tort of negligence (because it is not possible to order someone not to be careless).

---

15 For the defence of contributory negligence see Chapter 7.

A key feature of an injunction is that it is a discretionary remedy. A claimant who makes a successful claim does not have the right to demand an injunction. The court has a discretion whether or not to grant an injunction, and must be persuaded that it is an appropriate remedy in the circumstances.

A very common context in which injunctions are sought is in the tort of nuisance; and for that reason injunctions are covered further in Chapter 16, where the explanation is also applicable to injunctions in other contexts, such as trespass to land. Another common context in which injunctions may be sought is in the torts of defamation and misuse of private information. So, they are further mentioned in Chapters 19 and 20 dealing with those torts.

10.6 Causes of action other than claims in tort

As a final word on remedies, it is important to note that in some cases, where a remedy is not available in tort, some other claim might provide a remedy. For example, in product liability cases there may be a claim in contract rather than in tort. Similarly, some harms that fall outside tort law may have a remedy under the *Human Rights Act 1988*. So, for a lawyer analysing potential claims in tort, it would be important always to also have other potential alternative claims in mind.

Chapter 10 revision points

Remedies

Damages: Compensatory damages aim to put the claimant into the position they would have been in had the tort not occurred.

- Damages for personal injury – living claimant:
  - Financial loss – past and future
  - Pain, suffering, and loss of amenity
- Damages on death:
  - Estate – survival of deceased's cause of action
  - Dependants – statutory list and financially dependent
  - Bereavement – limited claimants and specified amount

Injunction:
  - An order of the court that directs the defendant to behave in a certain way
  - Discretionary remedy

Multiple choice questions for Part 6

1. A lorry driven negligently struck a pedestrian, Amelia, aged 27. She survived for one hour after the accident, during which time she was conscious and in pain, but she then died. Her funeral was paid for by her estate. Amelia had no children, spouse, or partner. Prior to her death, Amelia had been in full-time employment. Amelia's parents are wealthy and often lent her money. They now seek advice as to what claims, if any, may be brought against the lorry driver as a result of Amelia's death.

   Which one of the following best explains the advice that should be given to the parents?

   A. No claims arise from the death of Amelia.
   B. The only claim to arise from the death of Amelia is a claim on behalf of her parents for bereavement damages.
   C. The only claim to arise from the death of Amelia is a claim on behalf of her estate for the pain she suffered between the accident and death, and her funeral expenses.
   D. The only claim to arise from the death of Amelia is a claim on behalf of her estate for her pain and suffering up to death, her funeral expenses, and her future loss of earnings.
   E. The only claim to arise from the death of Amelia is a claim on behalf of her parents for loss of dependency since they fall within the statutory list of persons eligible to make such a claim.

2. A worker was seriously injured in a road accident caused by the negligence of a bus driver, who has admitted liability in full. Prior to the accident the worker earned a substantial salary from which he supported himself and his wife, and he had expected to work until aged 60. As a result of his injuries he can no longer work, and he is not expected to live beyond the age of 40. He is now aged 30, and his legal adviser is calculating his claim for loss of earnings from now onwards.

Which one of the following best explains the basis for this calculation?
(Assume that in each case adjustments will be made for the contingencies of life and investment of the damages awarded.)

A. Calculation of the worker's claim for loss of wages from now onwards should be based on the ten-year period of his current life expectancy. The calculation should be based on his net annual salary.
B. Calculation of the worker's claim for loss of wages from now onwards should be based on the ten-year period of his current life expectancy. The calculation should be based on his gross annual salary, less his own living expenses.
C. Calculation of the worker's claim for loss of wages from now onwards should be based on the 30-year period of his pre-accident life expectancy. For the whole period, the calculation should be based on his net annual salary.
D. Calculation of the worker's claim for loss of wages from now onwards should be based on the 30-year period of his pre-accident life expectancy. For the whole period, the calculation should be based on his net annual salary after deduction of his own living expenses.
E. Calculation of the worker's claim for loss of wages from now onwards should be based on the 30-year period of his pre-accident life expectancy. For the first ten years, the calculation should be based on his net annual salary. For the remaining 20 years, it should be based on his net annual salary after deduction of his own living expenses.

PART 7
Employers' liability and vicarious liability

11

Employers' liability

11.1 Chapter overview

This chapter deals with the employer's personal liability to their employees in the tort of negligence. A claim by an employee against their employer for injury, illness, or disease suffered at work follows the standard structure for a claim in negligence. The employee must establish:

- Duty of care
- Breach of duty
- Causation of damage.

The special principles applicable to employers' liability in negligence lie in the area of duty of care. This chapter examines the content of the employer's duty, dealing with the place of work, work equipment, the system of working, and competent fellow staff. It then explains the special non-delegable nature of the employer's duty.

This chapter does not re-visit the other elements of the claim (breach of duty, causation of damage, and defences) because they are fully covered in previous chapters. However, it is always necessary to complete the analysis of an employers' liability claim by considering those elements.

11.2 Duty of care

In the tort of negligence an employer owes their employees an **established duty of care**. So, an employer owes employees a duty to take **reasonable care** for their safety, which encompasses the following aspects:[1]

- Safe place of work
- Safe system of work
- Safe equipment
- Competent fellow staff.

It is important to remember that this is a duty to take **reasonable care**. It is not an absolute duty to ensure safety (see further Section 11.3).

---

1 See ***Wilsons & Clyde Coal Co Ltd v English*** [1938] AC 57 (HL) covered in Chapter 22.

DOI: 10.4324/9781003133698-19

The duty in relation to a **safe place of work** could, for example, cover features of the workplace such as lighting, tripping and slipping hazards, and hazardous substances.

The duty in relation to a **safe system of work** covers both setting up a safe system and ensuring that the system continues to be properly operated. It could, for example, require the employer to provide training for the employee, together with adequate supervision to ensure that such training is followed in practice. The employer's duty to operate a safe system of work can also extend not just to physical injuries but also to psychiatric illness caused by stress at work.[2]

The duty in relation to **safe equipment** could, for example, require both provision of personal protective equipment and ensuring that it is used.

The duty in relation to provision of **competent fellow staff** aims to protect employees from harm caused by those they work with. So, for example, it could cover selection of staff with adequate skills and experience, provision of training, and adequate supervision.

These are just some examples of the content of the employer's duty. Taken together these aspects of the employer's duty impose a positive obligation to take **reasonable care** to safeguard employees. The duty extends to taking positive steps to ensure safety (so, in this sense, an employer can be liable for an omission to act).

In the case of **defective equipment**, the employer's liability is even further extended.

> Suppose that an employee is supplied with a piece of equipment by his employer. The equipment contains a defect, caused by the fault of a third party (for example, the manufacturer). The defect causes an injury to the employee.

Statute[3] provides that, in such circumstances, the injury is *deemed* to be caused by the employer's negligence. This is despite the fact that the employer may, in fact, have taken reasonable care – for example, by purchasing from a reputable supplier. Note that the defect in the equipment must have been caused by *fault* on the part of someone (whether identified or not). The statute does not provide for liability without proof of fault. The purpose of the provision is to enable the injured

---

2 This is a complex area of law in which liability depends on whether the employer ought reasonably to have foreseen the risk of psychiatric illness to the employee concerned, and the steps the employer ought reasonably to have taken in response. See: **Walker v Northumberland CC** [1995] 1 All ER 737 (QBD); **Hatton v Sutherland** [2002] EWCA Civ 76, [2002] 2 All ER 1; **Barber v Somerset CC** [2004] UKHL 13, [2004] 2 All ER 385; **Hartman v South Essex Mental Health and Community Care NHS Trust** [2005] EWCA Civ 6, [2005] ICR 782.
3 *Employer's Liability (Defective Equipment) Act 1969*.

employee to pursue a claim against their employer, rather than against the third party whose fault, in fact, caused the defect.

11.2.1 Non-delegable duty

An individual employer, running a workplace, is likely to rely on its staff of managers and supervisors. Management of the workplace may be delegated, along with tasks such as selection, training, and supervision of staff, purchasing of equipment, etc. The employer may also rely on independent contractors for some tasks, for example, the installation of safety equipment.

Although the employer may delegate tasks to its own staff and to independent contractors, it cannot delegate the duty of care it owes to its employees. This means that the employer remains responsible for ensuring that reasonable care is taken.[4] For example:

> An employer employs a manager to run a new fast food outlet. It makes extensive checks to ensure that he is suitably qualified. The manager recruits an inexperienced teenager and puts him to work on the deep-fat fryer without any training. The teenager is burnt. The manager's failure to take reasonable care for the safety of the teenage employee will cause the employer to be in breach of its duty of care.

This is described by saying that:

- An employer owes its employees a **non-delegable** duty of care.

In the above example, the manager who caused the employer to be in breach of its duty was an employee. However, the same applies where an employer delegates a task to an independent contractor. Lack of care by an independent contractor may place the employer in breach of its own non-delegable duty. (Note: the employer is not being made liable for a tort committed by the independent contractor. The tort is that of the employer itself, in breaching its own duty).

11.3 Breach of duty

As usual in the tort of negligence, the claimant (employee) must show that the defendant (employer) breached its duty. The usual standard of care in negligence applies. That is:

- An employer is in breach of duty if it falls below a **reasonable standard of care**.[5]

---

4 See **Wilsons & Clyde Coal Co Ltd v English** [1938] AC 57 (HL) covered in Chapter 22.
5 Note, however, the specific case of defective work equipment (referred to in Section 11.2), where the **Employer's Liability (Defective Equipment) Act 1969** provides for the fault of a third party to be attributed to the employer, who is deemed to be negligent.

When determining what amounts to a reasonable standard of care, the standard which the employer must meet is that of a reasonable employer in the industry concerned.

11.4　Causation of damage and defences

Having established that the employer was in breach of its duty of care, the claimant must establish causation of damage in the usual way. It would then be open to the defendant to raise any applicable defences.

11.5　Other claims by employees

This chapter has dealt with the personal liability of an employer to employees in the tort of negligence. However, it is important to bear in mind that an employer can also incur vicarious liability for an injury caused by one employee to another.

Vicarious liability is covered in the next chapter. Under the principles of vicarious liability an employer can incur liability for a tort which is committed by an employee in the course of their employment. Since an employee owes an established duty of care to those with whom they work, an employee who negligently injures a fellow employee may commit the tort of negligence, for which the employer may be vicariously liable. So, when examining claims by an employee injured at work, it would be important to bear in mind both the employer's personal duty and their potential vicarious liability.

Finally, note that until 2013, in addition to a claim in negligence, an injured employee would often have relied on a claim for breach of the statutory duties imposed by health and safety legislation. However, statute now provides that such legislation is, in general, not actionable in a civil claim.[6]

Chapter 11 revision points

Employers' liability

Duty of care

- Scope
  - Safe place of work
  - Safe equipment
  - Safe system of work
  - Competent fellow staff
- Non-delegable

6　*Health and Safety at Work etc. Act 1974* s.47 amended by the *Enterprise and Regulatory Reform Act 2013* s.69.

After duty of care – complete analysis by considering:
- Breach of duty
- Causation of damage
- Defences

12 Vicarious liability

12.1 Chapter overview

This chapter begins by explaining what is meant by vicarious liability: the liability of one person for a tort committed by another.

It notes that vicarious liability most commonly arises in the context of liability of an employer for a tort committed by an employee in the course of their employment.

It also notes that this has now been extended to apply to torts committed by a person who is in a relationship 'akin' to employment.

So, the chapter is structured around the elements of vicarious liability:

- Tort
- Relationship – employment or 'akin' to employment
- Close connection between tort and relationship.

12.2 Introduction to vicarious liability

Consider this situation:

> A customer is shopping in a supermarket when an employee, refilling the shelves, carelessly drops a heavy box. The box strikes the customer and injures him.

In these circumstances, the customer is likely to wish to pursue a claim in tort against the supermarket, rather than against the individual employee (because the supermarket is more likely to have insurance). The principle of vicarious liability allows him to do so.

Vicarious liability is the liability of one person (in our example, the supermarket employer) for the tort of another person (in our example, the employee who dropped the box).

DOI: 10.4324/9781003133698-20

The most common example of vicarious liability is the liability of an employer for torts committed by employees during the course of their employment. So, we will focus on vicarious liability in the context of the employer/employee relationship. We will also see that this has recently been extended to include relationships which are 'akin' to employment.

For vicarious liability to arise the following must be satisfied:

- A tort must have been committed.
- There must be a relationship capable of giving rise to vicarious liability.
- There must be a sufficiently close connection between that relationship and the tort.

12.3 Tort

A claimant seeking to hold an employer vicariously liable must establish that the individual who injured them committed a tort. All of the elements of the tort must be established in the usual way. So, in the example above, the injured customer must show that the supermarket employee was liable to them in the tort of negligence.

A common factual situation in which vicarious liability arises is where one employee injures another. For example:

> Two employees are working together pulling a heavy trolley. One of them lets go of the trolley without checking, and the other is injured when the trolley runs away. In the tort of negligence, an established duty of care is owed by employees to each other. The duty was breached by letting go of the trolley without checking – a failure to take reasonable care. It is clear that the breach caused the damage.

In analysing a potential vicarious liability claim, it is important not to omit this first step of identifying the tort committed against the claimant and establishing its elements in the usual way.

Note also the fact that the employer is vicariously liable does not exonerate the tortfeasor. The employer is liable as well as the tortfeasor, not instead of them. So, the claimant could sue both of them, but could only recover their total damages once.

12.4 Relationship – employment or 'akin' to employment

A claimant seeking to hold an employer vicariously liable must establish that the relationship between the employer and the tortfeasor was capable of giving rise to vicarious liability.

The main relationship capable of giving rise to vicarious liability is that of employer and employee. However, recent cases have extended this to also cover relationships which are 'akin' to employment. So, we can summarise this by saying: an employer is not vicariously liable unless the tortfeasor was working under a contract of employment or 'akin' to employment. For example:

> A business owns a van whose brakes need repairing. The business does not employ its own maintenance staff, so it calls out a local self-employed mechanic. He repairs the brakes and is paid a fee for the job. The mechanic carries out the work negligently, causing the brakes to later fail, injuring a pedestrian. The mechanic is not an employee, so the business owner is not vicariously liable to the injured pedestrian for the mechanic's tort.

Compare:

> A business owns a fleet of vans and employs a full-time mechanic to carry out repairs and servicing. The mechanic repairs the brakes on one of the vans. He carries out the work negligently, causing the brakes to later fail, injuring a pedestrian. The mechanic is an employee, and the employer is liable to the injured pedestrian for his tort.

Sometimes it is clear from the facts that a person is (or is not) an employee (or 'akin' to an employee) – as in the two examples above.

However, the status of the tortfeasor may be disputed. An employer seeking to avoid vicarious liability may argue that the tortfeasor was not working under a contract of employment. In such a case, the court must determine the issue. Case law[1] shows that, to determine whether or not the tortfeasor was an employee, the court will consider a range of factors, including:

- Control: Did the employer tell the tortfeasor what to do and how to do it?
- Work equipment and materials: Were they provided by the employer or did the tortfeasor provide their own?
- Financial risk: Did the tortfeasor have any financial investment or financial risk in the work carried out?
- Payment: Was the tortfeasor paid regular wages? Was national insurance paid?
- Personal service: Was the tortfeasor expected to do the job personally, or were they free to delegate to someone else in their place?
- Integration: Was the tortfeasor's work an integral part of the employer's business?

---

1 See for example: ***Ready Mixed Concrete (South East) Ltd v Minister of Pensions and National Insurance*** [1968] 2 QB 497 (QBD).

None of these factors is conclusive by themselves – the court must look at the whole relationship.

Importantly, the label the parties have attached to their relationship is not conclusive. So, a contract for work to be carried out may designate the relationship as one of independent contracting parties rather than employer and employee; but if the above factors point to the relationship being one of employment, then the employer can still be vicariously liable.

We have already noted that vicarious liability now also extends to relationships which are 'akin' to employment. A relationship akin to employment is a relationship which is sufficiently analogous to employment to make it fair, just, and reasonable to impose vicarious liability. Case law[2] indicates that, in identifying whether a relationship is sufficiently 'akin' to employment, the following factors should be taken into account:

- The tort is committed as a result of an activity undertaken by the tortfeasor on behalf of the employer, and
- The tortfeasor was carrying on activities as an integral part of the employer's business activities and for its benefit (rather than as part of his own independent business), and
- The employer created the risk of the tort by assigning those activities to the tortfeasor.

The court may also consider the degree of control exercised by the employer over the tortfeasor, and whether the employer is more likely to have the means to compensate the victim than the tortfeasor. For example:[3]

> A prison authority requires prisoners to work during their sentence, in return for a nominal wage. A prisoner working in the prison kitchen negligently injures the catering manager. The prisoner has committed a tort, but is not an employee of the prison authorities. Nevertheless, the prisoner's work is an integral part of the operation of the prison. So, there is a relationship 'akin' to employment, and the prison authorities can be vicariously liable for the prisoner's tort.

12.4.1 Independent contractors

So far, we have seen that establishing vicarious liability depends on showing the necessary relationship between the employer and the tortfeasor. There must be a relationship of employment or 'akin' to employment. In contrast to this:

- A person is not vicariously liable for the torts of their independent contractor.[4]

---

2   See **Cox v Ministry of Justice** [2016] UKSC 10, [2016] AC 660, considered in **Various Claimants v Barclays Bank Plc** [2020] UKSC 13, [2020] 2 WLR. 960.
3   This example is based on **Cox v Ministry of Justice** [2016] UKSC 10, [2016] AC 660.
4   **Various Claimants v Barclays Bank Plc** [2020] UKSC 13, [2020] 2 WLR 960.

So, it is important to recognise when a person has been engaged to carry out work as an independent contractor (rather than under a contract of employment or 'akin' to employment).

- The distinguishing feature of an independent contractor is that they are someone who carries on business on their own account.

So, looking back to the examples considered in Section 12.4:

> A self-employed mechanic, in business on his own account, is engaged by a garage owner, in return for a fee, to repair the brakes on a van. He is an independent contractor, merely providing a service. When the work is carried out negligently, causing an accident, the garage owner is not liable for his tort.

> A mechanic is employed full time to service and repair vehicles as part of his employer's business operation. He is an employee, and when he carries out work negligently, causing an accident, the employer can be vicariously liable for his tort.

12.5 Close connection/course of employment

Establishing the necessary relationship between employer and tortfeasor is only one of the steps to establishing vicarious liability. There must also be a sufficiently close connection between that relationship and the tort which was committed.

Compare these problem scenarios:

> A factory worker is driving her own car to work. She is late and is driving too fast. Her carelessness causes an accident in which the claimant is injured. Clearly, there is no connection between the tort (negligence in driving too fast) and her employment. There are no grounds to hold the tortfeasor's employer vicariously liable.

> A delivery driver is driving his employer's vehicle, filled with parcels which he is delivering to various addresses. He is running late on his delivery schedule and so is driving too fast. His carelessness causes an accident in which the claimant is injured. Here, there is a clear connection between the tort (negligence in driving too fast) and his employment. The employer is likely to be vicariously liable.

As these examples show:

- A claimant seeking to hold an employer vicariously liable must establish that the tort had a sufficiently close connection to the relationship between the employer and the tortfeasor.

We usually refer to this by saying that the tort must have been committed during the course of employment – but remember that this now also includes relationships 'akin' to employment.

So, when does an employee act outside the course of their employment, and when do they remain within the course of employment? We can give some examples, drawn from case law as follows.

Carelessness
An employee who does their job, but does it carelessly, does not thereby cease to be acting in the course of employment. (We saw this in the example of the careless delivery driver above.)

Intentional wrongdoing
Employees who have carried out a deliberately wrongful act may still remain within the course of employment. For example:

> A staff member employed to care for children is guilty of sexually abusing them. The tort is closely connected with the work he is employed to do, so he is still acting in the course of employment.

Disobedience to instructions
An employee who fails to follow their employer's instructions and disobeys a direct prohibition may still remain within the course of their employment. Whether or not such disobedience places the employee outside the course of employment depends upon the nature of the prohibition. Does the prohibition limit the *scope* of the employment or just the *manner* in which it is carried out? Compare these problem scenarios:

> A bus conductor is employed to collect fares from passengers. The conductor is given an instruction – that he must not drive the bus. He disobeys this and drives the bus, and in doing so negligently causes an accident. It is likely that he is *not* acting in the course of employment so that the employer is not vicariously liable for his tort.[5]

> A bus driver is employed to drive buses. The driver is given an instruction – that he must not exceed the speed limit when driving the bus. He disobeys this and exceeds the speed limit. In doing so he negligently causes an accident. It is likely that he *is* acting in the course of employment so that the employer is vicariously liable for his tort.[6]

---

5 See ***Iqbal v London Transport Executive*** (1973) 16 KIR 329.
6 See ***Limpus v London General Omnibus Co*** (1862) 158 ER 993.

The difference between these two examples is in the nature of the instruction. Where an instruction limits the *scope* of the employment, disobedience will put the employee outside the course of employment (so, in our example, an instruction not to drive buses at all limits the scope of the conductor's employment).

Where an instruction only limits the *manner* in which employment is carried out, disobedience will not place the employee outside the course of employment (so, in our example, an instruction not to exceed the speed limit when driving the bus only limits the manner in which the bus driver's employment is carried out).

In analysing the facts of a case, it can be difficult to determine whether a particular prohibition limits the scope of employment or only the manner of employment. However, a significant factor is the extent to which the disobedient employee was acting to further the purposes of the employer's business. Where the prohibited conduct benefits the employer in some way it is more likely to remain within the course of employment.

These examples, based on decided cases, show us how some common employment situations have been dealt with. They should now be seen in the context of the overall test developed by the courts: the 'close connection' test.

Close connection test

Overall, the test which the courts have developed to determine whether or not a tort was committed within the course of employment is:

- Was the tort **so closely connected** with acts the employee was authorised to do that it may fairly and properly be regarded as done in the ordinary course of employment?[7]

In order to decide whether this close connection test is satisfied the court must consider the following:

- What functions or 'field of activities' were entrusted by the employer to the employee (i.e., what was the nature of the employee's job)? and
- Was there was a sufficiently close connection between the position in which the employee was employed and the tort for it to be right for the employer to be held liable?

This test also applies to determine whether or not a person in a relationship 'akin' to employment was acting in the course of that relationship, so as to make the employer vicariously liable for their tort.

---

7 See ***Various Claimants v Wm Morrison Supermarkets Plc*** [2020] UKSC 12, [2020] 2 WLR 941 covered in Chapter 22, and ***Mohamud v Wm Morrison Supermarkets Plc*** [2016] UKSC 11, [2016] AC 677.

Chapter 12 revision points

Vicarious liability

- Liability of one person for tort committed by another
- Most often: a tort committed by an employee in the course of their employment (and now extends to relationships 'akin' to employment)
- Elements:
  - Tort
  - Relationship – employment or 'akin' to employment
  - Close connection/course of employment
- Remember – a tort must have been committed before vicarious liability can arise

Multiple choice questions for Part 7

1. An employer engaged an independent contractor to design a production line. The employer took reasonable care to check that the contractor was competent. Despite this, when the production line was put into use, an employee suffered a serious injury caused by a design defect. An expert report shows that the design defect was due to the negligence of the contractor. The employee seeks damages for his injuries and wants to know against whom he should claim.

   Which one of the following best sets out the correct advice to the employee?
   A. The employee should claim only against the contractor. The employer is not liable because it took reasonable care to select a competent contractor.
   B. The employee should claim against both the contractor and the employer since both are liable.
   C. The employee should claim only against the contractor. The employer is not liable because it is not vicariously liable for the negligence of its independent contractor.
   D. The employee should claim only against the employer since the employer is liable instead of the contractor.
   E. The employee should claim only against the contractor. The employer is not liable because it delegated the task of designing and installing the production line to the independent contractor.

2. An employer provided safety gloves for employees working with hot metal. When gloves became worn out, the employer provided replacements on request, but had no system for checking that worn-out gloves were replaced. A new employee was given a pair of gloves but was not given any safety training, so was unaware of the system for replacing them. When his gloves wore out, he continued to use them. As a result of the worn gloves, he suffered a severe burn to his hand. He now makes a claim for damages against the employer.

Which one of the following best explains the likely outcome of the claim?

A. The employer is liable because by failing to provide safety training to the injured member of staff it has failed to comply with its duty to provide competent staff.
B. The employer is not liable because it has complied with its duty to provide a safe system of work and safe equipment by making the gloves available.
C. The employer is not liable because the injured employee voluntarily accepted the risk of injury by continuing to wear the worn gloves.
D. The employer is liable because the duty to provide a safe system of work also extends to taking steps to ensure that the system is operated properly.
E. The employer is liable because statute imposes liability on the employer where equipment provided for work is defective.

3. A customer was walking across a supermarket car park when an employee of the supermarket saw that a car, being driven by another customer, was about to collide with her. He quickly pushed her out of the way and saved her from being run over. However, she fell to the ground and broke her wrist. She now makes a claim against the owner of the supermarket to recover damages for her broken wrist.

Which one of the following best explains the likely outcome of the customer's claim?

A. The owner of the supermarket is not liable because the employee did not commit any tort against the customer.
B. The owner of the supermarket is liable because the employee committed the tort of battery against the customer.
C. The owner of the supermarket is liable because the employee committed the tort of negligence against the customer.
D. The owner of the supermarket is liable because the employee committed the tort of assault against the customer.
E. The owner of the supermarket is not liable because the employee was not acting within the course of his employment since he had no authority to push the customer.

4. An employer employed a tanker driver to deliver fuel to petrol stations. The employer provided comprehensive health and safety training for the tanker driver. Despite this, during a delivery of fuel, the tanker driver negligently lit a cigarette. This ignited the vapors from the fuel, causing a fire which destroyed the petrol station.

In a claim by the petrol station owner against the employer, which one of the following best explains the likely outcome?

A. The employer is not liable because the tanker driver was not acting in the course of his employment.
B. The employer is not liable because it could not reasonably have foreseen that the tanker driver would disregard the safety training.
C. The employer is liable because it owed a non-delegable duty of care to the petrol station owner.
D. The employer is liable because it is vicariously liable for the actions of the tanker driver.
E. The employer is not liable because it took reasonable care to ensure that the tanker driver was properly trained.

PART 8

Occupiers' liability

13 Occupiers' liability: visitors

13.1 Chapter overview

This and the following chapter cover the liability a person may incur where someone comes on to their premises and is injured by the dangerous state of the premises.

Occupiers' liability to persons who enter the premises as lawful visitors is covered here. Liability to persons entering as trespassers is covered in the next chapter.

In order to put occupiers' liability in context, this chapter begins with an overview of some issues which are relevant to both visitors and trespassers. In particular, it notes that the occupier's duties are governed by statute.

Then, turning to the liability of an occupier to their visitors, it first identifies the parties to a claim: who is an occupier and who is a visitor? It then explains the nature and content of the occupier's statutory duty of care to their visitors. It outlines how that duty may be discharged so that the occupier is not in breach. It notes that the usual principles for causation of damage apply. Finally, it considers defences.

13.2 Introduction to occupiers' liability

Look at this problem scenario:

> A man owns a house with a large garden. He invites some friends to a garden party. Unfortunately, one of the guests trips over a defective paving slab and breaks her ankle.
> - Would the householder be liable to the friend for her injury?
> - Would it be different if the paving slab had been recently laid by a building contractor engaged by the householder?

Suppose that a neighbour of the householder is not an invited guest at the garden party but nevertheless sneaks into the garden uninvited. She cuts her hand on some barbed wire.

- Would the householder be liable for her injury?
- Would it be different if she had only torn her trousers rather than cutting her hand?

These examples illustrate some of the issues of occupiers' liability which we will consider in this chapter and the next.

The special rules for occupiers' liability are established by statute:

- The ***Occupiers' Liability Act 1957*** ('the 1957 Act') applies to visitors.
- The ***Occupiers' Liability Act 1984*** ('the 1984 Act') applies to persons other than visitors.

It is important to understand the distinction between these two classes of people because the rules for occupiers' liability are different for each class.

- A visitor is someone whom the occupier has invited or permitted to be on the premises (such as the invited guest in our example). The 1957 Act applies to these visitors.[1]
- People who enter premises other than as visitors (such as the uninvited neighbour in our example) fall within the 1984 Act.

Usually, a person who enters premises other than as a visitor is a trespasser.[2] So, from now on, we will use the terms 'visitor' and 'trespasser' to distinguish between the two classes of people covered by the 1957 Act and 1984 Act.

13.3 Liability to visitors – introduction

Under the ***Occupiers' Liability Act 1957*** an occupier of premises owes a duty of care to their visitors in respect of dangers due to the state of the premises. We will begin by considering the meaning of premises and the state of the premises.

We will then consider the parties to the claim: who is an occupier of premises and who is a visitor. (The 1957 Act does not define 'occupier' and 'visitor'; they are defined by case law.)

Finally, we will examine the content of the occupier's duty of care to their visitors.

---

1 The 1957 Act also applies (with some exceptions) to persons who enter premises in the exercise of a right conferred by law, since the Act provides that they are to be treated as having the occupier's permission to be there for that purpose.
2 Strictly speaking not everyone who enters premises other than as a visitor is a trespasser. A trespasser is someone who is present unlawfully. They have neither permission from the occupier nor any other legal right to be on the land. However, a person who enters premises pursuant to a private right of way is not a trespasser because they do have a legal right to be there. However, they are not visitors because they did not rely on an invitation or permission from the occupier. So, they are non-visitors, who come within the 1984 Act. The 1984 Act also applies to people exercising certain statutory rights of access to the countryside.

13.4 Liability for the state of the premises

13.4.1 Premises
Premises includes the land itself (for example, a garden, campsite, race track, or field) and buildings on the land (for example, a house, shopping centre, or office block). The occupier's duty also applies to structures on the land (for example, a climbing frame or a ladder).

13.4.2 State of the premises, not activities on premises
The principles for occupiers' liability only apply to damage caused by the state of the premises (for example, an injury caused by a defective paving slab, a steep staircase, a broken light fitting, or a slippery floor).

Of course, in contrast to being injured by the state of the premises, a person may also suffer damage on premises as a result of activities carried out there (for example, a lorry manoeuvring in a supermarket car park hits a car). In this case, since the injury has not been caused by the state of the premises, the ordinary rules of the tort of negligence apply, rather than the special rules for occupiers' liability.

13.5 Who is a visitor?
We saw above that:

- A visitor is someone whom the occupier has invited or permitted to be on the premises.

For example, a guest invited for dinner or shoppers visiting a store would be visitors.

A person who goes beyond the permission given by the occupier may cease to be a visitor. For instance, a customer who leaves the public area of a store and goes into an area marked 'private' would cease to be a visitor. They would no longer be owed a duty under the 1957 Act (but they could be owed the more limited duty under the 1984 Act, covered in Chapter 14).

13.5.1 Visitors who enter pursuant to a contract
Often, people enter premises under a contract made with the occupier. For example, people pay to enter cinemas, theme parks, and sports centres. If such a person suffers damage caused by the state of the premises, they could sue in contract as well as in tort (but would only recover damages once). In these circumstances the 1957 Act provides that an occupier's implied contractual duty regarding the state of the premises is the same as the duty in tort. So, whether a claim is in tort or under the implied contractual duty, the outcome should be the same. (Of course, a contract might contain an express term dealing with the

occupier's duty, rather than the implied term. However, statute severely limits the freedom of occupiers to set a *lower* standard of care – see Section 13.9.2 on exclusion of liability.)

13.6 Who is an occupier?

Case law establishes that:

- The occupier of premises is the person who exercises control over them.[3]

For example, the owner of a house, who lives there with her family, exercises control and so would be the occupier.

Premises can have more than one occupier at the same time, where more than one person exercises control over them. In such a case, each occupier owes visitors a duty of care.

13.7 The occupier's duty of care to visitors

The duty of care owed by an occupier to their visitors is specified in the statute. The statute says:

- 'An occupier of premises owes the same duty, the "common duty of care", to all his visitors ...'.[4]

Do not make the mistake of misreading this as if the Act said that occupiers owe a **common law** duty to their visitors. What the Act does say is that an occupier owes the *same* duty of care to **all visitors in common**. (Before the 1957 Act, an occupier owed *different* duties to different kinds of visitors.)

The Act also specifies the content of the occupier's duty. The common duty of care is:

- A duty to take such care as is reasonable in all the circumstances to see that the visitor will be reasonably safe in using the premises for the purposes for which they are invited or permitted to be there.

Look at this scenario:

> Aileen is the occupier of an ancient castle which she opens to visitors. A visitor fell down a narrow, steep staircase and was injured. Aileen can show that the staircase was well lit and had a handrail, and that a sign informed visitors that it was steep. So, Aileen may deny liability by arguing that she *did* take reasonable care for the visitor's safety.

---

3   See **Wheat v E Lacon & Co Ltd** [1966] AC 552 (HL) covered in Chapter 22.
4   *Occupiers' Liability Act 1957* s.2(1).

Now that we have noted the content of the occupier's duty of care, we need to consider in more detail how the occupier can comply with that duty.

First, it is important to note the terminology used. In the above example, Aileen argues that she complied with her duty of care. This is often expressed (e.g., in the 1957 Act itself) by saying that the occupier has *discharged* her duty of care. For example, we will look at how the occupier may discharge (i.e., comply with) her duty of care by giving a warning of the danger concerned.

Where an occupier denies liability, it is important to distinguish between an argument that the occupier is not liable because they have discharged their duty of care and an argument in which the occupier admits that the duty of care was breached but relies on a defence. For example, suppose that Aileen had not taken any precautions to safeguard visitors using the staircase, so was in breach of duty, but she relied on the partial defence of contributory negligence. So, we will first consider ways in which the occupier's duty can be discharged. Then, later, we will consider defences.

13.7.1 Discharging the duty

An occupier discharges their duty by complying with the obligation to take reasonable care. So, an occupier may simply argue that, on the facts of the case, the precautions taken were sufficient to amount to reasonable care. Just as in the tort of negligence, a court will need to consider the degree of risk to which the visitor was exposed and the adequacy of the precautions the occupier took in response to that risk.

In addition, the Act also specifies some specific factors to be taken into account when determining whether or not an occupier has discharged their duty by taking reasonable care. These factors are:

- The amount of care the visitor could be expected to take for themselves
- The effects of any warning given by the occupier
- The use of independent contractors to carry out work on the premises.

The following sections consider each of these in more detail.

The amount of care the visitor could be expected to take for themselves

The occupier can take into account the extent to which visitors might reasonably be expected to look after their own safety. This applies to all visitors, but the Act goes on to give two specific examples:

Children: The Act specifies that an occupier must be prepared for children to be less careful than adults. This would mean that an occupier might need to take extra precautions to protect child visitors. For example:

In a garden to which visitors have access, it might be obvious to an adult that a plant was poisonous, whereas a child might be unable to appreciate this. Thus the only way for the occupier to meet the standard of reasonable care might be to fence off the plant to prevent children from accessing it.

Professionals: Where a visitor comes to premises to carry out their trade or profession, the Act says that the occupier can expect them to take their own precautions against special risks that involves. For example:

A builder called to premises to fix a roof might be expected to check that no lose roof tiles would fall and injure him.

The effects of any warning given by the occupier

Suppose that Aileen, the owner of the castle in our example above, had put a notice above a steep staircase stating: 'Danger very steep steps.' Would that enable her to argue that she had discharged her duty by taking reasonable care?

The Act provides that just giving a warning of danger, without any other precautions, is not necessarily sufficient to discharge the occupier's duty. Giving a warning is only sufficient to discharge the duty if the warning would enable the visitor to be reasonably safe.

So, in our example, the warning of steep stairs might not, by itself, be sufficient to show that Aileen had exercised reasonable care. In contrast, a warning which directed visitors to avoid the steep stairs by taking an alternative route might be sufficient to discharge the duty because it could enable visitors to be reasonably safe.

The use of independent contractors to carry out work on the premises

What if premises are in a dangerous state because of faulty work by an independent contractor? Suppose that Aileen had engaged a contractor to fix a handrail on her stairs but it came loose when in use, causing a visitor to fall. Could Aileen argue that she had discharged her duty by employing the contractor to do the work?

The Act provides for situations like this. That is, where an occupier engages an independent contractor to carry out work of construction maintenance or repair and the contractor's faulty work creates a danger that damages a visitor. An occupier is *not* responsible for the danger created by the contractor provided *all* of the following are satisfied:

- The occupier acted reasonably in entrusting the work to a contractor.
- The occupier took reasonable steps to check that the contractor was competent.
- The occupier took reasonable steps to check that the work had been done properly.

The question of whether or not the occupier satisfied these conditions will be dependent on the facts of the case.

For example, acting reasonably in entrusting work to an independent contractor will require the occupier to take care in selecting the contractor, and might (depending on the circumstances) require the occupier to supervise the contractor's work.

Taking reasonable steps to check that a contractor is competent could, for example, require the occupier to check that the contractor is properly qualified to undertake the kind of work in question. For example:

> The occupier of a hotel engages a contractor to renew the electrical wiring but does not check that the contractor is a qualified electrician. The contractor, who is not qualified, incorrectly wires a light fitting. A guest suffers an electric shock when turning on the light and is injured.

Here, the hotel occupier has not discharged their duty to the guest because they did not take reasonable steps to check that the contractor was competent to undertake the work safely.

The occupier must also take reasonable steps to check that the contractor's work has been done properly. The checks it is reasonable for an occupier to make will depend on the nature and complexity of the work.

For example, it might be reasonable to expect Aileen to check that a handrail was firmly fixed to the wall because this is something she could see for herself. So, if she didn't check, she might not have discharged her duty of care and could be responsible for the damage to the visitor.

In contrast, suppose that a contractor is engaged to install a lift, on which the brakes then malfunction, injuring a visitor. It might not be reasonable to expect the occupier to be able to check the contractor's installation of the brakes because of the complexity of the task. (Though, as we noted above, the occupier would still be expected to take reasonable steps to check that the chosen contractor was competent to undertake the work.)

13.8 Causation of damage

As always, when analysing a potential claim, it is important to check that all elements are satisfied. We have examined the duty of care owed by an occupier to their visitor. If the visitor can establish that the duty has been breached, the next element to be considered is causation of damage. Can the visitor establish a causal link between the damage they suffered and the breach by the occupier?

Just as in the tort of negligence, the visitor would need to show that 'but for' the occupier's breach the damage would not have occurred and also, that the damage was a reasonably foreseeable consequence of the breach, and so not too remote.

Assuming that a duty has arisen, that it has been breached, and that the breach has caused damage, the final element to consider would be possible defences.

13.9 Defences

In this section we consider specific defences that might apply to allow an occupier who has breached their duty of care to their visitor to nevertheless escape liability (in whole or in part). Chapter 7 explained the defences available in an action for the tort of negligence. Those defences are also applicable in occupiers' liability claims. So, this section just focuses on the specific application of relevant defences to occupiers' liability claims.

13.9.1 Contributory negligence

The 1957 Act does not make any reference to contributory negligence; but it is clear from case law that this defence does apply to occupiers' liability claims.

Contributory negligence is only a partial defence. It allows the claimant's damages to be reduced. It does not extinguish the liability of the defendant entirely. (See further Chapter 7.)

13.9.2 Exclusion of liability

An occupier may try to exclude their liability, either by displaying a notice on the premises or by a term in the contract under which the visitor entered.

Effective notice

The first point to consider (as discussed in Chapter 7) is effective notice. For a non-contractual exclusion notice, reasonable steps must be taken to bring it to the claimant's attention. For a contractual term, it must be properly incorporated into the contract. Also, the wording of the notice (or term) must cover the damage caused.

Statutory controls

The wording of the 1957 Act itself does envisage that an occupier might exclude their liability. However, where the defendant acts in the course of a business, this is now subject to important controls imposed by later statutes.[5] Those statutory controls are explained in Chapter 7. As noted there:

---

5 **Consumer Rights Act 2015** ('CRA') and **Unfair Contract Terms Act 1977** ('UCTA'). Where the CRA and the UCTA refer to limits on excluding liability for negligence, that term is defined so as to include a breach of the occupier's duty of care under the *Occupiers' Liability Act 1957*. See UCTA s.1(1)(c) and CRA s.65(4)(c).

- **Death or personal injury** caused by negligence – liability cannot be excluded where the defendant acts in the course of a business.
- **Other loss or damage:**
  - Where both claimant and defendant act in the course of business, liability for negligence can only be excluded if the notice (or term) satisfies the requirement of reasonableness.[6]
  - Where the defendant acts in the course of a business but the claimant acts as a consumer, an unfair notice (or term) is not binding on the consumer.[7]

Where the defendant does not act in the course of a business, these statutory controls do not apply.

13.9.3 Voluntary assumption of risk

The wording of the 1957 Act[8] expressly recognises that the defence of voluntary assumption of risk applies. This defence is explained in Chapter 7.

Chapter 13 revision points

Occupiers' liability – visitors

- *Occupiers' Liability Act 1957* – duty of occupier to visitors
- Liability – dangers due to the state of the premises
- Visitor – person invited or permitted by the occupier
- Occupier – person with control over the premises
- Duty of care:
  - Occupier owes a "common duty of care" to all visitors
  - Duty to take reasonable care to see that the visitor will be reasonably safe in using the premises
- Discharging the duty:
  - Care expected from the visitor – e.g., children
  - Warnings
  - Employing independent contractors
- After duty of care and discharge of duty – complete analysis by considering:
  - Causation of damage
  - Defences

---

6 *Unfair Contract Terms Act 1977* s.2(2).
7 *Consumer Rights Act 2015* s.62.
8 Section 2(5).

14 Occupiers' liability: trespassers

14.1 Chapter overview

Before beginning this chapter, you may find it useful to refer to the general introduction to occupiers' liability in Section 13.2, noting in particular that the occupier's duty is imposed by statute.

This chapter considers the liability of an occupier of premises to people who enter the premises other than as lawful visitors.

This chapter first explains the limited duty of care owed by an occupier to such persons. It notes the conditions that must be satisfied before such duty can arise. Then it explains the limited scope of the duty once it has arisen.

It considers the standard of care the occupier is expected to meet when a duty does arise. It notes that the usual principles for causation of damage apply. Finally, it outlines possible defences.

14.2 Liability to trespassers – introduction

As explained in Chapter 13, we will use the terms 'visitor' and 'trespasser' to distinguish between the two classes of people covered by the **Occupiers' Liability Act 1957** and **Occupiers' Liability Act 1984** ('the 1957 Act' and 'the 1984 Act').[1]

As a reminder, a visitor (owed a duty under the 1957 Act) is a person who is invited or permitted by the occupier to be on the premises. In contrast, people may enter premises as trespassers in a wide range of circumstances. Look at these problem scenarios:

> An uninvited guest gate-crashes a party at a house and is injured when he falls downstairs.

---

1 As noted in Chapter 13, the 1984 Act also covers some classes of people who are not trespassers (e.g., those exercising a private right of way).

DOI: 10.4324/9781003133698-23

At a zoo, a young child wanders away from her parents and enters an area which is closed to the public, where she is injured when she falls through some railings.

A teenager cannot afford to buy a ticket to enter a theme park, so he sneaks in without paying but is injured when he falls from a defective carriage on one of the rides.

In each of these cases the person who is hurt is a trespasser on the premises. (In the case of the child, she becomes a trespasser when she wanders into an area where she had no right or permission to enter.) So, in cases like this, the question of the occupier's duty is governed by the 1984 Act.

14.3 Occupiers and premises

The 1984 Act says that an occupier is defined in the same way as for the 1957 Act. So, we know that an occupier is the person who exercises control over the premises.

Similarly, as under the 1957 Act, the duty is owed in respect of damage caused by the state of the premises. The duty does not cover activities carried out on the premises (but, of course, a claim in the tort of negligence could cover such activities).

14.4 The limited duty of care

If you invite or permit someone to come on to your premises as your visitor you have voluntarily entered into that relationship with them. So, it seems reasonable that you should be under a duty to take care for their safety. However, the relationship between an occupier and a trespasser is different. Looking back at the examples in Section 14.2, should the occupier of a theme park owe a duty of care to a person who enters without paying? If a guest comes to a party uninvited, can the occupier be expected to take care for their safety?

The 1984 Act deals with these issues by placing two limitations on the occupier's duty of care to trespassers:

- A duty is only owed if certain preconditions are met. So, we first need to ask: *when* is a duty owed?
- If a duty is owed, the content of the duty is limited. So, we then need to examine: *what is the scope* of the duty owed?

When looking at an occupier's duty to trespassers, a common mistake is to only consider the three factors that determine *when* a duty is owed, and to assume that if a duty is owed the defendant is liable. This is a mistake because, if a duty is owed, it is important to go on to consider the *scope* of the duty and determine whether or not the defendant is in breach of it.

14.4.1 When is a duty owed?

Where a trespasser is injured by a danger in the state of the premises, the occupier only owes a duty of care if *all* of the following are satisfied:[2]

- The occupier is aware of the danger (or has reasonable grounds to believe it exists).
- The occupier knows that the trespasser is in the vicinity of the danger (or has reasonable grounds to believe he may come into the vicinity).
- It would be reasonable in all the circumstances to expect the occupier to offer the trespasser some protection against the danger.

If all three of these conditions are satisfied, the occupier owes a duty of care.

Look at this problem scenario:

> A large tree stands on land belonging to a farmer. The tree is old and its branches are in a dangerous condition, so the farmer has prohibited anyone from going near it. Despite this, local children often play under the tree and the farmer has to chase them off his land. Recently a child was sitting under the tree when a branch fell and seriously injured him. Did the farmer owe a duty of care to the child?

Clearly, the farmer knew about the danger from the tree, and that trespassers (the children) were likely to come into the vicinity. However, could he argue that it would not be reasonable in all the circumstances to expect him to offer trespassers protection against the danger posed by the tree? If that argument succeeded, he would not owe a duty of care to the child.

If that argument were not successful, so that the farmer was held to owe a duty of care, the next step would be to consider the content, or scope, of the farmer's duty to determine whether or not he was in breach of it.

14.4.2 What is the scope of the duty?

The occupier's duty to a trespasser is:

- To take reasonable care to see that the trespasser does not suffer injury from the danger on the premises.

This is a limited duty, as we can see by comparing it with the duty owed to a lawful visitor. For a lawful visitor, the occupier – having taken the positive step of inviting or permitting them to be there – has a positive duty to see that they will be reasonably safe in using the premises. In contrast, the occupier's duty to a trespasser is limited to avoiding injury.

---

2 For a case illustrating the limitations on when a duty of care is owed see ***Tomlinson v Congleton BC*** [2003] UKHL 47, [2004] 1 AC 46 covered in Chapter 22.

Warnings

The 1984 Act provides that the occupier's duty to take reasonable care to see that the trespasser does not suffer injury may be discharged by taking such steps as are reasonable in all the circumstances of the case to give a warning of the danger, or to discourage them from incurring the risk.

Damage to property

The 1984 Act expressly excludes damage to property from the scope of the occupier's duty. So, an occupier is not liable under the Act for damage caused to a trespasser's property. For example:

> A person entering a garden party uninvited cuts her hand and tears her trousers. The occupier might owe a duty in respect of the cut hand, but would not be liable for the damaged trousers.

So, to conclude on the issue of duty of care, look back at the example in Section 14.4.1 of a child injured by a dangerous tree. If the farmer *did* owe a duty of care, was he in breach of it? Did he fail to take reasonable care to see that the child did not suffer injury from the dangerous tree? Of course, we need to know more about the facts to answer this, but the farmer might argue that he *did* exercise reasonable care (for example, by constantly warning the children of the danger and chasing them off the land). If this argument were to be accepted, the farmer would not be in breach of duty and would escape liability.

14.5 Causation of damage

The principles for causation of damage in relation to trespassers are the same as those for claims by lawful visitors. So, the injured trespasser would need to show that 'but for' the occupier's breach the injury would not have occurred and also, that the injury was a reasonably foreseeable consequence of the breach, and so not too remote.

14.6 Defences

The general defences discussed in Chapter 7 may also be relevant to a claim in occupiers' liability, and you should refer back to that chapter for further explanation. In this section we will just outline issues of specific relevance to the liability of an occupier to a trespasser.

14.6.1 Contributory negligence

The 1984 Act does not make any reference to contributory negligence, but it is clear from case law that this defence does apply to occupiers' liability claims.

Contributory negligence is only a partial defence. It allows the claimant's damages to be reduced. It does not extinguish the liability of the defendant entirely. (See further Chapter 7.)

14.6.2 Exclusion of liability

In contrast to the 1957 Act,[3] the 1984 Act does not say that an occupier's liability to a trespasser can be excluded. This difference makes it unclear whether an occupier can effectively exclude their liability to a trespasser.

14.6.3 Voluntary assumption of risk

The wording of the 1984 Act[4] expressly recognises that the defence of voluntary assumption of risk applies. This defence is explained in Section 7.6.

14.6.4 Illegality

The defence of illegality may apply where the claimant was engaged in an illegal activity.[5] Of course, a person who enters someone else's land as a trespasser is not acting legally. However, it is important to appreciate that this does not mean that the defence of illegality automatically applies to a trespasser. This would be contrary to the purpose of the 1984 Act. So, the mere fact of being a trespasser does not give rise to the defence of illegality.

As explained in Chapter 7, for the defence of illegality to arise, the claimant must have been engaged in serious wrongdoing such that it would be viewed as offensive and unfair for him to receive compensation for the consequences of his own illegal conduct. So, the defence of illegality could apply where a trespasser is engaged in really serious wrongdoing. However, case law[6] suggests that even trespassing on premises with the intention of carrying out a burglary may not be serious enough to give rise to the defence.

> **Chapter 14 revision points**
>
> **Occupiers' liability – trespassers**
>
> - *Occupiers' Liability Act 1984* – duty of occupiers to persons other than visitors ('trespassers')
> - Liability – dangers due to the state of the premises
> - Occupier – person with control over the premises

---

3 Which allows for exclusion of liability, subject to the statutory restrictions explained in Chapter 13.
4 Section 1(6).
5 See further Chapter 7.
6 *Revill v Newberry* [1996] QB 567 (CA).

Duty of care

- No duty owed unless:
  - Occupier is aware of the danger
  - Occupier knows the trespasser may encounter the danger
  - Reasonable to expect occupier to offer some protection against the danger
- Where duty is owed, limited to:
  - Reasonable care to see that the trespasser does not suffer injury
- After duty of care – complete analysis by considering:
  - Breach of duty
  - Causation of damage
  - Defences

Multiple choice questions for Part 8

1. A local authority school held an open evening for parents. A worn carpet presented a possible tripping hazard, so a notice was displayed stating, 'Danger worn floor.' However, parents still had to pass over the area to reach the open evening. A parent who was late hurried in without watching where she was walking, tripped on the worn carpet and was injured. She now brings a claim against the local authority ('LA') as occupier of the school.

   Which one of the following best states the likely outcome of the claim?

   A. The LA is liable to the parent because it owed her a common law duty of care, which it breached, causing her injury.
   B. The LA is not liable because the accident arose due to a failure to repair the carpet, and no duty of care is owed in respect of an omission to act.
   C. The LA is not liable because, although it owed the parent a duty of care, it discharged the duty by giving a warning of the danger.
   D. The LA is liable in full to the parent because, as occupier of the premises, it owed her a statutory duty of care, which it breached, causing her injury.
   E. The LA is liable to the parent, but her damages are likely to be reduced because she was not looking where she was going.

2. An occupier of land knew that there was a building on his land in a dangerously dilapidated condition. He knew that local teenagers gathered there. So, he put up a prominent notice which read: 'Danger. Keep Out.' He also erected a substantial fence around the area of danger. Despite this, a group of teenagers climbed over the fence and entered the building. One of them was seriously injured when part of the roof collapsed. The teenager now brings a claim against the occupier.

   Which one of the following best explains the likely outcome of the claim?

   A. The occupier is not liable. The occupier did not owe the teenager any duty of care because the teenager entered the land without permission.
   B. The occupier is not liable. The occupier did not owe the teenager any duty of care because the statutory conditions for a duty of care to arise were not satisfied.
   C. The occupier is not liable. The occupier did owe the teenager a duty of care but has discharged the duty by the precautions he took.
   D. The occupier is not liable. The occupier did owe the teenager a duty of care, and was in breach, but can rely on the defence of illegality.
   E. The occupier is liable. The occupier did owe the teenager a duty of care and was in breach, and no relevant defence applies.

3. A father took his son, aged six, to a shop. Whilst the father was shopping, he carelessly failed to supervise his son. The son wandered off to the toy department, where children often went to look at the toys. In the middle of the toy department the son reached a cordoned-off area, where a notice read: 'No entry, installation of shop fittings in progress.' The son went under the cordon and entered the area. A heavy shop fitting, which had been left only partially secured to the floor, fell on to him, causing serious injury. The company that runs the shop seeks advice as to its liability to the son.

Which one of the following best represents the advice that should be given to the company?

A. The company is liable. It was in breach of its duty of care owed to the son under the *Occupiers' Liability Act 1957*.
B. The company is not liable. It owed the son a duty of care under the *Occupiers' Liability Act 1984* but was not in breach of that duty.
C. The company is not liable. The father is liable instead of the company because the father owed his son a duty of care and was in breach of that duty.
D. The company is liable in addition to the father. It was in breach of its duty of care to the son, but can recover from the father a contribution to the damages payable.
E. The company is not liable. The *Occupiers' Liability Act 1984* applied, but the statutory conditions for a duty of care to arise were not met.

4. A householder held a party at his home. A guest arrived in a car with an uninvited friend. The householder welcomed the friend and showed him where to park his car. The householder moved his own car to make space. Unfortunately, in doing so, he carelessly collided with the friend's car and damaged it. The friend's car was an extremely expensive model, so cost substantially more to repair than a normal car.

In a claim by the friend against the householder, which one of the following best states the likely outcome?

A. The householder is liable because he is in breach of his duty of care in common law negligence.
B. The householder is liable because he is in breach of his duty of care under the *Occupiers' Liability Act 1957*.
C. The householder is liable because he is in breach of his duty of care under the *Occupiers' Liability Act 1984*.
D. The householder is not liable because an occupier's duty of care does not cover damage to property.
E. The householder is not liable because the high cost of repairs to the car was not foreseeable and so is too remote.

PART 9
Product liability

15

Product liability

15.1 Chapter overview

This chapter examines possible claims in tort where damage is caused by a defective product. It begins by outlining the application of the tort of negligence to claims arising from defective products. It sets out the duty of care owed by a manufacturer to a consumer, noting the conditions that must be satisfied for such duty to arise. It then turns to breach of duty, noting that, since a claim in negligence is based on *fault*, the claimant must show that the defendant manufacturer fell below a reasonable standard of care.

Next, it notes that the difficulties faced by consumers in establishing such fault led to the introduction of the statutory regime of liability without fault in the **Consumer Protection Act 1987** ('CPA').[1]

The second part of the chapter examines claims under the strict liability regime of the CPA for damage caused by defective products. It outlines:

- Who may be a defendant under the CPA
- The definition of when a product is defective
- The principle of strict liability for damage caused by a defective product
- Possible defences under the CPA.

15.2 Why claim in tort rather than in contract?

A defect in a product may cause:

- Damage to the product itself
- Damage to other property
- Personal injury.

---

[1] For a case illustrating how a claimant may fail to establish a claim in negligence but succeed under the **Consumer Protection Act** see *Abouzaid v Mothercare (UK) Ltd* [2000] All ER (D) 2436 (CA), [2001] CLY 920 (CA) covered in Chapter 22.

DOI: 10.4324/9781003133698-25

In tort, only personal injury and damage to other property are recoverable. Damage to the defective product itself is classed as pure economic loss and is not recoverable in tort. However, damage to the product itself would be covered under a claim in contract. So, it is important to view claims in tort against the background of possible claims in contract.

Where the claimant is able to pursue a claim in contract, that claim can cover damage to the defective product itself as well as personal injury and damage to other property caused by the defective product. So, if a claim in contract is available, it is usually more advantageous than a claim in tort.

However, the rules of privity of contract mean that a claim in contract is usually only available as between the purchaser of the defective product and its seller.[2] So, usually, if harm is suffered by someone other than the purchaser, the claim must be in tort.

The need to claim in tort, rather than contract, may also arise where the seller of the product is insolvent or has ceased to trade. Where this happens, instead of pursuing a contractual claim against the seller, the consumer may consider a claim against the manufacturer. Since the claimant has no contract with the manufacturer, this claim would need to be in tort.

15.3 Claims in negligence

When considering a potential claim in negligence against the manufacturer of a defective product you should keep in mind the basic structure for a claim in the tort of negligence:

- Duty of care
- Breach of duty
- Causation of damage
- Defences.

So, turning to the manufacturer's **duty of care**: manufacturer to consumer is an established duty situation.[3] The manufacturer owes a duty of care to the ultimate consumer where:

---

2 However, be aware of the **Contracts (Rights of Third Parties) Act 1999**. This Act may allow a non-party to enforce the terms of a contract if the contract expressly provides that he may do so or if the term purports to confer a benefit on him, provided that the non-party is identified by name, or as a member of a class, or by description.
3 See **Donoghue v Stevenson** [1932] AC 562 (HL).

- The manufacture puts the goods into circulation intending them to reach the consumer in the same form as they left the manufacturer,
- with no reasonable expectation of an intermediate examination between the goods leaving the manufacturer and reaching the consumer.[4]

'Manufacturer' has been given a wide interpretation, so that a duty of care is also owed, for example, by those who repair or install products.

A mere supplier, who could not reasonably be expected to examine the product, would not usually be subject to this duty of care. However, there may be circumstances in which a supplier reasonably ought to examine the product before supplying it – for example, if the supplier has to assemble the product or if the product has an obvious defect the supplier could have seen. In those circumstances, the supplier could owe the consumer a duty of care.

'Consumer' has also been interpreted widely, so that the duty is owed to anyone who comes into contact with the product and suffers personal injury or damage to property.

The next element to be established for a successful claim in negligence is **breach of duty**. The consumer must show that the manufacturer fell below a reasonable standard of care. That is, the standard to be expected of a reasonable manufacturer of the type of product in question. However, an individual consumer may find it difficult to obtain evidence of a lack of reasonable care (for example, where the defendant has control over the manufacturing process to which the consumer has no access). Such difficulties led to the introduction of the statutory regime of strict liability, discussed below.

If breach is established, the claimant must then establish causation of **damage** in the usual way. It would then be open to the defendant to raise any applicable **defences**.[5]

---

4 We have used the words 'reasonable *expectation*' of intermediate examination. In ***Donoghue v Stevenson*** [1932] AC 562 (HL), Lord Atkin used the words: 'no reasonable *possibility* of intermediate examination'. However, subsequent case law suggests that the mere *possibility* of an intermediate examination would not be sufficient to absolve the manufacturer. There must be a reasonable *probability* that such examination will take place. In other words, a manufacturer would owe a duty unless they reasonably expected that the product would be examined before reaching the consumer.
5 For defences in negligence see Chapter 7.

15.4 Consumer Protection Act 1987 – strict liability

The **Consumer Protection Act 1987** ('CPA') established a statutory regime of product liability. Liability under the CPA is in addition to liability in the tort of negligence, not instead of it (see further Section 15.5, 'Which claim to bring').

- The CPA imposes liability where: **damage** is caused by a **defect** in a **product**.

'Product' essentially means goods, including component parts and raw materials.

15.4.1 Who may claim?

Any person who suffers damage caused by a defect in a product may claim.[6]

15.4.2 Who is the claim against?

A claim may be brought against:

- The **producer** of the product (usually, the person who manufactured it).
- A person who held themselves out as the producer by putting their name or mark on the product (usually referred to as an **'own brander'**).
- A person who imports the product into the United Kingdom in order to supply it in the course of his business (usually referred to as the **'importer'**).

In limited circumstances, a claim may be brought against the supplier of a product. In summary, this applies where the claimant is unable to identify the producer, own brander, or importer, and asks the supplier to identify those persons. The supplier must then either identify the producer, own brander, or importer, or provide details of the person who supplied the product to them. If the supplier fails to supply that information, the supplier becomes a potential defendant. This is often referred to as the **'forgetful supplier'** (since the supplier can avoid becoming a defendant by 'remembering' the above details). If the supplier does provide details of their own supplier or the producer, etc., this should enable the consumer to follow the supply chain and identify a relevant defendant.

15.4.3 Strict liability for defective products

The CPA imposes strict liability. This means that where a product is defective, it is not necessary for the claimant to show that the defect was caused by a lack of reasonable care.

However, although liability is strict, it is not absolute. It is not sufficient for the claimant to show that the product caused damage. The claimant must show that the product was defective, as defined in the CPA.

- A product is **defective** if: the safety of the product is not such as persons generally are entitled to expect.

---

6 Subject to the exclusion of certain types of damage – see further below.

All of the circumstances are to be taken into account, including any instructions or warnings given with the product. For example:

> A customer purchases a kettle and uses it to boil water. She suffers burns when she places her hand on the outside of the kettle. The court may find that the kettle was not defective because people would expect it to become hot during use.

15.4.4 Meaning of damage

As we have seen, the CPA provides a remedy for damage caused by a defect in a product.

- Damage means: personal injury, death, or damage to property.

However, the CPA excludes the following instances of damage. In the following cases compensation cannot be recovered under the CPA.

Low-value property damage

No damages can be awarded under the CPA for property damage which does not exceed £275.[7]

Business property

There is no liability under the CPA for damage to property which is used for business purposes.[8]

Not the product itself

There is no liability under the CPA for damage to the defective product itself.[9] (This is consistent with the position in the tort of negligence where, as noted above, damage to the product itself is classed as pure economic loss and is not recoverable.)

15.4.5 Defences

The CPA provides specific defences to a claim under the Act.[10] Key defences are outlined below.

---

7 CPA s.5(4). However, a claim in negligence might be possible in respect of such damage – see further below.
8 The CPA s.5(3) provides that the CPA does not impose liability for damage to property unless the property is both intended by the claimant for their own private use and also of a type usually intended for private use. In other words, damage to business property is not covered. (However, a claim in negligence might be possible in respect of such damage – see further below).
9 CPA s.5(2).
10 CPA s.4.

State of scientific knowledge
Under the CPA it is a defence for the defendant to show that:

- At the time when the product was supplied by the producer, the state of scientific and technical knowledge was such that a producer of goods of that kind could not have been expected to discover the defect.

This defence has been criticised as inconsistent with the strict liability imposed by the CPA. So, it is interpreted narrowly. For this defence to apply the state of scientific knowledge must be such that the possibility of the defect could not have been discovered. So, the defence could not be relied on where there was *known risk* that the defect could arise, even if the producer could not have discovered that defect in the individual product that caused the harm.[11]

Product not supplied in course of business
Under the CPA it is a defence for the defendant to show that:

- He did not supply the product in the course of a business *and* either:
  - He was not the producer (or 'own-brander' or importer) of the product, or
  - He was not acting with a view to profit.

Suppose, for example, that a man makes a home-made pie and gives it to friend as a gift. The pie is defective and causes the friend to suffer damage. In this example the defence could apply. The man is the producer of the pie; but he did not supply it to the friend in the course of a business, and he was not acting with a view to profit.

Compare the situation where a man enjoys baking and makes home-made pies which he sells for a small profit to fund his hobby. Here, the man is the producer of the pies. He does not sell them in the course of a business, but he does sell them with a view to profit. So, if a pie is defective and causes damage, he could not rely on this defence.

Product not defective when first put into circulation
It is a defence for the defendant to show that:

- The defect in the product did not exist at the time when it was supplied by the producer (or 'own brander' or importer).

So, this defence would cover a situation in which goods are manufactured and supplied without any defect, but a defect develops at a later time – for example, because of wear and tear whilst in use.

No exclusion of liability
Liability arising under the CPA cannot be excluded.[12]

---

11 See ***A v National Blood Authority*** [2001] 3 All ER 289 (QBD).
12 CPA s.7.

15.5 Which claim to bring?

As noted above, where a consumer has been harmed by a defective product, the starting point is likely to be a claim in contract, if available. This is because a claim in contract can cover all relevant damage, including damage to the defective product itself as well as damage to other property and personal injury. However, where a claim in contract is not available, it may be necessary to claim in tort.

In tort, a claim under the CPA is likely to be the starting point. This is because its strict liability provisions avoid the need to prove a lack of reasonable care.

However, as noted above, in some circumstances a claim under the CPA is not available (e.g., for low-value property damage and damage to business property). So, the claimant would then consider a claim in the tort of negligence.

Sometimes, the facts could give rise to a claim both under the CPA and in the tort of negligence. In that case, the claimant may bring both claims. However, even if both claims succeed, the claimant can only recover their damages once.

Chapter 15 revision points

Product liability

Negligence

- Duty of care: owed by manufacturer to consumer
- Breach of duty: fault based – claimant must establish that defendant failed to take reasonable care
- Complete analysis by considering:
  - Causation of damage
  - Defences

Consumer Protection Act 1987

- Strict liability
- Damage caused by a defect in a product
- Defect – the safety of the product is not such as persons generally are entitled to expect
- Defences – e.g., state of scientific knowledge

Damage to the defective product itself

- Pure economic loss
- Not covered in negligence
- Not covered under ***Consumer Protection Act 1987***

Multiple choice questions for Part 9

1. A café owner purchased a new coffee machine from a supplier and placed it on an expensive glass counter in his café. When first turned on, the machine overheated and cracked the counter top, causing substantial damage. An expert examination revealed that a component inside the sealed body of the machine had been negligently assembled in the factory, and this caused the overheating. The supplier of the machine is no longer in business, so the café owner wishes to recover damages for the broken counter top from the manufacturer.

   Which one of the following best explains the correct advice that should be given to the café owner?

   A. He should pursue a claim against the manufacturer under the *Consumer Protection Act 1987* because, under the statute, the manufacturer will incur strict liability for the damage to the counter top.
   B. He should not pursue any claim against the manufacture, since his only valid claim would be in contract against the supplier who sold him the machine.
   C. He should pursue a claim against the manufacturer in the tort of negligence because the manufacturer owed him a duty of care, which it has breached, causing the damage to the counter top.
   D. He should not pursue a claim in the tort of negligence because the manufacturer did not owe him a duty of care since it did not supply the product to him.
   E. He should not pursue a claim in the tort of negligence because the manufacturer did not owe him a duty of care since the damaged property was used for business.

2. A man bought a bag of dried pasta, branded with the name of the manufacturer. He cooked it and served it to his family. When his daughter ate the pasta, she broke her tooth on a small stone which had somehow got mixed into the packet of pasta during the manufacturing process.

Which one of the following best explains why the manufacturer of the pasta is liable to the daughter for her injury?

A. The manufacturer of the pasta is liable because, but for eating the pasta, the daughter would not have been injured.
B. The manufacturer of the pasta is liable because strict liability arises where a product causes injury.
C. The manufacturer of the pasta is liable because the injury from the stone was reasonably foreseeable.
D. The manufacturer of the pasta is liable because it put its own brand on the pasta.
E. The manufacturer of the pasta is liable because the safety of the pasta was not such as persons generally are entitled to expect.

3. A teenager was given a new mountain bike with an ultra-light metal alloy frame for his birthday. The first time he rode it, the frame snapped as he descended a bumpy track at speed. He was thrown from the bike and suffered a serious injury. Evidence later showed that the frame snapped because of a latent weakness in the metal, which the manufacturer's equipment was not capable of detecting. The teenager now brings a claim against the manufacturer under the ***Consumer Protection Act 1987*** ('CPA').

Which one of the following best explains the advice that should be given to the manufacturer as to its liability?

A. The manufacturer will be liable, unless it can show that the safety of its product met the standard that persons generally are entitled to expect.
B. The manufacturer will not be liable. It has a defence because the state of its scientific and technical knowledge meant that its equipment was not capable of discovering the latent weakness.
C. The manufacturer will not be liable because, given that its equipment could not discover the latent weakness, the product was not defective.
D. The manufacturer will have a defence, provided it can show that the state of scientific and technical knowledge meant that no bike producer could have discovered the latent weakness.
E. The manufacturer will be liable because the CPA imposes strict liability in such circumstances, so discoverability of the defect is not relevant.

4. A businesswoman purchased an expensive leather bag to carry her laptop computer when travelling for work. After only a short period of use, the bag strap broke as she was carrying it. The bag fell to the floor and the laptop inside was damaged. The retailer who supplied the bag has closed down. However, the woman has traced the manufacturer and has obtained evidence showing that the strap broke because of a failure to exercise reasonable care during the manufacturing process. The woman seeks damages from the manufacturer for the cost of repairs to the bag and the laptop.

Which one of the following best describes the advice that should be given to the businesswoman regarding potential claims in tort against the manufacturer?

A. The woman can claim for the damage to the laptop in the tort of negligence but has no claim for the damage to the bag, either in negligence or under the *Consumer Protection Act 1987*.
B. The woman can claim all of her losses under the *Consumer Protection Act 1987*.
C. The woman can claim all of her losses in the tort of negligence.
D. The woman cannot claim for any of her losses, either in negligence or under the *Consumer Protection Act 1987*.
E. The woman can claim for the damage to laptop under the *Consumer Protection Act 1987* but has no claim for the damage to the bag, either in negligence or under the *Consumer Protection Act 1987*.

PART 10
Nuisance

16 Private nuisance

16.1 Chapter overview

Chapters 16, 17, and 18 all deal with aspects of nuisance: private nuisance, the rule in *Rylands v Fletcher*, and public nuisance.

To put this into context, it is important to be aware that harms which amount to a nuisance at common law may also be subject to statutory controls. However, we will not discuss statutory nuisance since our focus is on claims in tort.

This chapter covers private nuisance, and begins by introducing what is meant by private nuisance: an unlawful interference with the claimant's use or enjoyment of land.

It first examines who may sue in private nuisance (who can be a claimant?) and who may be sued (who is the relevant defendant?). Next, it examines the elements of a claim in private nuisance.

Then, it then considers the possible defences to a claim in nuisance. Finally, the chapter outlines remedies for a claim in nuisance.

16.2 Introduction to private nuisance

A private nuisance is:

- An unlawful interference with the claimant's use or enjoyment of land.

Look at the following problem scenarios and in each one identify the interference with land and think about the remedies that might be sought. (Consider also how these interferences differ from the intentional and direct interferences actionable as trespass to land.)

> A householder in a busy city cannot sleep because a nightclub next door regularly plays loud music until late at night.

An extra storey is added to a tower block. The leaseholder of a neighbouring building complains that it blocks out the light entering the windows.

A factory processing fish emits a strong smell which is so bad that the tenants of nearby flats cannot open their windows.

In each of these examples someone is complaining about an interference with their land caused by a conflicting use of their neighbour's land. They could consider bringing a claim in private nuisance. The principles of private nuisance are the means by which the law of tort regulates conflicts that arise between neighbours over their use of land.

The interferences with use and enjoyment of land falling within nuisance can include:

- Encroachment – e.g., tree roots growing into neighbouring land
- Tangible damage – e.g., damage to plants by harmful chemicals
- Intangible damage – interference with amenity, such as noise or smells.

The fact that tort of private nuisance provides a remedy for interference with the claimant's land means that there is an important restriction on the type of harm covered:

- Damages cannot be recovered in private nuisance for personal injury.[1]

16.3 Who may sue for private nuisance?

Private nuisance provides a remedy for interference with land. So, in order to be able to bring a claim in private nuisance:

- The claimant must have an interest in the land affected.[2]

Clearly, a person who owns the freehold title to land will satisfy this requirement (for example, a person who owns and occupies a house).

A person who holds a lease or tenancy of land also satisfies this (for example, a company that holds a long lease on an office block, or a tenant who rents a flat monthly).

The holder of a licence granting them exclusive possession of land also satisfies this requirement and could sue in nuisance.[3]

---

1 Where personal injury is suffered, remember to consider the possibility of a claim in negligence.
2 *Hunter v Canary Wharf Ltd* [1997] AC 655 (HL).
3 See *Tinseltime Limited v Roberts* 2011 EWHC 1199 (TCC), [2011] CLY 2272.

Even a person who has exclusive possession of land simply as a matter of fact, without any permission to be there, may have a sufficient interest in the land to bring a claim in nuisance.[4]

However, a person who merely has permission to occupy land without having exclusive possession does not have a sufficient interest in the land to be able to bring a claim. For example, a person occupying a house solely owned by their spouse could not bring a claim. A child occupying a house where the tenancy was held by their parents could not bring a claim. A lodger renting a room in a house could not bring a claim.

16.4 Who may be sued?

16.4.1 The creator of the nuisance

The person who creates a nuisance can be sued. For example, a builder engaged to construct an extension on a house makes an unreasonable level of noise and works at unreasonable hours. The builder is not the owner of the land where the nuisance is being created, but he can still be sued by neighbours who are affected by it.

16.4.2 The occupier of the land where the nuisance occurs

Of course, the occupier of the land where the nuisance occurs may be the **creator** of the nuisance. For example, a householder who regularly plays loud music late at night is both the occupier of the land and the creator of the nuisance. However, what happens if the nuisance is created by someone other than the occupier? Can the occupier of the land be sued?

Nuisances created by persons under the occupier's control

The occupier can be sued if the nuisance is created by someone under his control. This could apply, for example, to nuisances created by his employees or by visitors whom he authorises to come on to the premises.

Nuisances created by independent contractors

If an occupier employs an independent contractor to carry out work which results in a nuisance, the landowner is *not* liable *unless* the nature of the work is such that it is inherently likely to give rise to a nuisance. For example:

> The owner of a multistorey building engages a contractor to carry out work on the ground floor. The work will inevitably cause noise and dust on the floors above, sufficient to amount to a nuisance. Here, the building owner can be liable for the nuisance created by the contractor whom he has engaged.

---

4   See ***Foster v Warblington UDC*** [1906] 1 KB 648 (CA).

Nuisances created by third parties or acts of nature

An occupier can also be sued where they have **adopted** or **continued** a nuisance created on their land by someone else.

- An occupier **adopts** a nuisance where they make use of it for their own purposes.

For example:

> A local authority installs a drain on land without authority from the occupier. Instead of requiring the removal of the drain pipe, the occupier uses it to drain the water from his land. If the drain becomes blocked and overflows, causing a nuisance to adjoining land, the occupier can be liable.

- An occupier **continues** a nuisance where he is aware of it and fails to take reasonable steps to bring it to an end.

This is particularly relevant where a nuisance is created on the defendant's land by an act of nature. For example:

> A naturally occurring hill on the defendant's land is eroded by the weather and begins to collapse on to the claimant's land.[5]

In cases like this, liability depends on whether the defendant has taken **reasonable steps** to deal with the nuisance. Since the defendant did not create or adopt the nuisance, they are only expected to do what would be **reasonable**, and this can take into account the resources they have available to deal with the nuisance.

In assessing whether the defendant failed to take reasonable care, the court will have regard to: whether the risk of nuisance caused by the natural occurrence could reasonably have been foreseen; the magnitude of the foreseeable risk; and the precautions the defendant ought to have taken to deal with such risk.

In assessing the precautions the defendant ought reasonably to have taken, the court will take into account the financial resources available to the defendant (as well as those of the neighbour whose land is affected). For example:

> A local authority owns land on which a line of trees is growing close to the boundary with neighbouring land. The tree roots have gradually grown over the boundary, encroaching beneath the neighbour's land and causing subsidence to buildings located there. The question of whether or not the local authority is liable for the damage depends on whether it took reasonable care. So, the court will consider whether the damage from the tree roots was reasonably foreseeable, and, if so, what steps ought reasonably to have been taken to deal with it.

---

5   See *Leakey v National Trust* [1980] QB 485 (CA).

16.4.3 Landlords

A landlord who has let premises and parted with possession is not liable for a nuisance created by the tenant (unless the purpose for which the premises were let was likely to cause a nuisance).

However, where a nuisance already exists on the premises before the premises are let to a tenant, the landlord can continue to be liable (otherwise a landlord would be able to escape liability in nuisance by letting the premises to someone else).

Also, where a nuisance is caused by premises falling into disrepair, the landlord can be liable if they had a duty or a power to carry out repairs to the premises.

16.5 Continuing state of affairs

For a claim in nuisance there must be a continuing state of affairs, not just a single event. For example:

> A householder demolishes a wooden building on their property, and then burns all the wood on a bonfire. The resulting smoke drifts across a neighbour's garden whilst the fire is burning. After a few hours, the fire burns out and the smoke ceases.

This is not a continuing state of affairs, so the neighbour would not have a claim in nuisance. (Compare this with the situation in which a householder regularly creates smoke by burning a garden bonfire every week. Here, there is a continuing state of affairs, which could be actionable in nuisance.)

16.6 Intangible damage – interference with amenity

As noted above, one of the forms in which private nuisance may arise is intangible damage from things such as smoke, smells, and noise that interfere with the claimant's amenity in using and enjoying their land.

Where the claim in nuisance is based upon intangible amenity damage, the law has to balance conflicting rights. That is, the right of the defendant to use their land as they wish, and the rights of neighbouring landowners not to suffer interference. The law must strike a balance between these conflicting rights, and it does this by holding that an interference is unlawful if it is **unreasonable**.[6]

---

6   See ***Bamford v Turnley*** (1862) 3 B & S 66; ***Sedleigh-Denfield v O'Callaghan*** [1940] AC 880 (HL); and, for an illustrative case, see ***Coventry v Lawrence*** [2014] UKSC 13, [2014] AC 822 covered in Chapter 22.

So, whether or not intangible amenity damage is sufficient to constitute an actionable nuisance depends upon a range of factors used to determine whether the interference is unreasonable.

16.6.1 Reasonableness factors

Substantial interference

For an interference to be unreasonable it must be substantial. That is, something which any ordinary person occupying the affected property would find to be a substantial interference with their comfort and convenience.

Character of the neighbourhood

What is reasonable will differ according to the character of the neighbourhood where the activities are taking place. For example:

> A defendant uses their land as the location for a nightclub that plays loud music every evening. The music disturbs the occupiers of neighbouring residential premises.

If the nightclub is situated in a busy city centre, this may not be an unreasonable use of the land, since people who live in a city centre should expect to encounter this kind of noise. On the other hand, if the same nightclub, making the same noise, were to be located in a quiet country village, this could be an unreasonable use of the land – so leading to successful claims in nuisance by neighbours who were disturbed.

Intensity and duration

In assessing whether the defendant's use of land is unreasonable, the court will have regard to the intensity of the disturbance caused to neighbours as well as the duration of the disturbance. For example:

> A defendant needs to demolish a building on their land. The work is extremely noisy but only lasts for two days. This intense disturbance over a very short period may not amount to an actionable nuisance.

> A defendant wishes to carry out essential building works on their land, which will inevitably create loud noise at times. The builder restricts his work to reasonable hours on weekdays only so as to reduce the intensity of the interference. The work lasts for six weeks. This less intense disturbance over a longer period may not amount to an actionable nuisance.

Abnormal sensitivity of the claimant

Whether or not the defendant's use of land is reasonable is measured against the standards of ordinary people living as neighbours. If the defendant's activities only affect their neighbour's premises because the neighbour is abnormally sensitive, this may not amount to a nuisance. For example:

> Two businesses occupy neighbouring buildings on an industrial estate. One of the businesses specialises in making sound recordings which require exceptionally delicate tuning of electronic equipment. The neighbouring business is a wholesaler and receives regular deliveries of goods. The sound recording business complains that vibration from the wholesaler's delivery vehicles interferes with the tuning of their electronic equipment.

If the delivery vehicles would *not* interfere with the ordinary use of a building situated on an industrial estate, there may be no actionable nuisance.

On the other hand, if the interference from delivery vehicles is so bad that it would adversely affect any ordinary normal use of neighbouring land, then it could amount to a nuisance. (So, in these circumstances, once it has been established that the interference does amount to a nuisance, the sound recording business could then recover damages for the interference with their equipment.)

Malice on the part of the defendant

If the defendant acts maliciously – carrying out an activity on his land in order to cause annoyance or interference with the claimant's land – then it is likely that this will be an unreasonable use, amounting to an actionable nuisance. For example:

> A householder objects to the breeding of animals for fur. Her neighbour runs a small business breeding rabbits for their fur. The householder deliberately makes a lot of noise on her land, intending to frighten the rabbits and stop them from breeding.

This is likely to be an actionable nuisance. This is so even if the same noise made for a legitimate purpose, in the ordinary use of the householder's land, would not be unreasonable.

Is negligence a factor?

If the defendant's actions on his land have resulted in the creation of an unreasonable interference with the claimant's land, then the fact that the defendant took reasonable care will not excuse him. This is because, rather than assessing the standard of the defendant's behaviour, nuisance assesses the reasonableness of the interference. For example:

> The operator of a factory processing fish takes all reasonably possible steps to reduce the smell emitted from the factory. Despite this, if the irreducible

minimum smell which is emitted still amounts to an unreasonable interference with neighbouring land, the factory operator can be liable in nuisance.

However, compare this with the situation in which a landowner is faced with a nuisance he did not create. As noted in Section 16.4 ('Who may be sued?'), where a nuisance is created on the defendant's land by a third party or an act of nature, the defendant is only liable where he has **continued** the nuisance by failing to take reasonable steps to bring it to an end. So, in these circumstances, liability does depend on the defendant's exercise of reasonable care.

16.6.2 Factors that do not excuse a nuisance

Case law shows that defendants have sought to rely on certain arguments to defeat a claim in nuisance which the courts have held not to be a valid excuse. These are planning permission and coming to a nuisance.

Planning permission

Look at these two problem scenarios:

> A farmer obtains planning permission to extend his pig farm by constructing extra pig shelters closer to his boundary with neighbouring land. Once the new shelters are built, the neighbours complain that the smell from the pigs has substantially increased and is interfering with their use of their land.

Does the fact that planning permission was granted mean that the farmer's use of his land is not an actionable nuisance?

> A business man buys a house and obtains planning permission to convert it to a bar and restaurant. When the new bar and restaurant is opened the occupiers of neighbouring properties complain about interference from the noise.

Does the fact that planning permission was granted mean that the businessman's use of his land is not an actionable nuisance?

The answer in each case is that a grant of planning permission does not authorise a nuisance. So, if a defendant makes an unreasonable use of their land which interferes with the comfort and convenience of neighbouring occupiers, the fact that planning permission was granted for that use does not exonerate the defendant. He can still be liable in nuisance.

Coming to a nuisance

Look at this problem scenario:

> A musician owns a house and, until recently, used an upstairs room as a recording studio. The house is situated next to a small factory that uses heavy

machinery, causing vibrations. Until now, this has not caused any concern to the musician. However, recently, he built an extension to his house and moved his recording studio downstairs into the new extension. He now complains that the vibrations interfere with his music recording and are damaging the foundations of the extension. Given that the factory owner's activities were in existence before the musician moved his recording studio into the vicinity, can the factory owner escape liability?

The answer here is that a defendant is not excused from liability in nuisance just because they were already carrying out the activity before the claimant came to the land affected by it.[7]

16.6.3 Proof of damage

An essential element of a claim in private nuisance is that the claimant has suffered damage.

Where the complaint is one of intangible amenity damage, the damage consists of the interference with the claimant's comfort and convenience in using their land.

So, proof that such interference has occurred is sufficient. The claimant does not need to go further and prove that any injury to health or financial or physical damage has been suffered.

16.7 Tangible damage and encroachment

As noted above, a claim in nuisance may also be based on:

- encroachment on to the claimant's land or
- tangible damage to the land (including things on the land, such as buildings and plants).

A landowner does not have the right to inflict this kind of damage on land belonging to another. So, where the interference with land is caused by encroachment or tangible damage, it is not usually relevant to consider whether or not that interference is reasonable.

---

[7] See, for example, **Sturges v Bridgman** (1879) 11 Ch D 852 (CA). However, in **Coventry v Lawrence** [2014] UKSC 13, [2014] AC 822 the Supreme Court suggested that the position might be different where the nuisance consists only of amenity damage (such as noise) and the defendant's existing activity only became a nuisance because the claimant changed the use of their land. In this case, the existing activity might form part of the character of the neighbourhood.

In particular, the character of the neighbourhood is not considered.[8] So, for example:

> A defendant whose factory has emitted noxious fumes causing the claimant's neighbouring trees to die is not excused by the fact that the claimant's land is situated in an industrial area.

As an exception, however, the reasonableness of the defendant's conduct does become relevant where the encroachment or tangible damage is caused by something naturally occurring on the defendant's land. As noted in Section 16.4 ('Who may be sued?'), where a nuisance is caused by something naturally occurring on the land, the defendant is not under an absolute duty to prevent it. Instead, the defendant is only liable if they have failed to take reasonable care to deal with the naturally occurring nuisance.[9]

16.7.1 Proof of damage

We have seen that an essential element of a claim in private nuisance is that the claimant has suffered damage. So, where the complaint is of tangible damage to the claimant's land, the claimant must prove that such damage has occurred. Where the claimant complains of an encroachment on to their land, proof that the encroachment has occurred is sufficient, since it is presumed that the encroachment causes damage.

16.8 Causation and remoteness of damage

We have noted that a claimant in private nuisance needs to prove damage, as an essential element of the tort. So, the claimant must establish a causal link between the defendant's conduct and the damage suffered.

However, even where factual causation is established, damage will not be recoverable if it is too remote a consequence of the defendant's tort. The test for remoteness of damage is one of reasonable foreseeability:

- Damage which was not a reasonably foreseeable consequence of the nuisance created by the defendant is too remote and so not recoverable.[10]

16.9 Defences to nuisance

Where the claimant is able to establish that the defendant has caused a nuisance, the defendant may nevertheless seek to escape liability by relying on one of the following defences: consent, statutory authority, or prescription.

---

8 See **St. Helen's Smelting Company v Tipping** (1865) 11 HLC 642, on which the following example is based.
9 See **Leakey v National Trust** [1980] QB 485 (CA).
10 **Cambridge Water Co Ltd v Eastern Counties Leather Plc** [1994] 2 AC 264 (HL).

16.9.1 Consent

A defendant carrying out an activity on their land will not be liable in nuisance if the occupiers of the land affected by the activity have given their consent to it. For example:

> A businessman purchases the top-storey flat in a block of flats. He wishes to carry out extensive renovations, which will inevitably cause a lot of noise and dust. He contacts the occupiers of the flats likely to be affected and negotiates an agreed duration for the works and acceptable working hours.

This would avoid claims in nuisance by the affected occupiers in respect of the works to which they gave their consent.

16.9.2 Statutory authority

Look at this problem scenario:

> A local authority is authorised by statute to construct and operate a waste disposal incineration plant. Pursuant to the statutory authority, land is purchased, and the plant is built and put into operation. The owner of a hotel located next to the new plant complains that the plant emits bad smells and smoke, which is interfering with the use and enjoyment of the hotel, causing it to lose business. The local authority may seek to rely on statutory authority as a defence to the claim.

The fact that activities on land have been authorised by statute can provide a defence to claims in nuisance. For the statute to operate as a defence, the activities must fall within the scope of the authority conferred by the statute. They must also be carried out taking reasonable care.

16.9.3 Prescription

Where activities on the defendant's land have caused a nuisance to neighbouring land for more than 20 years, the defendant's land may have the benefit of a prescriptive right over the neighbouring land to carry out the activity in question.[11] This would then be a defence to a claim in nuisance in respect of that activity.

For such a right to arise, the activity must have been carried out without force, without secrecy, and without permission. If objections are raised to the activity but they are disregarded and the activity carried on, the prescriptive right cannot be established because the activity is then being carried on by force.

---

11 The land affected by the nuisance may have been owned and occupied by different people during the 20-year period. See: *Peires v Bickerton's Aerodromes Ltd* [2016] EWHC 560 (Ch).

A prescriptive right to commit a nuisance can only arise if the activity has amounted to an actionable nuisance throughout the 20 years. So, a defendant may be carrying on activities which would amount to a nuisance, but the 20-year period does not begin to run until the neighbouring occupier is actually affected by the activities and suffers damage.[12]

16.10 Remedies for private nuisance

16.10.1 Damages

In private nuisance the function of an award of damages is to compensate the claimant for the effects of the nuisance on their land.

Where the effect of the nuisance is to reduce the value of the land, the claimant should recover damages for that diminution in value. For example, where the nuisance takes the form of tangible damage to the land or encroachment on to the land, damages should reflect the difference between the original value of the land and the reduced value after the interference. This measure of damages could also apply in a case of intangible amenity damage where the damage has been so serious as to cause a reduction in the value of the land.

In other cases of intangible amenity damage, where the effect of the nuisance is just to interfere with comfort and convenience in the use and enjoyment of the land, damages will be assessed to reflect this loss of amenity.

Where the nuisance has interfered with the claimant's ability to use the land for their business, damages can also cover the financial loss caused (provided that the damage is not too remote, as explained above).

16.10.2 Injunctions

Whereas an award of damages may compensate for harm already caused, claimants in a nuisance action very often seek a remedy which will prevent the defendant from causing harm in the future. This is the remedy of an injunction.

An injunction is an order of the court that directs the defendant to behave in a certain way. The most usual form of an injunction is one that orders the defendant to stop doing something (a prohibitory injunction). More rarely, it may take the form of an order requiring the defendant to take some positive action (a mandatory injunction).

Usually, the defendant has already begun to commit the tort and the claimant wants an injunction to prevent it from continuing. However, it is also possible for

---

12 See, for example, *Sturges v Bridgman* (1879) 11 Ch D 852 (CA).

an injunction to be granted where a future tort is likely to occur. This kind of injunction (called a *quia timet* injunction) will only be granted where there is an imminent danger of serious damage.

Discretion

An injunction is a discretionary remedy. So, the court must decide whether or not to grant an injunction, taking into account all of the circumstances – including the conduct of the claimant themselves. For example:

> The defendant begins to build a house which will interfere with the claimant's right to light, so committing the tort of nuisance. Instead of objecting immediately, the claimant waits until the building is completed. Then he begins negotiations with a view to a financial settlement. Only when negotiations break down does he begin proceedings for an injunction to force the defendant to demolish the house. Taking into account all of these circumstances, the court, in the exercise of its discretion, is likely to refuse to grant the injunction.

Where the court has the power to grant an injunction but, in the exercise of its discretion, decides not to do so, it may award damages instead.

These damages, granted in lieu of an injunction, can compensate the claimant for future recurring or continuing harm that the injunction would have prevented had it been granted. Of course, where damages are granted in lieu of an injunction, the claimant has not succeeded in stopping the defendant from causing harm. However, the claimant will be compensated now for likely future damage, rather than having to bring a new claim each time fresh harm occurs. The disadvantage for the claimant is that the defendant is, in effect, able to continue with the harmful conduct in return for the payment of damages.

So, in summary, an injunction is a powerful remedy whose effect is to stop the defendant from causing harm to the claimant. However, it is a discretionary remedy, and the court must be satisfied that grant of an injunction is appropriate.[13]

16.10.3 Abatement

Instead of seeking a remedy by pursuing a legal claim against the defendant, a claimant might take action themselves to stop the nuisance. This is the self-help remedy of abatement. However, this is a very limited remedy because it carries a risk that the landowner seeking to stop the nuisance might themselves commit a tort – for example, trespass to their neighbour's land. So, in practice, it is of very limited application. One context in which it might be used is where a landowner cuts back

---

13 For further discussion see ***Coventry v Lawrence*** [2014] UKSC 13, [2014] AC 822.

branches from his neighbour's trees which are overhanging his land.[14] (However, he is not entitled to keep the branches because they belong to his neighbour.)

16.11 Nuisance, trespass, and negligence – which claim to bring?

We have seen that the tort of nuisance protects rights in land. Rights in land are also protected by the tort of trespass to land.[15] Trespass is an unlawful interference with the claimant's possession of land. It is intentional and direct. So, if you were analysing a dispute concerning land, how would you decide which tort would be applicable: nuisance or trespass? You would also need to take into account the possibility of a claim in negligence, where tangible damage has been caused by a lack of reasonable care.

Look at the following problem scenarios. What claims would you advise the party who suffers harm to pursue?

> Neighbouring properties (owned by Tom and Mary) are separated by a line of trees planted on Tom's side of the boundary and belonging to him. The tree branches have grown over the boundary and are now overshadowing Mary's garden. She objects and wants Tom to cut them back.

> Neighbouring properties (owned by Mike and Jean) are separated by an old fence, belonging to Mike. He replaces the old fence with a new one. However, Jean objects, claiming that the new fence has been erected in the wrong place so that it now stands on her property.

> Neighbouring properties (owned by Dhruv and Alisha) are separated by a wooden fence erected on Dhruv's side of the boundary and belonging to him. Alisha is burning rubbish in her garden when she carelessly allows the fire to get out of control, and it badly damages Dhruv's fence. Alisha regularly burns rubbish in her garden, and this often causes smoke to drift over Dhruv's, garden making it impossible for him to sit outside. Dhruv would like Alisha to pay for the damage to the fence and to stop burning rubbish.

In the case of the tree branches growing over the boundary, the appropriate claim to consider would be in nuisance. The branches are interfering with Mary's use of her land by encroaching on it, and the interference is indirect (because the branches have grown over the boundary gradually over the course of time).

Contrast this with the case of the new fence erected on Jean's land. The fence interferes with Jean's possession of land. The interference is direct and intentional.

---

14 See, for example, **Lemmon v Webb** [1895] AC 1 (HL) covered in Chapter 22.
15 Trespass to land is covered in Chapter 2.

So, the relevant tort to consider would be trespass to land. (For a claim in trespass Mike must have acted intentionally. This is satisfied by the fact that he intended his actions in erecting the fence, even if he made a mistake about the location and did not intend to erect it on Jean's land.)

The final scenario, concerning Dhruv and Alisha, involves claims in both nuisance and negligence. Alisha caused damage to Dhruv's fence carelessly, so here you should consider a claim in negligence. (The damage to the fence is not trespass because Alisha's actions were not intentional. It is not nuisance because it is a single event rather than a continuing state of affairs.)

In contrast to this, Alisha's regular burning of rubbish – causing smoke and ash – is likely to be a nuisance. It is a continuing state of affairs and is likely to amount to an unreasonable interference with Dhruv's use and enjoyment of his land. (The smoke cannot give rise to a claim in negligence because it is intangible, and so does not amount to the kind of damage necessary for a claim in negligence.)

Chapter 16 revision points

Private nuisance

- Private nuisance: unlawful interference with the claimant's use or enjoyment of land
- Protects land: claimant must have an interest in the land affected
- Interference with land includes:
  - Encroachment – e.g., tree roots
  - Tangible damage – e.g., damage to plants
  - Interference with amenity – intangible damage from, e.g., noise, smells
- Requires a continuing state of affairs
- Intangible amenity damage: unlawful if unreasonable; reasonableness factors:
  - Substantial interference
  - Character of neighbourhood
  - Intensity and duration
  - Abnormal sensitivity
  - Malice
- Naturally occurring nuisances – reasonable care
- Causation of damage must be established
- Damage must not be too remote
- Consider Defences
- Remedies:
  - Damages
  - Injunction
  - Abatement

17 The rule in *Rylands v Fletcher*

17.1 Chapter overview

This chapter explains the rule in **Rylands v Fletcher** – a special principle, within the tort of private nuisance, dealing with the escape of dangerous things from land. (Its name comes from the case in which the rule was established.)[1]

It looks at who can make a claim, noting the nature of the claim as protecting land, resulting in the requirement for the claimant to have an interest in the land affected.

Then it explains the elements of the claim noting that liability arises where:

- The defendant made a non-natural use of their land
- By bringing a dangerous thing on to the land
- Which escapes and causes damage,

The chapter explains that liability under the rule is strict, so that where the elements of the claim are established the defendant is liable without proof of fault.

17.2 Introduction to the rule in *Rylands v Fletcher*

The rule in **Rylands v Fletcher** is a special rule, within nuisance, to deal with isolated escapes of dangerous things from land. Where the rule applies, it imposes strict liability (that is, liability without proof of fault). Look at this problem scenario:

> A landowner stores a large quantity of a dangerous substance on her land for the purposes of her business. She exercises reasonable care to ensure that the substance is stored correctly. Nevertheless, one day, without any fault on her part, some of the substance escapes and causes damage to neighbouring land.

---

1 *Rylands v Fletcher* (1868) LR 3 HL 330 (HL).

This is the kind of scenario that may fall within the rule in **Rylands v Fletcher**. (Of course, we would need to know more about this particular case to be able to say whether the rule does apply on the facts.)

17.3 Parties to the claim

In order to bring a claim under the rule in **Rylands v Fletcher**:

- The claimant needs to have an interest in the land affected.

This is the same as in the ordinary rules of private nuisance.[2]

As to who may be sued:

- Liability is imposed on the person who owns or controls the dangerous thing that has escaped from the land.

This could be the owner of the land, if they accumulated the thing themselves or allowed someone else to do so. Alternatively, it could be a non-owner licensed to use the land and responsible for the accumulation.

17.4 Elements of the claim

The rule in **Rylands v Fletcher** is the principle that:

- A person is liable, without proof of fault, if they make a non-natural use of their land by bringing a dangerous thing on to the land, which escapes and causes damage.

We will examine each of these aspects of the rule in turn.

17.4.1 Dangerous thing

- A dangerous thing is one which is likely to cause damage if it escapes.

An example might be large quantities of a substance poisonous to plants on neighbouring land.

Whether or not the thing a defendant has accumulated on land does amount to a dangerous thing for the purposes of this rule is a question of fact in each case.

Note: the mere storage of something flammable, leading to a fire which spreads to neighbouring land, does not attract strict liability under the rule in **Rylands v Fletcher**. This is because things which are flammable are not necessarily dangerous

---

2   Older case law allowed claims by persons affected by the escape, even without an interest in land; but the more modern view is that an interest in land is required. See **Transco Plc v Stockport MBC** [2003] UKHL 61, [2004] 2 AC 1.

in themselves; and, for the rule to apply, it is a dangerous thing itself that must escape, not the fire.[3]

The rule does not apply if the dangerous thing is present naturally on the land (rather than having been brought there by the defendant).

17.4.2 Non-natural use of land

- A non-natural use of land is some special use, different from the ordinary use of land, which involves some special danger of causing harm.

An example might be storage of large quantities of harmful chemicals.[4]

Whether a particular use of land amounts to a non-natural use within the rule is to be decided as a question of fact in each case, taking into account all the circumstances.

17.4.3 Strict liability

Liability under the rule in **Rylands v Fletcher** is strict. This means that the defendant is liable without proof of fault. So, it is not necessary to show that the escape of the dangerous substance resulted from any lack of care on the part of the defendant.

This means that it is not necessary to show that defendant ought to have foreseen the possible escape of the dangerous substance; nor that the defendant failed to take reasonable care to prevent the escape. The mere fact that the dangerous substance was brought on to the land in the course of a non-natural use is sufficient.

Note, however, that a defendant has a defence where the escape of the dangerous thing was caused by the deliberate independent act of a third party, with no negligence on the part of the defendant.

17.4.4 Damage

Liability under the rule in **Rylands v Fletcher** provides a remedy for damage caused to the land affected by the escape. The rule does not provide a remedy for personal injury.[5]

---

3 See **Gore v Stannard** [2012] EWCA Civ 1248, [2014] QB 1. Where a fire starts and spreads as a result of a failure to exercise reasonable care, a claim in negligence should be considered.
4 For an example in which the claimant failed to establish a non-natural use of land see **Transco Plc v Stockport MBC** [2003] UKHL 61, [2004] 2 AC 1.
5 Older case law did allow recovery for personal injury caused by an escape from land, but the more modern view is that personal injury is not covered. See **Transco Plc v Stockport MBC** [2003] UKHL 61, [2004] 2 AC 1. Where a person suffers injury caused by an escape from land, it would therefore be necessary to consider a claim in negligence based on lack of reasonable care, rather than under the strict liability regime of **Rylands v Fletcher**.

Recoverable damage is further limited by the principle of remoteness of damage. The same rule for remoteness of damage applies as in ordinary nuisance (and negligence):

- Damage is too remote, and not recoverable, if it is not a reasonably foreseeable consequence of the escape.[6]

17.5 Nuisance, negligence, and *Rylands v Fletcher* – which claim to bring?

You may now be asking: when should a claim be made under the ordinary rules of private nuisance and when it should be pursued under the rule in *Rylands v Fletcher*?

In principle, we can distinguish between the ordinary rules of private nuisance and the special rule in *Rylands v Fletcher* by saying that the rule in *Rylands v Fletcher* applies to an isolated escape, whereas a claim under the ordinary rules of private nuisance requires there to be a continuing state of affairs. However, this distinction is not always easy to apply on the facts of a particular case. For example:

> Suppose a person carries out activities on their land over a long period which involve the use and storage of a dangerous substance. Usually, the substance is confined to use on the land, but then an incident occurs in which some of the substance escapes and causes damage to neighbouring land.

Should these facts be interpreted as an underlying continuing state of affairs (within the ordinary rules of private nuisance) or as an isolated escape (potentially within the rule in *Rylands v Fletcher*)? Additionally, where there has been a lack of reasonable care on the part of the defendant, resulting in physical damage, there may also be an overlap with the tort of negligence.

This means that lawyers representing a claimant in such a dispute are likely to plead more than one cause of action in their client's claim. Depending on their interpretation of the facts, they are likely to argue that the facts give rise to a claim, either in nuisance generally and/or under the rule in *Rylands v Fletcher* and/or in negligence. The court will then decide which causes of action have been successful. Of course, damages for the claimant's loss can only be awarded once, even if more than one cause of action is successfully established.

It is of course possible to envisage a situation in which neither the ordinary rules of private nuisance nor the special rule in *Rylands v Fletcher* would apply. For example:

> Suppose that a neighbour suffered damage caused by a single isolated escape from the defendant's land of a substance which is not normally dangerous.

---

6   *Cambridge Water Co Ltd v Eastern Counties Leather Plc* [1994] 2 AC 264 (HL).

Since there was clearly no continuing state of affairs, the ordinary rules of private nuisance would not apply. Additionally, these circumstances would not satisfy the conditions for **Rylands v Fletcher** to apply. So, in a case like this, the relevant tort to consider would be negligence. The person responsible for the escape could only be liable if they had failed to exercise reasonable care.

Chapter 17 revision points

The rule in *Rylands v Fletcher*

- A special rule, within nuisance, to deal with isolated escapes of dangerous things from land
- Where the rule applies, it imposes strict liability
- The rule in **Rylands v Fletcher** is the principle that:
  - A person is liable, without proof of fault, if they make a non-natural use of their land by bringing a dangerous thing on to the land, which escapes and causes damage
  - Dangerous thing – one which is likely to cause damage if it escapes
  - Non-natural use of land – some special use, different from the ordinary use of land, which involves some special danger of causing harm

18 Public nuisance

18.1 Chapter overview

This chapter outlines the tort of public nuisance. It notes that public nuisance arises from an unreasonable interference with the comfort and convenience of a class of the public. It notes that an individual can claim in public nuisance only if they have suffered particular damage, over and above that suffered by the public in general.

18.2 The nature of public nuisance

Look at the following problem scenarios, and in each one identify whose rights appear to have been interfered with:

> A local authority is operating a land reclamation site on the edge of a large town. The land on the site is contaminated by chemicals which are injurious to health. The operations on the site cause contaminated mud and dust to spread across the town, so endangering the health of the public. A number of individual claimants suffer personal injury as a result of this contamination, and they seek damages in compensation for their injury.[1]

> A building contractor excavates a hole in a public highway outside the main entrance to a shop. The hole blocks the highway for a number of months, causing inconvenience to the public by preventing them from passing by. The owner of the shop also suffers a loss of profits because the interference with the highway substantially reduces the number of customers coming to the shop, and she seeks damages for this loss.

In cases like these, consideration would be given to a claim in public nuisance. The key feature of these cases is that the defendant's activities have interfered with the comfort and convenience of a whole class of the public.

---

1 See ***Corby Group Litigation v Corby DC*** [2009] EWHC 1944 (TCC), [2010] Env LR D2, on which this example is based.

18.3 Definition

- A public nuisance is something which interferes with the reasonable comfort and convenience of a class of the public.[2]

The requirement for the interference to affect a **class of the public** means that a sufficiently large number of people must be affected. Whether a sufficient class of the public has been affected for the interference to amount to a public nuisance is a question of fact in each case.

To amount to a public nuisance, the interference must be **unreasonable**. Consider, for example, disruption caused by the creation of an obstruction or danger on the public highway (as in our example in Section 18.2). For this to be actionable as a public nuisance the interference with the highway must be unreasonable.

Other examples of public nuisance could include: the spread of contaminated materials (such as the mud in our example above); excessive noise and vibrations (for instance, from heavy goods vehicles accessing premises); and the creation of dust or smells. This is provided that in each case the interference is **unreasonable** and affects a sufficient number of people to constitute a **class of the public**.

The same facts can be both a public and a private nuisance. This will be the case where the interference is with the rights of a class of the public (public nuisance) but also affects individuals' use and enjoyment of their land (private nuisance).

18.4 Who can sue in public nuisance?

18.3.1 Attorney General

Where a remedy is sought on behalf of the public generally, this can be done by the Attorney General, who may seek an injunction to prevent the public nuisance from continuing.[3]

18.4.2 Individuals

An individual member of the public may wish to seek damages for harm they have suffered. However, a person cannot make an individual claim for damages if they have only suffered the same general harm as the rest of the affected class of the public.

For an individual to be able to make a claim for damages in public nuisance, they must show that they have suffered **particular damage** over and above that suf-

---

2 See ***Attorney General v PYA Quarries Ltd*** (No.1) [1957] 2 QB 169 (CA).
3 A local authority also has power to apply for an injunction to protect the inhabitants of its area against a public nuisance.

fered by the public in general.[4] In the examples in Section 18.2, this would be satisfied by the individuals who suffered personal injury from contaminated mud and dust, and by the shop owner who suffered a loss of profits.

In contrast to private nuisance, public nuisance does cover personal injury, and it is not necessary for the claimant to have an interest in land.

Chapter 18 revision points

Public nuisance

- Interference with the reasonable comfort and convenience of a class of the public
- Must affect a class of the public
- Must be unreasonable
- Individual claimant: must have suffered particular damage over and above that suffered by the public in general

---

[4] For an example see *Castle v St Augustine's Links Ltd* (1922) 38 TLR 615.

Multiple choice questions for Part 10

1. An environmental pressure group formed a private company. The company leased an empty plot of land on an industrial estate in order to create an urban farm. The farm grew a good crop of tomato plants. Unfortunately, the factory next door then introduced a new process which gave off toxic fumes. The fumes killed all the tomato plants and polluted the soil. The factory owner can show that, despite the use of reasonable care in the design of the new process, it was not possible to eliminate the toxic fumes. The company seeks compensation for the damaged crop and would like to prevent the emission of fumes in future.

   If the company brings a claim in private nuisance against the factory owner, which of the following best explains the likely outcome?

   A. The company cannot bring a successful action in nuisance because it is only leasing the land.
   B. The company can bring a successful action in nuisance, and can seek both damages and an injunction.
   C. The company cannot bring a successful action in nuisance because the factory owner took reasonable care.
   D. The company can bring a successful action in nuisance, but must choose between claiming damages and asking the court to grant an injunction.
   E. The company cannot bring a successful action in nuisance because the interference from the fumes is not unreasonable given the character of the neighbourhood.

2. A man erected a fence along the boundary between his land and that of his neighbour. The fence posts were erected on his land but, over time, the fence has gradually deteriorated until it leans over boundary line. Also, bits of wood sometimes fall from the fence onto the neighbour's land, although they do not cause any damage.

Which one of the following best explains the position of the neighbour?

A. The neighbour could pursue a successful claim in the tort of negligence on grounds that the man has fallen below a reasonable standard of care in not maintaining the fence.
B. The neighbour could pursue a successful claim in trespass to land because there is an interference with his possession of land.
C. The neighbour could pursue a successful claim under the rule in *Rylands v Fletcher* because of the bits of wood which are escaping from the fence onto his land.
D. The neighbour could not pursue any successful claim because the fence has not caused any tangible damage to his land.
E. The neighbour could pursue a successful claim in nuisance because the fence is gradually encroaching onto his land.

3. A company stored large quantities of a harmful chemical on its land for use in an industrial process. The company took all reasonable care to store the chemical safely. However, despite this, one of the chemical containers suddenly ruptured and its contents leaked out. The chemical flowed onto the surface of a neighbouring field and contaminated the soil. Some of the chemical also flowed down a drain and contaminated a pond a substantial distance away. No one had been aware of the presence of the drain and the risk to the pond.

Which one of the following best explains the liability of the company to the owner of the field and the owner of the pond?

A. The company is liable to the owner of the field, but not to the owner of the pond, because only the owner of the field was a foreseeable victim to whom a duty of care was owed.
B. The company is not liable to either owner because it exercised all reasonable care to store the chemicals safely, so was not in breach of any duty of care.
C. The company is not liable to either owner because the leak of chemicals was a single sudden event rather than an ongoing state of affairs.
D. The company is liable to both owners because, in these circumstances, liability is strict, so the absence of fault is no defence.
E. The company is liable to the owner of the field. However, it is not liable to the owner of the pond because the damage to the pond was not reasonably foreseeable.

4. A restaurant was undergoing refurbishment, and the owner hired a rubbish skip which was placed outside the premises on the public highway, where it was left for an unreasonably long period of time. The skip hindered the passage of both pedestrians and motorists. Also, the owner of the flower shop next door to the restaurant suffered a loss of business profits because customers could not easily access the shop.

Which one of the following best explains the liability of the restaurant owner in tort?

A. Given that the flower shop owner has suffered special damage, the restaurant owner is liable to her because he owed her a duty of care which he has breached by leaving the skip in position for so long.
B. Given that a wide class of people have all been affected by the skip, each individual can make a claim against the restaurant owner for the disruption they have suffered.
C. Given that a wide class of people have all been affected by the skip, no one can make an individual claim for compensation against the restaurant owner.
D. Given that the flower shop owner has suffered more damage than other persons, the restaurant owner is liable to her for her loss of business profits.
E. Given that the flower shop owner has suffered only a financial loss of business profits, the restaurant owner is not liable to her because this is pure economic loss.

PART 11
Protections for reputation and private information

19

Defamation

19.1 Chapter overview

This chapter outlines the elements of the tort of defamation:

- Publication
- Of a statement which is defamatory
- Which refers to the claimant.

It then outlines key defences:

- Truth
- Honest opinion
- Publication on a matter of public interest
- Privilege.

Having established the elements of defamation and key defences, the chapter then explains the distinction between libel and slander:

- Libel – a defamatory statement in permanent form (such as writing)
- Slander – a defamatory statement in transient form (such as the spoken word).

Finally, it considers the remedies for defamation.

19.2 Introduction

For a successful action in defamation the claimant must show that the statement made by the defendant:

- Was defamatory
- Referred to the claimant
- Was published.

If these elements are established, the defendant may seek to establish a defence.

These elements and defences apply to both libel and slander.[1]

---

1 The differences between libel and slander are explained later in this chapter.

19.3 Defamatory statement

Look at the following statements. Each of them could be considered defamatory:

- A student is accused of cheating in an exam.
- It is reported that a businessman has cheated his customers.
- A politician is said to have taken bribes.
- A sports personality is said to have acted immorally.

There is no single definition of a defamatory statement, but case law shows that:

- A statement is defamatory if:
  - It would lower the claimant in the estimation of right-thinking people, or
  - It would cause the claimant to be shunned or avoided, or
  - It would expose the claimant to hatred, ridicule, or contempt.

In addition, statute[2] has now imposed a further requirement:

- A statement is not defamatory unless its publication has caused or is likely to cause **serious harm** to the reputation of the claimant.[3]

So, this statutory provision imposes a **threshold of seriousness**. It means that trivial allegations that do no real harm will not give rise to a successful claim in defamation.

19.4 Statement referring to the claimant

The defamatory statement must refer to the claimant. This does not mean that the statement must name the claimant. The overall test to determine whether the statement refers to the claimant is:

- Would a reasonable person understand the defamatory statement to refer to the claimant?

For example, the claimant could be referred to by their description (e.g., 'the prime minister'), and this would be sufficient if a reasonable person would understand this to refer to the claimant.

19.5 Publication of a defamatory statement

The defamatory statement must be published to someone other than the claimant themselves. For example:

> A manager calls an employee into their office and tells them, in private, that the manger suspects them of dishonesty. This would not give rise to a claim in defamation. The statement is defamatory, but it has not been published to anyone other than the employee themselves.

---

2 *Defamation Act 2013* s.1.
3 For the effects of this provision see *Lachaux v Independent Print Ltd* [2019] UKSC 27, [2020] AC 612.

Publication simply means:

- The statement must be communicated to someone other than the claimant.

So, each of the following would be an example of publication of a defamatory statement: sending it in a letter; reading it aloud; writing it on a wall; transmitting it via the internet; or printing it in a book or newspaper.

If one person publishes a defamatory statement and another person then **repeats** it, both of them have published it. For example, a letter printed in a newspaper is published *both* by the writer of the letter *and* by the publisher of the newspaper.[4]

19.6 Defences to defamation

Once the claimant has established the elements of defamation, the onus shifts to the defendant to establish a defence.[5] We will consider here the most important of these defences: truth; honest opinion; publication on a matter of public interest; privilege; and limitation.[6]

19.6.1 Truth

- It is a complete defence to a claim in defamation that the defamatory statement is **true**.[7]

Once the claimant has established that the statement was defamatory, referred to the claimant, and was published, the defendant has the burden of proving that the statement was true.

19.6.2 Honest opinion

This defence protects statements of opinion, as opposed to statements of fact.

The defence of **honest opinion** applies if the defendant can show that the defamatory statement satisfied all of the following:[8]

- It was a statement of **opinion**.
- It indicated the **basis** of that opinion.
- An **honest person** could have held that opinion on the basis of facts existing at the time of publication.

The defence is defeated if the claimant shows that the defendant did *not* hold the opinion.

---

4 So, for example, a claim might be brought against both the original author and the commercial publisher. However, there are limitations on claiming against a person who repeats a defamatory statement but is not the original author, editor, or commercial publisher – see *Defamation Act 2013* s.10.
5 Some of the defences to defamation are now codified by statute (as indicated below).
6 It is *not* our aim here to outline *all* defences to defamation.
7 See: *Defamation Act 2013* s.2.
8 See: *Defamation Act 2013* s.3.

The rationale for this defence is that a person should be free to express their opinion, provided that it is based upon true facts – but the statement should indicate the basis on which the opinion was formed, so that readers can evaluate the opinion for themselves.

It is important to note that the defence does not require the defendant's opinion to be reasonable. A defendant who is unreasonably prejudiced can still rely on the defence if they held the opinion honestly and satisfy the requirements set out above.

19.6.3 Publication on a matter of public interest

This defence applies to both statements of fact and statements of opinion.

It is a defence for the defendant to show that both of the following are satisfied:[9]

- The defamatory statement was **on a matter of public interest**.
- The defendant reasonably believed that **publishing** the statement was **in the public interest**.

In deciding whether these requirements are satisfied, the court must have regard to all the circumstances of the case.

Statute does not define what is a matter of public interest. It is not possible to give an exhaustive definition or list. However, case law indicates that it could include matters such as: the conduct of government and politicians; the conduct of public bodies; the conduct of the police; and issues such as crime and terrorism, and the use of drugs in sport.

19.6.4 Privilege

A person who makes an untrue defamatory statement may nevertheless be protected from liability in defamation if they make the statement in circumstances where the defence of privilege applies. Privilege may be absolute or qualified.

Absolute privilege

Where the defendant makes a statement in circumstances of absolute privilege, they are protected from an action in defamation *even if* the statement was made maliciously. (In this context, maliciously means that the statement was made for an improper motive.)

Situations in which absolute privilege applies include:

- Statements made during **judicial proceedings** (for example, by the parties or by witnesses or by the judge) and
- Statements made in **parliament**.

---

9   See: ***Defamation Act 2013*** s.4.

Qualified privilege

Where the defendant makes a statement in circumstances of qualified privilege, they are protected from an action in defamation *unless* the claimant can show that the defendant made the statement *maliciously* (i.e., for an improper motive).

Qualified privilege arises where:

- The maker of the defamatory statement has a **legal, social, or moral duty or interest** to make the statement, and
- The person to whom the statement is made has a **corresponding duty or interest** in receiving it.

Examples could include reporting someone suspected of crime to the police, or providing a reference for someone to a prospective employer.[10] For example:

> A householder witnesses a burglary. In response to police questions, she suggests that her neighbour could be guilty of the crime (because the burglar wore a distinctive coat similar to one belonging to the neighbour). The householder made the statement to the police honestly and without malice. Further investigations later revealed that the neighbour was not guilty of any crime.

Clearly, it is defamatory to accuse someone of committing a crime.[11] The statement was later shown to be untrue (so the defence of truth could not apply). However, the householder had a social duty to give the information to the police, and the police had a corresponding interest in receiving it. Therefore, the defence of qualified privilege would apply.

19.6.5 Limitation

It is a general defence to claims in tort that the claim has been brought after the expiry of the limitation period under the **Limitation Act 1980**.[12] Such claims are said to be statute barred.

- The limitation period for claims in defamation is **one year** from the date on which the cause of action accrued.

In practical terms, this is quite a short period within which to investigate the claim, gather evidence, notify the claim to the defendant, and issue proceedings in court.

---

10 Statute also creates some other instances of qualified privilege, e.g., for reports of public proceedings and statements in scientific or academic journals. See **Defamation Act 2013** and **Defamation Act 1996**.
11 Subject to satisfying the threshold of seriousness imposed by the **Defamation Act 2013** s.1.
12 See further Chapter 7.

We saw above that each **repetition** of a defamatory statement can give rise to a new cause of action. However, special rules on limitation apply where a statement is repeated by the *same person* who originally published it. For example:

> A newspaper publishes defamatory material in its daily edition, and then continues to make the material available via the internet.

In a case of this kind, the limitation period is one year from the date of the first publication.[13]

19.7 Libel and slander – damage in defamation claims

There are two forms of defamation:

- **Libel** – where the defamatory statement is in permanent form, such as in writing, and
- **Slander** – where the defamatory statement is in transient form, such as the spoken word.

Libel and slander differ as to the **damage** a claimant needs to prove:

- Libel is **actionable per se**.
- Slander requires proof of special damage.[14]

Special damage is loss of money or loss of something which has a monetary value.

This is contrasted with **general damage**, which is damage to reputation itself.

So, applying this to distinguish between libel and slander:

- To say that libel is actionable per se means that general damage to the claimant's reputation itself is sufficient. Proof of financial loss is not required.
- To say that slander requires proof of special damage means that the damage to the claimant's reputation must have caused the claimant to suffer a loss of money or monetary value.

It is important to note that the requirement of serious harm to reputation under s.1 of the **Defamation Act 2013**[15] does not change the fact that libel is actionable per se.

---

13 This is the 'single publication' rule under s.8 of the **Defamation Act 2013**. Where it applies, this section provides that, for the purposes of the limitation period under the **Limitation Act 1980**, the cause of action accrues on the date of first publication.
14 As an exception to the general rule, slander is actionable per se where the defamatory statement implies that the claimant was guilty of a criminal offence punishable by imprisonment, or where the defamatory statement damages the claimant's reputation in their trade profession or business.
15 Covered above – Section 19.3.

As we have just seen, 'actionable per se' means that **general damage** to reputation is sufficient. The effect of the **Defamation Act 2013** is simply to require that this general damage must reach the threshold level of serious harm.[16]

19.8 Remedies for defamation

19.8.1 Damages

In a claim for **libel**, the function of an award of damages is:

- To **vindicate** the claimant's reputation (by publicly confirming that the defamatory statement was untrue), and
- To **compensate** for distress and loss caused by the defamatory statement.

So, the claimant should recover compensation for the general damage to their reputation as well as for any special damage (quantifiable financial loss) they specifically claim and prove.

A claim for **slander** requires the claimant to prove **special damage** (quantifiable financial loss), and the purpose of the award of damages is to compensate for such loss.

19.8.2 Injunction

In an action for defamation an injunction may be used to prevent publication of a defamatory statement. An injunction is a discretionary remedy, so the court must be persuaded that it is an appropriate remedy in the circumstances.

Final injunction

An injunction may be granted as a final remedy following a trial in which the claimant establishes a successful claim. So, this could be applicable where it is necessary to restrain the defendant from continuing to publish the defamatory statement in future.

Interim injunction

An injunction may (in some very limited circumstances) be granted as an interim remedy. An interim remedy is one the court grants before the matter has come to trial, for an interim period, pending the full trial of the matter. The circumstances in which an interim injunction can be granted are limited by the following:

- The matter must be urgent.
- The claimant must demonstrate that there is no defence to the claim with a realistic prospect of success. (So, if the defendant intends to rely on a defence such as truth, the interim injunction will *not* be granted unless the claimant shows that the defence is certain to fail.)[17]

---

16 See: ***Lachaux v Independent Print Ltd*** [2019] UKSC 27, [2020] AC 612.
17 See: ***Bonnard v Perryman*** [1891] 2 Ch 269 (CA), applied in ***Greene v Associated Newspapers Ltd*** [2004] EWCA Civ 1462, [2005] QB 972.

If the claimant can meet the stringent requirements for grant of an interim injunction, this remedy could be appropriate where:

- The defamatory statement has already been published, but the injunction could effectively prevent further publication, or
- The defamatory statement has not yet been published, but there is threat of publication. In this case, the injunction would be known as a *quia timet* injunction.[18]

The ability of a claimant to obtain an injunction to prevent publication poses a potential threat to the defendant's freedom of expression. Therefore, safeguards are imposed by the **Human Rights Act 1998** s.12. This applies where the court is considering granting relief (such as an injunction) which could affect the defendant's right to freedom of expression. In particular it provides that:

- When deciding whether to grant the relief, the court must have particular regard to the importance of freedom of expression.
- Where the proceedings relate to journalistic, literary, or artistic material, the court must also consider the extent to which it would be in the public interest for the material to be published.
- Relief restraining publication before trial (i.e., an interim injunction) should not be granted unless the court is satisfied that the applicant is likely to establish that publication should not be allowed.

Chapter 19 revision points

Defamation

- Publication
- Defamatory statement
- Refers to the claimant

Defamatory

- A statement is defamatory if it would lower the claimant in the estimation of right-thinking people
- A statement is not defamatory unless its publication has caused or is likely to cause serious harm to the reputation of the claimant

Key defences to defamation

- Truth
- Honest opinion
- Publication on a matter of public interest
- Privilege
- Limitation

---

18 That is, an injunction granted to restrain a threatened wrongful act.

20

Misuse of private information

20.1 Chapter overview

This chapter outlines the tort of misuse of private information. It explains the elements of the tort:

- Disclosure of information in which the claimant has a reasonable expectation of privacy
- In circumstances where the claimant's right to privacy is not outweighed by the defendant's right to freedom of expression.

It notes how the tort seeks to balance conflicting rights from the European Convention on Human Rights ('ECHR'): the claimant's right to privacy (Article 8) and the defendant's right to freedom of expression (Article 10).

20.2 Introduction

To illustrate the context of the tort of misuse of private information, look at the following problem situation:

> A prominent Member of Parliament (MP) has publicly campaigned against drinking alcohol and taking illegal drugs. Recently a journalist discovered that the politician had attended several private parties at which he had drunk alcohol to excess and taken illegal drugs. The journalist's story has been published in a national newspaper.
>
> The politician accepts that the story is true (so there is no possibility of a claim for defamation). However, he claims that the parties were not part of his public duties as a politician, and that he should be entitled to respect for his private life in accordance with ECHR Article 8. So, he may consider bringing a claim for misuse of private information.
>
> The journalist and the newspaper argue that there should be respect for the right to freedom of expression under ECHR Article 10. They say that this right should prevail because there is a legitimate public interest in disclosing

information which shows that the politician is not respecting, in private, the claims he makes in public. So, they would argue that the politician's claim for misuse of private information should not succeed.

We will return to this example later when we consider the balance that the tort of misuse of private information seeks to strike between these conflicting rights.

20.3 Elements of the tort

The tort of misuse of private information has developed to provide a remedy where private information about the claimant has been wrongfully disclosed by the defendant. It needs to strike a balance between the claimant's ECHR Article 8 right to respect for private life and the defendant's ECHR Article 10 right to freedom of expression.[1] So, where a claim is made the court must consider the following questions:

- Was the information of a kind in which the claimant had a reasonable expectation of privacy?
- In all the circumstances, should the defendant's right to freedom of expression outweigh the claimant's right to privacy? In particular, was it in the public interest for the information to be disclosed, despite the interference with the claimant's privacy?

If the claimant cannot show that they had a reasonable expectation of privacy in the information, then the claim fails at that first stage.

Even if there was a reasonable expectation of privacy, the claim will still fail at the second stage if the court finds that the defendant's right to freedom of expression should outweigh the claimant's right to privacy.

20.3.1 Reasonable expectation of privacy

So, what kind of information might come within a reasonable expectation of privacy? There is no fixed definition, but case law suggests that this would include matters such as the claimant's health, personal relationships, and financial affairs.

20.3.2 Balancing freedom of expression

What factors and circumstances might lead the court to conclude that the defendant's freedom of expression should outweigh the claimant's privacy? An important factor is whether disclosure of the claimant's private information was in the public

---

1 For a case illustrating this balancing of rights see **Campbell v Mirror Group Newspapers Ltd** [2004] UKHL 22, [2004] 2 All ER 995 covered in Chapter 22.

interest. It would also be relevant to consider how the information was obtained and the impact of the disclosure on the claimant.

We can illustrate this by returning to the example in Section 20.2:

> A journalist discloses information that a politician who publicly campaigns against drinking alcohol and taking drugs has privately done so himself.
>
> - It is possible that the politician could have a reasonable expectation of privacy in his private social life.
> - However, when that is balanced against the defendant's freedom of expression, the court may conclude that, in the circumstances, this should prevail.

On the facts, it seems clear that there was a public interest in disclosure of the information because it shows that the politician is not respecting, in private, the claims he makes in public. So, in this example, the politician is unlikely to have a successful claim for misuse of private information.

20.4 Remedies for misuse of private information

20.4.1 Damages

Where there is a successful claim for misuse of private information, the court may award damages to the claimant to compensate for the infringement of their rights and the distress caused.[2]

20.4.2 Injunction

In an action for misuse of private information, an injunction may be used to prevent the defendant from disclosing (or further disclosing) the claimant's private information.

An injunction may be a final remedy (granted once the claimant has established a successful claim) or an interim remedy (granted pending trial of the matter).

An injunction is a discretionary remedy, so the court must be persuaded that it is an appropriate remedy in the circumstances.

---

2 For examples see *Richard v BBC* [2018] EWHC 1837, [2019] 2 All ER 105 and *Ali v Channel 5 Broadcasting Ltd* [2019] EWCA Civ 677, [2019] All ER (D) 128 (Apr).

An injunction granted to safeguard the claimant's right to privacy is likely to have the effect of limiting the defendant's right to freedom of expression. Therefore, the safeguards imposed by s.12 of the **Human Rights Act 1988** apply:

- When deciding whether to grant the relief (i.e., the injunction preventing disclosure of the private information), the court must have particular regard to the importance of freedom of expression.
- Where the proceedings relate to journalistic, literary, or artistic material, the court must also consider the extent to which it would be in the public interest for the material to be published.
- Relief restraining publication before trial (i.e., an interim injunction) should not be granted unless the court is satisfied that the applicant is likely to establish that publication should not be allowed.[3]

Chapter 20 revision points

Misuse of private information

- Disclosure of information in which the claimant had a reasonable expectation of privacy
- In circumstances where this is not outweighed by the defendant's right to freedom of expression

Balancing of rights

- Respect for private and family life (ECHR Art 8)
- Freedom of expression (ECHR Art 10)

---

3 On interim injunctions in privacy cases see **PJS v News Group Newspapers Ltd** [2016] UKSC 26, [2016] AC 1081 (applying the interpretation of s.12 from **Cream Holdings Ltd v Banerjee** [2004] UKHL 44, [2005] 1 AC 253).

Multiple choice questions for Part 11

1. The assistant to a football club manager became convinced that the manager was accepting bribes to influence the result of matches. As she was accompanying him to a match as a passenger in his car, she spoke to him about her suspicions. He has produced conclusive evidence that the accusation was not true. He is very angry, but has been advised that a claim in defamation against the assistant is not likely to succeed.

   Which one of the following best states the reason why the claim is not likely to succeed?

   A. The statement was not published.
   B. The statement was privileged.
   C. The statement was made in the public interest.
   D. The statement was the assistant's honest opinion.
   E. The statement was not defamatory.

2. The secretary to a construction company manager found evidence suggesting that the manager was dishonestly accepting payments in return for allocating work to contractors. The secretary explained these suspicions to the company chairman in private, ensuring that no one else was able to overhear their conversation. The chairman found the secretary's evidence convincing. However, investigations later showed that the manager had not acted dishonestly. The manager now seeks advice as to his chances of pursuing a successful claim in defamation against the secretary.

   Which one of the following best explains the advice that should be given to the manager?

   A. The claim is likely to succeed because the manager was able to show that the statement was untrue.
   B. The claim is not likely to succeed because the defamatory statement was not published since the secretary only spoke to one other person in private.
   C. The claim is not likely to succeed because the secretary can rely on the defence of qualified privilege.
   D. The claim is likely to succeed because the secretary's conversation with the chairman was the publication of a defamatory statement that referred to the manager.
   E. The claim is not likely to succeed because the secretary can rely on the defence of absolute privilege.

3. A journalist discovered that a prominent politician, active in formulating educational policy, recently cheated in public exams leading to a professional qualification. The journalist published the story in a national newspaper. He has proof that the statement is true. The politician now seeks advice on whether she has any claims in tort in respect of the publication.

Which one of the following best represents the advice that should be given to the politician?

A. A claim in defamation would not succeed because the statement is true. However, a claim for misuse of private information is likely to succeed.
B. Both claims in defamation and misuse of private information are likely to succeed because the statement is defamatory and the information was private.
C. A claim for misuse of private information would not succeed because the politician had no reasonable expectation of privacy in the information published. However, a claim in defamation is likely to succeed.
D. A claim in defamation would not succeed because the statement is not defamatory. However, a claim for misuse of private information is likely to succeed.
E. Neither a claim in defamation nor a claim for misuse of private information is likely to succeed.

4. A journalist published a true story stating that a prominent sportsperson had an extramarital affair. The sportsperson has never discussed their family life in public, having only ever given interviews relating specifically to their sporting performance.

If the sportsperson seeks a remedy in tort in respect of the publication of the story, which one of the following best describes the likely outcome?

A. A claim for misuse of private information is not likely to succeed, but a claim for defamation is likely to succeed.
B. Neither a claim in defamation nor a claim in misuse of private information is likely to succeed because the information published was true.
C. Both a claim in defamation and a claim for misuse of private information are likely to succeed because the story is defamatory and the information was private.
D. The only claim likely to succeed is a claim for misuse of private information.
E. Both a claim in defamation and a claim for misuse of private information are likely to succeed, unless the journalist can show that the story was on a matter of public interest and that he reasonably believed that publishing it was in the public interest.

PART 12
Client case analysis in tort

21 Client case analysis skills in tort

21.1 Chapter overview

This and the following chapter focus on developing client case analysis skills.

This chapter begins with a reminder of a clear client case analysis structure. It explores the skill of client case analysis as the foundation for litigation. It shows how a clear structured analysis of the client's prospects of success (either as claimant or defendant) enables the assessment of litigation risk. This in turn provides a structured approach to considering a negotiated settlement of the claim.

The chapter then turns to consideration of client case analysis in the context of reported cases. It explains how the legal issues which have come before the courts for determination were selected and shaped by the case analysis carried out by the parties themselves.

Chapter 22 then presents a selection of reported cases that illustrate the principles of tort law discussed in the preceding chapters. Structured questions for each case enable the reader to analyse the principles of tort law applied in each case.

21.2 Client case analysis

A clear client case analysis structure needs to: identify the relevant tort; identify the parties to the claim; establish the elements of the claim; and identify potential defences.

21.2.1 Identify the relevant tort
This is done by asking:

- What harm has claimant has suffered?
- Which tort might provide a remedy for harm of that type?

You have studied a range of torts. You have focused on the rights, interests, and harms protected by each one. So, you are now in a position to determine which tort might be applicable to the facts of a claim.

21.2.2 Identify the parties to the claim

This is done by asking:

- Who has suffered harm? (identifying the claimant)
- Who appears to be responsible for the harm? (identifying the defendant)

When identifying who is responsible for the harm, bear in mind the principles of vicarious liability (see Chapter 12). Where these are applicable, it may be appropriate for both an employee, committing a tort, and an employer to be identified as defendants.

21.2.3 Establish the elements of the claim

Having identified the relevant tort to provide a remedy for the harm suffered, the next step is to ask:

- What are the elements of that tort? (i.e., what does the claimant need to prove to establish a claim?)
- What potential defences might the defendant rely on?

In this stage of the analysis, you will draw upon your knowledge of the elements of each tort and potential defences covered in the preceding chapters.

The client case analysis process described here can provide a foundation for the conduct of litigation.

21.3 Litigation risk

Litigation is expensive. Usually, both parties will incur the cost of instructing lawyers.[1] There are also expenses, such as the cost of instructing expert witnesses. Broadly speaking, the further the case proceeds towards trial, the more preparatory work is completed and the more the costs increase.

Both claimant and defendant should be conscious of the costs of litigation. Very often the parties will seek a negotiated settlement of the claim in order to reduce those costs. So, each party's lawyers need to advise: should the claim be settled or should it be allowed to proceed to trial?

To be able to advise, both parties need to assess their chances of making a successful claim (or putting forward a successful defence). What is the risk that the claim (or defence) will not be successful if it proceeds to trial? Lawyers in practice often refer to this as assessing the litigation risk. Effective client case analysis skills are crucial to this process.

---

1 It is beyond the scope of this book to discuss the rules for costs in civil litigation. Readers should note that the rules as to costs can differ according to the type of claim. So, the extent to which a party may incur liability for costs depends on both the type of claim and on the type of funding arrangement entered into.

21.4 Assessing the evidence

So far, our discussion of client case analysis and litigation risk has focused on identification of the legal issues. However, another important factor is consideration of the evidence.

Client case analysis involves answering questions such as:

- What happened?
- What harm did this cause?
- Who was involved?
- How did they behave (e.g., in a negligence claim, was reasonable care exercised)?

When you study problem scenarios, the answers to these questions are usually given to you as part of the facts of the scenario. However, in reality, client case analysis and assessment of litigation risk have to take into account that these matters are very often disputed between the parties. Such disputes are resolved by assessing the credibility of the evidence presented by each party. A typical tort claim is likely to involve various kinds of evidence, such as from lay witnesses or experts.[2]

21.4.1 Lay witnesses

In order to answer the factual question of what happened, the parties will rely on evidence from witnesses.

In some cases, there may be independent witnesses who saw what happened. Often, however, the only people who saw what happened are the parties themselves. It is important to appreciate that each party's own account of what happened is part of the evidence.

Very often the parties will disagree on what exactly happened. For example, in a road accident the injured claimant might assert that the defendant's car was travelling in excess of the speed limit, but the defendant may deny this.

Where the parties do not agree on what happened, if the matter proceeds to trial the court will decide the issue by judging which witnesses are most credible. So, each party needs to assess the strength of their own and the opposing evidence. What is the risk that the court will prefer the evidence of the opposing party's witnesses? This is an important question in assessing litigation risk.

21.4.2 Expert evidence

Expert evidence may also be required. For example, in a personal injury case medical evidence will be required to establish the extent of the claimant's injuries, the treatment required, and the prognosis for recovery. In some cases, expert

---

2 The term 'lay witness' is used to distinguish ordinary witnesses of fact from expert witnesses.

evidence may help establish how the claimant's damage was caused. For example, in a claim arising from an industrial accident, an expert engineer may be required to examine and report on defects in machinery.

A witness who qualifies as an expert is permitted to give their **opinion**.[3] For example, a medical expert may give an opinion on what caused the claimant to develop an industrial disease. So, where expert evidence is obtained, the parties will need to assess how far the expert's opinion supports or undermines their claim or defence. This is a further aspect of assessing litigation risk.[4]

21.5 Advising and settlement

The greater the litigation risk (the risk that the claim or defence will be unsuccessful at trial), the more the party at risk should consider agreeing to a negotiated settlement.

So, a lawyer advising a party to litigation in a tort claim will need to answer the following questions:

- What does the claimant need to prove (and what defences might be raised)? This depends on a clear analysis of the legal issues.
- How likely is it that the claimant will be able to prove this (or the defendant establish a defence)? This depends on a clear analysis of the evidence.

Then, when seeking or offering a negotiated settlement, the lawyer will also need to answer this question:

- What remedy can the claimant expect to receive if the claim is successful?

A lawyer acting for a claimant must give the claimant a realistic assessment of what the claim can achieve for them. So, a clear understanding of the remedies available for each tort is essential.

21.5.1 What remedy?

The client's lawyer must advise on what kind of remedy may be available for the claim.

For example, in a negligence claim, where the client has suffered personal injury, it is not uncommon for the client to want not just damages but also an admission of liability and an apology. They may also wish to force the defendant to behave differently in future so as to avoid similar harm happening to others. However, their lawyer, familiar with remedies for the tort of negligence, would need to advise

---

3   In contrast to lay witnesses of fact, who are not permitted to give their opinion.
4   The rules of civil procedure are designed to minimise disputes between the parties on the expert evidence. They may, for example, require both parties to instruct a single joint expert. However, each party still needs to assess how helpful the expert evidence is to their case.

that a claim in negligence can only result in an award of damages. A defendant cannot be forced to apologise or make changes for the future.

This can be compared with the remedy of an injunction (for example, in trespass, nuisance, or defamation) which could, for example, order the defendant not to continue with certain activities.[5]

21.5.2 How much?

Next, where the appropriate remedy is an award of damages, the lawyers for both parties will need to assess the likely amount of damages (often referred to as the quantum of damages). How much is the court likely to award if the claim proceeds to trial and succeeds in full?

Both parties need to make this assessment because each needs to know how much to offer or accept when considering a negotiated settlement. A clear understanding of the principles applied to determine the amount of damages is essential to this part of the analysis.[6]

Finally, the lawyers for both parties will bring together their assessment of damages and their analysis of the degree of litigation risk so as to advise on settlement of the claim. For example:

> The claimant's lawyer has determined that, if the claim were to succeed at trial, damages would be very substantial. However, their assessment of the evidence indicates that there is a significant litigation risk that the claim may not succeed. Therefore, they advise the claimant to accept a negotiated settlement in which damages are reduced by an amount that reflects this litigation risk.

So, we have seen that a clear understanding of the principles of tort law is an essential foundation for litigation. Client case analysis, identifying the legal issues, enables the lawyer to determine what must be proved for a successful claim (or what is required for a successful defence). This is the foundation for consideration of the evidence, leading to the assessment of litigation risk as the basis for a negotiated settlement of the claim.

21.6 Decided cases – precedents in practice

Having considered how the parties to a claim use client case analysis to assess litigation risk, we can move on to look at how this works in decided cases which are reported and relied on as precedents for the future.

---

5   See further Section 10.5.
6   Chapter 10 explains the principles for the assessment of damages.

21.6.1 Principles drawn from litigated cases – piecemeal development

In this book, we have set out principles of tort law. We have focused on gaining a clear understanding of the current law, rather than examining how the law has developed over time. We have imposed a systematic structure to enable us to set down those legal principles as clearly and concisely as possible. However, tort law did not develop as a unified and coherent body of law set down in a systematic way. The principles of tort law have grown incrementally over time as a result of individual cases.

In each case, an individual claimant seeks a remedy for the particular harm they have suffered. If the case proceeds to a trial (rather than a negotiated settlement), the court pronounces its judgment – on the law as applied to the facts.

Where the judgment involves a ruling on issues of legal principle (rather than merely resolving a factual dispute), lawyers and commentators may consider it to determine what effect it has on the existing body of tort law. So, tort law is formed bit by bit over time, and is constantly being adjusted and developed through individual cases.

It helps to understand that, as a result of this process, the law is not always consistent or coherent. This means that it is not always possible to rationalise decided cases which appear to conflict in their application of the principles to their facts. This is something which should be kept in mind when reading and analysing decided cases.

21.6.2 Issues in litigated cases – chosen by the parties

When a case is litigated, the parties decide how the claim will be presented or defended. For example, a defendant could decide that the very strongest aspect of their case was breach of duty. So, they could admit that a duty of care was owed and focus only on breach. This means that the parties themselves determine the issues on which the court will be asked to adjudicate.

The issues on which the parties focus may also be determined by the remedy which is sought. For example, a claimant might seek to frame a case as one of trespass, rather than negligence, because they seek an injunction (which would not be available in a negligence claim).

So, when reading a report of a decided case, keep in mind that the issues on which it was decided were determined by the parties themselves, according to their assessment of the facts and the evidence, and what remedy they were seeking to achieve. (This does mean that, sometimes, the issues reported in a case may not be those which one would necessarily have expected just from reading the facts.)

21.6.3 Limiting the issues – trial on preliminary issue only

When reading decided cases, it is important to be aware that the court may not have been asked to adjudicate on all of the issues. In some cases the parties may ask the court to determine a preliminary issue which they have identified as the crux of their dispute.

For example, a defendant may deny liability on grounds that no duty of care was owed to the claimant (and, alternatively, that if a duty was owed, it was not breached). The parties recognise that, if it is found that the defendant did *not* owe a duty of care to the claimant, the claim will fail. (It will be unnecessary to determine the issue of breach.) So, they may ask the court to determine the duty of care question as a preliminary issue.

Cases of this kind are often reported at this stage. So, the reports record only the outcome on the preliminary issue, rather than the final outcome of the dispute between the parties. It is important to be aware of this when reading the case reports. Do not make the mistake of assuming, for example, that a finding that a duty of care was owed means that the claimant was ultimately successful in their claim.

For example, the parties identify the issue of duty of care as a preliminary issue:

- If the court finds that no duty of care was owed, the claim will end at that stage. The claimant has been unsuccessful.
- On the other hand, if the court finds that a duty of care *was* owed, the claim continues. The claimant must then establish breach of duty, and if they are unable to do so, the claim fails at that stage.

Often, once the preliminary issue has been determined by the court, the rest of the claim will be resolved by negotiated settlement. Where this happens, the final outcome of the dispute is never reported.

21.6.4 Using decided cases as a tool in client case analysis

We have outlined above the role that decided cases play in developing the principles of tort law. We have also shown how they may assist a lawyer in assessing their client's prospect of success.

From this we should see that, when a lawyer uses a precedent from a decided case, they will focus less on the outcome of the case on its particular facts and more on the legal principles established or applied in the case.

The decided cases in the following chapter will illustrate this focus on identifying the legal principles established or applied.

Chapter 21 revision points

Client case analysis skills in tort

Use a clear structure to analyse claims:

- Identify the claimant – who has been harmed?
- Identify the defendant(s) – who is responsible for the harm?
- Identify the relevant tort – what harm has the claimant suffered?
- What are the elements of the tort – how do they apply on the facts?
- Does the defendant have a defence?
- If liability is established, what remedies may be available?

Consider practical issues:

- Evidence
- Litigation risk
- Negotiated settlement

Understand value of precedents from case reports:

- Decisions may not always appear consistent
- Issues determined by the parties
- May be decided on a preliminary issue

22 Key cases in tort law

22.1 Chapter overview

This chapter sets out a selection of cases that illustrate the principles of tort law discussed in the preceding chapters.[1]

Each case has a summary of the facts, followed by focused questions. This enables the reader to identify the key principles in each case, using their knowledge and client case analysis skills. Each case concludes with a summary of the outcome, showing how the principles were applied to the facts.

The cases are set out in the same order as the topics appear in the preceding chapters.

22.2 Application of client case analysis skills to decided cases

Reading the decided cases in this chapter will help you:

- Consolidate your understanding of the principles of tort law discussed in preceding chapters
- Develop your skills of client case analysis.
    - For each case, you will read an outline of the key facts. This is followed by a summary of the issues in dispute.
    - You will then consider the questions provided with each case. This will enable you to analyse the legal issues and apply your knowledge of the principles of tort law.
    - You will then be able to check your understanding by reading a summary of the principles established or applied in the case.
    - Finally, you will read a summary of the outcome of the case. This will show how the principles were applied to the facts.

---

1 Do, however, be aware that no selection of cases can provide a comprehensive list of *all* key cases, so that is not the aim here.

DOI: 10.4324/9781003133698-35

22.3 Trespass

22.3.1 Trespass to land

Lemmon v Webb [1895] AC 1 (HL)

The facts were:

The claimant and defendant were neighbouring landowners. On the claimant's land a number of mature trees grew close to the boundary. Their branches projected over the boundary into the airspace above the defendant's land. The defendant cut off some of the overhanging branches so that they no longer overhung the boundary.

The dispute to be decided by the court was:

Was the defendant entitled to cut the branches off the claimant's trees without first giving notice to the claimant?

Use these questions to analyse the legal issues:

- What cause of action might be appropriate to provide a remedy for the harm suffered by the claimant – damage to trees?
- What argument might the defendant have relied on to deny liability?

The principle of law applied/established was:

The cause of action relied on by the claimant was trespass to land. The trees growing on his land formed part of the land. So, the damage caused by the defendant would come within the tort of trespass to land.

However, the trees constituted a nuisance since they were encroaching into the airspace that formed part of the defendant's land. The defendant was able to rely on the self-help remedy for nuisance – abatement.

The outcome (the principle applied to the facts) was:

The defendant was not liable to the claimant for cutting back the tree branches. He was entitled to do so without first giving notice to the claimant.

Notes:

In practice, the use of the self-help remedy of abatement is very limited. However, this case illustrates the way in which the torts of trespass to land and nuisance may interact.

***

22.3.2 Trespass to the person

Walker v Commissioner of Police of the Metropolis [2014] EWCA Civ 897, [2015] 1 WLR 312

The facts were:

The claimant had been involved in an incident of domestic violence and the police were called. A police officer wished to speak to the claimant and detained him in a doorway. For a very brief period the claimant was unable to leave. It was accepted that the officer was not in the course of arresting the claimant at the time when he initially detained him. However, after the initial very brief detention, the officer did arrest the claimant (and the Court of Appeal held that this arrest was lawful).

The dispute to be decided by the court was:

Did the police officer commit a tort by detaining the claimant in the doorway for a very brief period prior to the formal arrest?

Use these questions to analyse the legal issues:

- What tort might provide a remedy for the claimant's momentary detention?
- Why is it relevant that the police officer was not exercising any power of arrest at the point when the claimant was detained?

The principle of law applied/established was:

The claimant relied on the tort of trespass to the person – false imprisonment. The officer had imposed a complete restriction on the claimant's freedom to move from the doorway where he was confined.

The fact that the period of detention was very short (only a few moments) did not prevent it from amounting to a false imprisonment.

Lawful arrest provides a defence to false imprisonment. So, once the officer did arrest the claimant, the tort was no longer being committed. However, the brief period of detention prior to the formal arrest was unlawful.

The outcome (the principle applied to the facts) was:

The defendant (the Commissioner of Police) was liable to the claimant. Damages were awarded, as this was necessary to recognise the infringement of the claimant's rights. However, the amount of damages was very small (nominal damages of £5) to reflect the very short period of detention.

Notes:

You will note that proceedings were brought against the Commissioner of Police of the Metropolis. This is because the chief officer of police is vicariously liable for torts committed by police officers in their area. (A police officer is not an employee, but statute imposes vicarious liability in the same way as for employees.[2])

This case is important because it illustrates the function of trespass to the person in protecting individual liberty. It also shows how an understanding of trespass to the person can be required in order to analyse some vicarious liability claims.

***

22.4 Negligence

22.4.1 Duty of care

Donoghue v Stevenson [1932] AC 562 (HL)

The facts were:

The claimant and a friend visited a café. The friend bought a drink of ginger beer for the claimant. It was contained in a sealed opaque bottle. Some of the drink was poured into a glass and the claimant consumed some of it. The claimant's case was that, as the remainder of the drink was poured out, a decomposing snail floated out of the bottle. As a result, the claimant suffered shock and sickness. The case in the House of Lords concerned the claimant's claim against the manufacturer of the ginger beer.

The dispute to be decided by the court was:

Even if the facts alleged by the claimant were true, would this be sufficient for the manufacturer of the bottle of ginger beer to owe any obligation to the claimant, given that the manufacturer did not sell the drink to the claimant?

Use these questions to analyse the legal issues:

- What tort would the claimant rely on to pursue her claim against the manufacturer of the drink?
- What may have been the legal basis for the manufacturer's denial of liability?

---

2 *Police Act 1996* s.88.

The principle of law applied/established was:

The claim was based on the tort of negligence. The manufacturer's denial of liability turned on the question of whether any duty of care could be owed to the claimant in these circumstances.

The court held that the manufacturer owes a duty of care to the ultimate consumer where:

- The manufacture puts the goods into circulation intending them to reach the consumer in the same form as they left the manufacturer,
- with no reasonable expectation of an intermediate examination between the goods leaving the manufacturer and reaching the consumer.

This is the **narrow ratio** of the case, and it established the foundation for the common law principles of product liability.

The case is also authority for the wider principle, that a duty of care is owed to anyone whom the defendant ought reasonably to have foreseen as likely to be affected by a lack of care on his part. This is the **wide ratio** of the case, referred to as the neighbour principle, and it established the original foundation for the principles of duty of care in the tort of negligence.

The outcome (the principle applied to the facts) was:

The manufacturer did owe a duty of care to the claimant.

In this case, the existence of a duty of care was tried as a preliminary issue, so the findings of the House of Lords did not determine the final outcome of the dispute between the parties.

Notes:

The principles for duty of care in negligence were developed further in later cases, in particular **Caparo Industries Plc v Dickman and Others**, which is considered next.

***

Caparo Industries Plc v Dickman and Others [1990] 2 AC 605 (HL)

The facts were:

A firm of accountants was engaged to carry out a statutory audit of the annual accounts of a company (Fidelity Plc). The audited accounts were prepared for Fidelity's shareholders and were issued to them in preparation for Fidelity's annual general meeting.

The accounts showed that Fidelity was in a good financial condition. The claimant company (Caparo) held shares in Fidelity and, in reliance on the accounts, purchased more shares.

It was then discovered that the accounts were not accurate. The financial position of Fidelity was not as good as shown in the accounts. Therefore, the shares purchased by Caparo, in reliance on the accounts, were worth less than Caparo had paid for them.

Caparo brought an action in negligence in which the auditors (the firm of accountants) were one of the defendants. It was alleged that the audit of the accounts had been carried out negligently, so causing the loss suffered by Caparo.

The dispute to be decided by the court was:

Did the auditors have any obligations towards Caparo in respect of the losses suffered?

The accounts had been prepared for existing shareholders (of which Caparo was one), but could they also be relied on by Caparo in its capacity as an investor purchasing an additional shareholding?

Use these questions to analyse the legal issues:

- *This was a trial of a preliminary issue. How would you describe that issue in legal terms?*
- *What kind of loss was suffered by Caparo?*
- *What features of the relationship between the auditors and Caparo are likely to have been particularly significant?*

The principle of law applied/established was:

This was a claim in the tort of negligence, and the **preliminary issue** was whether or not the auditors owed a duty of care to investors who relied on their audited accounts.

The loss suffered was **pure economic loss**. The court held that, in cases of pure economic loss, the existence of a duty of care depended on the relationship between the parties. There must be a relationship of sufficient proximity between the claimant and the defendant. For such a relationship of proximity to arise, the following factors must be satisfied:

- The adviser (defendant) knows the purpose for which the advice is required.
- The adviser knows that his advice will be communicated to the advisee (claimant), either individually or as a member of an identifiable class, in order to be used for that purpose.
- The adviser knows that the advisee is likely to rely on the advice without making further independent enquiries.
- It is reasonable for the advisee to rely on the advice.
- The advisee does rely on the advice and suffers loss.

These were the findings of the court on the particular issue in the case.

However, the judgments in the case also discussed the **wider issue** of duty of care in **novel duty situations** (that is, a situation in which it is not clearly established by previous case law whether or not a duty of care is owed). The case is regarded as authority for the principle that, in a novel duty situation, the following factors are to be taken into account:

- Foreseeability – was the claimant a reasonably foreseeable victim of the defendant's negligence?
- Proximity – was there a sufficiently close relationship between claimant and defendant?
- Fair, just and reasonable – would it be fair, just and reasonable to impose a duty of care on the defendant?

The judgments in the case make clear, however, that the courts should only develop new duties of care incrementally and by analogy with existing duty situations.

The outcome (the principle applied to the facts) was:

The auditors did not owe a duty of care to Caparo in respect of the losses it suffered as an investor relying on the accounts.

Notes:

It is important to remember that in an **established duty** situation, where previous case law already establishes that a duty of care is owed, the Caparo factors for novel duties have no application. For example, in a road accident case it would be wrong to apply the Caparo factors to the issue of duty of care because it is already clearly established that road users owe a duty of care to other road users.

For example, ***Robinson v Chief Constable of West Yorkshire*** [2018] UKSC 4, [2018] AC 736 concerned an injury caused to a member of the public by the actions of police officers whilst struggling to arrest a suspect. One of the issues was whether or not the police owed a duty of care in these circumstances. The Caparo factor of 'fair, just and reasonable' was relied on to deny the existence of a duty. The Supreme Court held that the police *did* owe a duty of care in respect of their positive actions that created a risk of harm (as opposed to an omission to prevent harm caused by others). In particular, the court said that this was an **established** duty of care owed by the police to members of the public, so it would be unnecessary and inappropriate to seek to apply the Caparo factors for novel duties.

For a useful contrast in which a truly novel duty situation did arise, so that the Caparo factors were relevant, see *James-Bowen v Commissioner of Police of the Metropolis* [2018] UKSC 40, [2018] 4 All ER 1007. The Commissioner of Police was defendant in a claim based on vicarious liability for the actions of police officers. The Commissioner settled the claim in a way which involved accepting that the officers had been at fault. The officers then alleged that the Commissioner's actions had been negligent and had caused them economic and reputational harm. The court applied the Caparo factors to this novel duty of care situation, and held that it would not be fair, just and reasonable to impose a duty of care on the Commissioner in these circumstances.

***

22.4.2 Breach of duty

Bolton v Stone [1951] AC 850 (HL)

The facts were:

The claimant, Miss Bolton, lived near a cricket ground. She was standing in the street outside her house when she was struck and injured by a cricket ball hit out of the ground. She brought a claim for damages for her injury against the members and committee of the cricket club.

The evidence showed that cricket had been played at the ground for many years, and it was very rare for a batsman to hit the ball out of the ground. The cricket pitch had a very high fence, and the evidence showed that the batsman was wholly exceptional in managing to hit the ball over the fence, out of the ground, to reach the place where the claimant was standing.

The dispute to be decided by the court was:

The claim was pleaded in both nuisance and negligence. It was held that nuisance had not been established, so the appeal to the House of Lords focused on the claim in negligence.

To succeed, the claimant needed to show that the defendant was in breach of the duty of care owed to her. It was not disputed that a duty of care was owed to the claimant, so the argument focused on the question of breach.

The claimant alleged that the defendant had been negligent in the arrangements they made for playing cricket on the ground, in that they had made the cricket pitch too near the road, failed to erect a fence of sufficient height, and failed to prevent balls from being hit out of the ground into the road.

Use these questions to analyse the legal issues:

- What standard of care would the defendant be expected to meet?
- What is the significance of the fact that the batsman's hit was wholly exceptional?

The principle of law applied/established was:

The court applied the well-established principle that a claimant in negligence must show that the defendant's behaviour fell below a reasonable standard of care. It was held that, in assessing what would amount to reasonable care, the court should consider the degree of risk created by the defendant's actions and the precautions the defendant ought to have taken in response to that risk. It was not sufficient to show that an accident *could* occur. The claimant must show that the risk was such that it was reasonably foreseeable that an accident *was likely* to occur, so that the defendant ought to have taken precautions to prevent it.

The outcome (the principle applied to the facts) was:

It was significant that the batsman's hit was wholly exceptional because this showed that the risks created by playing cricket on the ground were low. Therefore, it could not be said that the defendants had failed to exercise reasonable care by not erecting a higher fence, etc. So, the claim failed.

***

Nettleship v Weston [1971] 2 QB 691 (CA)

The facts were:

The defendant wished to learn to drive and the claimant, a friend, agreed to teach her. During a driving lesson the defendant made an error in steering and controlling the car and the car hit a lamp post, injuring the claimant. The claimant made a claim in negligence. (The defendant was covered by a policy of motor insurance.)

The dispute to be decided by the court was:

In driving the car, the defendant owed a well-established duty of care to her passenger, the claimant. The defendant had done her best to drive the car safely, but, as a beginner learning to drive, she lacked sufficient skill. In those circumstances, could a claim in negligence succeed?

Use these questions to analyse the legal issues:

- *In a negligence claim, what must a claimant show to establish that the defendant was in breach of duty?*
- *Does the standard of care the defendant must meet depend on the individual defendant's level of skill?*

The principle of law applied/established was:

The court applied the well-established principle that a claimant in negligence must show that the defendant's behaviour fell below a reasonable standard of care. In assessing what would amount to reasonable care, the court held that a defendant who undertakes an activity (such as driving a car) must meet the standard of care of a reasonably competent person undertaking that activity. The fact that the defendant is a learner who lacks skill does not lower the standard of care they are expected to meet. The standard of care is **objective** and **impersonal**.

The outcome (the principle applied to the facts) was:

The defendant, as a learner driver, was required to meet the same standard as a competent qualified driver. Despite the fact that she had done her best to control the car, she had fallen below this objective reasonable standard of care, and so was in breach of duty. Therefore, she was liable to the claimant for the injury her breach of duty had caused.

Notes:

Remember, that the defendant was covered by a policy of motor insurance; so, although she was found liable to the claimant, the damages would be paid by her insurer.

***

Bolam v Friern Hospital Management Committee [1957] 2 All ER 118 (QB)

The facts were:

The claimant was a voluntary patient at a mental hospital. (The claim was brought against the hospital management committee, as defendants responsible for the actions of the doctor who treated the claimant.) The doctor treating the claimant administered electro-convulsive therapy ('ECT'), which consisted of passing an electric current through the claimant's brain. During the treatment, the claimant suffered violent muscle spasms and convulsions that caused fractures of his pelvis.

It was known that ECT could cause convulsions, so that the treatment carried a risk of causing fractures. The medical evidence showed that there were different opinions on how the treatment should be administered to reduce the risk of such fractures. Some doctors would have administered a muscle relaxant drug or used some form of physical restraint. However, there was also a firm body of opinion that relaxant drugs should not be used, and nor should physical restraint. The doctor treating the claimant followed this practice and used neither drugs nor restraint.

The dispute to be decided by the court was:

The claimant alleged that the doctor was negligent by failing to administer a relaxant drug and/or apply a physical restraint.

Use these questions to analyse the legal issues:

- Would the doctor owe a duty of care to the claimant in these circumstances?
- What is the standard of care imposed on a defendant who exercises a special skill?
- What is the significance of the existence of different bodies of opinion on how to administer the treatment?

The principle of law applied/established was:

It was not in dispute that the doctor owed the claimant a duty of care. The issue was whether or not the doctor had breached the duty owed. The duty of care would be breached if the doctor had fallen below a reasonable standard of care. Since the doctor was exercising a special skill, a reasonable standard of care was to be judged according to the standard of the ordinary skilled person exercising that special skill. That is, in this case, the standard of the ordinary reasonable doctor carrying out the treatment. However, how was that standard to be applied where there were differing bodies of professional opinion? In answer to this it was held that a doctor is not negligent if he has acted in accordance with a responsible body of professional opinion, even if there is a conflicting body of opinion that would have acted differently.[3]

The outcome (the principle applied to the facts) was:

The doctor was not in breach of the duty of care owed to the claimant (because he had acted in accordance with a responsible body of professional opinion). So, the claim failed.

Notes:

The principle in this case was decided in the context of a doctor administering medical treatment, but it would apply equally to other professions.

***

---

3 Note, however, the different principles applied where the alleged negligence consists in the doctor's failure to disclose the risks of medical treatment. See: **Montgomery v Lanarkshire Health Board** [2015] UKSC 11, [2015] AC 1430, noted in Chapter 5.

22.4.3 Causation of damage

Barnett v Chelsea & Kensington Hospital Management Committee [1969] 1 QB 428 (QB)

The facts were:

The claimant was the wife of a workman who had died after attending hospital. (She made the claim for damages on behalf of the deceased's estate as well as for herself and her children as dependants.)

The workman had become ill after drinking tea, and had been vomiting. He attended the casualty department of the defendant hospital. The doctor on duty decided not to examine the workman. Instead, he was sent home and told to see his own local doctor. The workman later died of arsenic poisoning.

It was discovered that the tea was contaminated with the arsenic from an unknown source. The evidence showed that, even if the doctor had examined the workman and admitted him to hospital, the effects of the arsenic were such that it would have been too late to save his life.

The dispute to be decided by the court was:

The workman's wife claimed that the hospital was liable in negligence because of the doctor's failure to examine him. Could the hospital escape liability by relying on the fact that the workman would have died in any event?

Use these questions to analyse the legal issues:
- *Do the facts suggest that a duty of care was owed to the workman?*
- *Do the facts suggest that the doctor's conduct fell below a reasonable standard of care?*
- *What is the significance of the fact that the workman could not have been saved even if he had been examined and admitted to hospital?*

The principle of law applied/established was:

It was held that the hospital and the doctor owed a duty of care to the workman, which the doctor had breached by failing to examine him and admit him for treatment.

However, for a successful claim in negligence, it was not sufficient to establish duty of care and breach. It was also necessary to establish that the harm suffered was caused by the breach.

The outcome (the principle applied to the facts) was:

On the facts, the workman's wife had failed to establish, on the balance of probabilities, that the doctor's breach had caused the workman's death. So, although the doctor had acted negligently, the claim for damages failed.

Notes:

This case demonstrates the application of the 'but for' test for factual causation. On the facts, the claim failed because it could not be said that 'but for' the doctor's breach of duty the workman would not have died.

***

Bonnington Castings Ltd v Wardlaw [1956] AC 613 (HL)

The facts were:

The claimant contracted lung disease during his employment at the defendant's factory. The disease was caused by exposure to silica dust. There were multiple sources of silica dust in the defendant's factory. These were grinding machines ('grinder dust') and pneumatic hammers ('hammer dust'). Exposure to grinder dust could have been prevented if the dust extraction equipment had been properly maintained. So, the employer was in breach of its duty under industrial safety regulations in respect of this dust.

However, exposure to the hammer dust could not have been prevented, so the employer was not in breach of duty as regards the claimant's exposure to this dust.

As the employee had been exposed to both sources of dust, he was unable to prove that his lung disease was caused by the grinder dust. The most that could be proved was that the grinder dust had contributed to causing the disease.

The dispute to be decided by the court was:

For a successful claim, the claimant needed to establish a sufficient causal link between his lung disease and the employer's breach of duty. Was the contribution made by the grinder dust sufficient?

Use these questions to analyse the legal issues:

- What is the basic test used to establish that the defendant's breach of duty was the cause of the claimant's damage?
- How is causation established where multiple causes combine together to cause the claimant's damage?

The principle of law applied/established was:

The basic test to establish causation of damage is the 'but for' test. Can it be said that 'but for' the defendant's breach the claimant would not have suffered harm?

However, the rules are modified where the defendant's breach of duty has combined with other causes to cause the claimant's harm. In such a case, although it is not possible for the claimant to prove that 'but for' the defendant's breach the claimant would not have been harmed, the claimant can establish causation provided that he can show that the defendant's breach made at least a material contribution to the harm.

The outcome (the principle applied to the facts) was:

The facts showed that the claimant had suffered one injury (lung disease) caused by multiple causes combining together (the grinder dust and the hammer dust). Therefore, he could not prove that 'but for' the employer's breach of duty in exposing him to the grinder dust he would not have contracted the disease. However, he could prove that the employer's breach had made a material contribution to causing the disease. That was sufficient to establish the necessary causal link, and the claim was successful.

Notes:

For other important cases dealing with causation of damage you may wish to look at:

McGhee v National Coal Board [1972] 3 All ER 1008 (HL)
Wilsher v Essex AHA [1988] AC 1074 (HL)
Fairchild v Glenhaven Funeral Services Ltd [2002] UKHL 22, [2003] 1 AC 32
Barker v Corus (UK) Plc [2006] UKHL 20, [2006] 2 AC 572, and **Compensation Act 2006** s.3
Clough v First Choice Holidays and Flights Ltd [2006] EWCA Civ 15, [2006] PIQR P22
International Energy Group Ltd v Zurich Insurance Plc UK [2015] UKSC 33, [2016] AC 509

***

22.4.4 Remoteness of damage

Overseas Tankship (UK) Ltd v Morts Dock & Engineering Co (The Wagon Mound), (No.1) [1961] AC 388 (PC)

The facts were:

The defendant's ship (SS *Wagon Mound*) was in harbour taking on fuel oil. The defendant's employees negligently allowed a large quantity of the oil to spill into the water of the harbour. The claimant company owned a wharf in the harbour where it repaired ships. The spilled oil floated on the water and reached the claimant's wharf. The claimant was carrying out welding on a ship being repaired at the wharf. Hot metal fell from the wharf and ignited the oil. The oil had soaked into a cotton rag floating on the water and this acted as wick, allowing the oil to ignite. The fire damaged the wharf and the equipment on it.

The dispute to be decided by the court was:

The fire damage was a direct result of the oil spillage caused by the negligence of the defendant's employees. However, it was not reasonably foreseeable that oil floating on water could catch fire, so the damage was not reasonably foreseeable. In those circumstances, was the claimant entitled to recover damages for the harm caused?

Use these questions to analyse the legal issues:

- On these facts, was the claimant able to show that 'but for' the defendant's negligence the claimant would not have suffered the harm? (factual causation)
- Where factual causation is established, what limitation does the law place on the extent of recoverable damage?

The principle of law applied/established was:

Damage is not recoverable if it was not a **reasonably foreseeable** consequence of the defendant's negligence.

The outcome (the principle applied to the facts) was:

Although the claimant could show that 'but for' the negligence the harm would not have occurred, the damage was not recoverable because it was too remote a consequence of the negligence. Even where factual causation is established, damage is too remote if it was not reasonably foreseeable. Therefore, although the negligence of the defendant's employees in spilling the oil did cause the fire damage to the claimant's wharf and equipment, the claimant was unable to recover compensation for that harm.

Notes:

It is important not to confuse **The Wagon Mound (No.1)** with **Overseas Tankship (UK) Ltd v The Miller Steamship Co Pty and Another (The Wagon Mound), (No.2)** [1967] 1 AC 617 (PC). **The Wagon Mound (No.2)** dealt with different claims arising from the same fire. The claimants were the owners of the ships undergoing repairs and damaged in the fire. This case was decided on different issues and did not affect the principles established in **The Wagon Mound (No.1)**.

***

22.5 Defences

Froom v Butcher [1976] 1 QB 286 (CA)

The facts were:

The claimant was injured whilst driving his car, in an accident caused wholly by the negligence of the defendant. The claimant had chosen not to wear a seatbelt.

The claimant suffered head and chest injuries which would probably have been prevented if he had worn the seatbelt.

So, the accident was caused by the defendant; but the claimant's injuries were caused in part by the claimant's failure to wear the seatbelt

The dispute to be decided by the court was:

The defendant admitted liability for the accident but argued that the defendant's damages should be reduced because his injuries were the result of his failure to wear a seatbelt.

Use these questions to analyse the legal issues:

- What defence is relevant where the defendant alleges that the claimant has failed to take reasonable care for their own safety?
- Could that defence apply despite the fact that the claimant's carelessness did not contribute to causing the accident to happen?

The principle of law applied/established was:

A claimant who has failed to take reasonable care for their own safety is guilty of contributory negligence. Failure to wear a seat belt amounts to contributory negligence where it contributed to the claimant's injuries.

In determining whether contributory negligence applies, the question is whether the claimant's carelessness contributed to the harm he suffered (not whether it contributed to causing the accident).

The outcome (the principle applied to the facts) was:

The claimant was guilty of contributory negligence. Therefore, in accordance with the **Law Reform (Contributory Negligence) Act 1945**, the claimant's damages were reduced.

Notes:

Contributory negligence operates as a partial defence to the claim. It does not defeat the claim entirely, but does reduce the claimant's damages. Under the

Law Reform (Contributory Negligence) Act 1945, damages are to be reduced to such extent as the court thinks just and equitable having regard to the claimant's share in responsibility for the damage. In *Froom*, the court gave guidance as to the appropriate reductions for failure to wear a seatbelt:

- If the injuries would have been prevented altogether by wearing a seat belt, damages should be reduced by 25 per cent.
- If the injuries would have been less severe had a seat belt been worn, damages should be reduced by 15 per cent.
- Where wearing a seat belt would not have made any difference, so that the injuries would have been the same, damages will not be reduced (because the claimant's carelessness has not contributed to the damage suffered).

***

22.6 Economic loss

22.6.1 Negligent statements

Caparo Industries Plc v Dickman and Others [1990] 2 AC 605 (HL)

Caparo developed the principles for duty of care in cases of pure economic loss arising from negligent statements. This case was considered above (at Section 22.4.1), and you will find it useful to refer back to it here.

For an important case predating *Caparo* and establishing principles subsequently developed in *Caparo* and later cases see *Hedley Byrne & Co Ltd v Heller & Partners Ltd* [1964] AC 465 (HL).

For a recent case applying those principles you may wish to read *Playboy Club London Ltd v Banca Nazionale del Lavoro SpA* [2018] UKSC 43, [2019] 2 All ER 478.

22.6.2 Acquisition of a defective product

Muirhead v Industrial Tank Specialities Ltd and Others [1986] QB 507 (CA)

The facts were:

The claimant was a fish merchant. He purchased water tanks in which to store live lobsters. The tanks were fitted with water pumps to provide oxygen to keep the lobsters alive. Whilst the tanks were in use the water pumps failed and all the lobsters died. The claimant suffered losses which included:

- The cost of the defective pumps (and other economic loss resulting from failure of the pumps).
- The physical damage to the lobsters.

The claimant had a valid claim (in contract) against the company that supplied the tanks and pumps, and obtained a judgment for damages. However, the supplier became insolvent, so the damages were not paid. Therefore, the claimant pursued the claim against the original manufacturer of the electric motors that had caused the pumps to fail (with whom he had no contractual relationship).

The dispute to be decided by the court was:

The claim against the manufacturer was pursued in the tort of negligence. Could the claimant recover all of his losses from the manufacturer?

Use these questions to analyse the legal issues:

- A manufacturer owes a duty of care in respect of damage caused by a defective product; but what kind of damage does this cover?
- What was the difference between the damage suffered by the pumps themselves and the damage caused to the lobsters that died?

The principle of law applied/established was:

No duty of care is owed in respect of damage to the product *itself* (since this is pure economic loss).

However, where damage is cause *by* a defective product to *other property* owned by the claimant, a duty of care can be owed in respect of that damage.

The outcome (the principle applied to the facts) was:

It was necessary to distinguish between damage suffered by the pumps *themselves* and damage caused by the pumps to the claimant's *other property*, the lobsters.

The damage suffered by the pumps themselves was pure economic loss, so the manufacturer did not owe the claimant a duty of care in respect of that damage. Thus, the claimant was not able to recover the purchase cost of the pumps (and other financial losses resulting from their failure). However, the claimant was able to recover damages for the physical damage caused to the lobsters (including any *consequential* economic loss flowing from that physical damage).

Notes:

For a further important case on pure economic loss caused by acquisition of a defective product (in this case a badly constructed house) see **Murphy v Brentwood DC** [1991] 1 AC 398 (HL).

It is important to distinguish pure economic loss caused by the acquisition of a defective product (as above) from pure economic loss caused by damage to property belonging to someone else (as explained in Chapter 8). For a key case on this kind of pure economic loss see **Spartan Steel & Alloys Ltd v Martin & Co (Contractors) Ltd** [1973] QB 27 (CA).

***

22.7 Psychiatric harm

22.7.1 Primary victims

Page v Smith [1996] AC 155 (HL)

The facts were:

The claimant was involved in a car accident caused by the negligence of the defendant. The claimant did not suffer any physical injury in the accident. However, prior to the accident he had been suffering from a medically recognised condition (known as 'ME'). He claimed that the accident had caused the ME to become worse, and he sought damages for this aggravation of his condition.

This was a case of pure psychiatric harm because the claimant's medical condition was caused by the shock of the accident rather than by any physical injury sustained in the accident.

The claimant was a **primary victim** because he was within the actual area of danger created by the defendant's negligence.

The dispute to be decided by the court was:

It was argued that the defendant did not owe the claimant a duty of care in respect of injury caused by shock because, in the circumstances, injury by shock was not reasonably foreseeable.

Use these questions to analyse the legal issues:

- What is the test used to determine whether a duty of care is owed to a primary victim?
- How does this test differ from that applied to the issue of duty of care in relation to secondary victims?

The principle of law applied/established was:

When considering the duty of care owed in respect of injuries caused by shock, it is necessary to distinguish between primary and secondary victims.

For a primary victim, establishing a duty of care does not depend on showing that injury by shock was reasonably foreseeable. For primary victims, a medically recognised illness caused by shock is treated in the same way as physical injury. Therefore, primary victims are owed a duty of care provided they were placed at a foreseeable risk of physical injury.

The outcome (the principle applied to the facts) was:

Although the issue of duty of care was resolved as above, there remained the issue of causation of damage. The defendant did not accept that the exacerbation of the claimant's ME had in fact been caused by the accident. This issue was sent back to the Court of Appeal, which upheld the finding that the claimant's ME had been aggravated by the trauma of the accident. Therefore, the claimant was entitled to damages for the exacerbation of his condition. See **Page v Smith** (No.2) [1996] 1 WLR 855.

Notes:

Contrast the findings in this case with the position on secondary victims. A secondary victim suffers a medically recognised psychiatric illness but is not in the area of danger caused by the defendant's negligence. In **Page**, the court pointed out that secondary victims are not exposed to a foreseeable risk of physical injury (because they are outside the area of danger). Therefore, **foreseeability of psychiatric injury** *is* required for a duty of care to be owed to a **secondary victim**. Note also the further conditions to be satisfied for a duty of care to be owed to a secondary victim, set out in **Alcock v Chief Constable of South Yorkshire**, below.

***

22.7.2 Secondary victims

Alcock v Chief Constable of South Yorkshire [1992] 1 AC 310 (HL)

The facts were:

The case arose from a disaster at the Hillsborough football stadium. The defendant was responsible for policing a match at the stadium. As a result of the defendant's negligence, overcrowding occurred; 95 people died, and many others were injured.

This case concerned claims by people who witnessed the events. It was admitted that the defendant's negligence had caused the shocking events witnessed by the claimants. For the purpose of giving judgment on the issues it was assumed that each claimant could prove they had suffered a medically recognised psychiatric illness caused by the shock of witnessing those events.

There were a number of claimants who had witnessed the events in different ways. None of them were in the area where the disaster occurred. Some of them were present in other parts of the football ground. Some witnessed events on television (live or recorded).

Each of the claimants was a relative of one of the immediate victims involved in the disaster (except for one who was the fiancé of an immediate victim).

The dispute to be decided by the court was:

Whilst it was accepted that the defendant had been negligent, the defendant denied that he was liable to compensate these claimants for the harm they had suffered.

Use these questions to analyse the legal issues:

- Which of the elements of a claim in negligence was disputed by the defendant in this case?
- How did the victims in this case differ from those who were killed or injured in the disaster?
- What conditions need to be satisfied for the defendant to be liable to victims of this kind?

The principle of law applied/established was:

The defendant denied that he owed a duty of care to the claimants.

The findings in the case established that, for a duty of care to be owed to a **secondary victim** suffering psychiatric illness caused by shock, it was necessary to show not only that such injury was **reasonably foreseeable**, but also that the claimant satisfied the following conditions:

- Close ties of love and affection with the immediate victim
- Proximity to the accident
- Direct perception of events by sight or hearing.

The outcome (the principle applied to the facts) was:

None of the claimants were able to satisfy all of these conditions. The claimants who were present at the ground (so in proximity to the accident and with direct perception of events) had not demonstrated close ties of love and affection with an immediate victim. Some of the claimants did satisfy the requirement of close ties of love and affection with an immediate victim. However, they had witnessed events on television, and so did not meet the requirements for proximity to the accident and direct perception of events.

Therefore, no duty of care was owed to the secondary victims in this case. So, they did not receive compensation for the harm they suffered.

Notes:

See also **McLoughlin v O'Brian** [1983] 1 AC 410 (HL), on witnessing not the accident itself, but the immediate aftermath.

***

22.8 Remedies

Hicks and Others v Chief Constable of the South Yorkshire Police [1992] 2 All ER 65 (HL)

The facts were:

The case arose from a disaster at the Hillsborough football stadium. The defendant was responsible for policing a match at the stadium. As a result of the defendant's negligence, overcrowding occurred and many people were killed or injured. This case concerned two sisters who died during the disaster. The sisters died when they were caught in the crush caused by the overcrowding. They were aged 19 and 15.

The claim was brought by their parents. The parents sought an award of damages for pain and suffering of the sisters prior to their death.

The medical evidence showed that, in the crush, the sisters would have lost consciousness within seconds and died within five minutes. The judge at trial found that the sisters had not suffered any physical injury before they died.

The dispute to be decided by the court was:

The dispute in this case was one of fact. The parents sought to persuade the House of Lords that, on the facts, the sisters had suffered injuries causing considerable pain and suffering. On this issue of fact, the House of Lords held that it could not depart from the findings of the judge at trial. It also confirmed that fear of death was not, in itself, capable of giving rise to a claim.

Use these questions to analyse the legal issues:

- What potential claims might have arisen from the death of the two girls?
- On the facts as found by the court, which (if any) of those claims could succeed?

The principle of law applied/established was:

This case did not establish any new law, but it is a very useful illustration of the rules for awarding damages on death.

The sisters did not have any dependants. Therefore, there could be no claim for damages for loss of dependency under the *Fatal Accidents Act 1976* ('FAA').

Their parents had suffered bereavement. However, damages for bereavement under the FAA are only payable to bereaved parents where the deceased was aged under 18 (and unmarried). Therefore, only the death of the younger sister attracted the fixed statutory sum for bereavement damages.

The only claim the parents could bring was under the *Law Reform (Miscellaneous Provisions) Act 1934*, in their capacity as administrators of the girls' estates. The 1934 Act would have allowed any cause of action the sisters had prior to their death to survive for the benefit of their estate. However, because it could not be proved that the sisters had suffered injury before their death, no cause of action had arisen.

The outcome (the principle applied to the facts) was:

Since it could not be shown that the sisters had suffered injury prior to their death, no cause of action had arisen prior to their death. Therefore, no cause of action could survive their death for the benefit of their estate. So, no award of damages could be made.

Notes:

This case illustrates very starkly the fact that, in the tort of negligence, damage is an essential element of the claim. If the claimant cannot establish that the defendant's negligence caused them to suffer actionable damage, compensation cannot be awarded. The court noted that the claim was not brought for financial reasons. Its aim was to demonstrate the anger felt by the parents at the negligence which had occurred. However, the court pointed out that in a civil action for negligence damages are compensatory, not punitive.

***

22.9 Employers' liability

Wilsons & Clyde Coal Co Ltd v English [1938] AC 57 (HL)

The facts were:

The defendant was a company that owned a coal mine. The claimant was an employee at the defendant's coal mine. He was injured whilst working down the mine.

Statute prevented the defendant company itself from taking part in the technical management of the mine. Statute required the technical management of the mine to be entrusted to a qualified mine manager.

On the facts, it was found that the system of working at the mine was not reasonably safe, and that this was the cause of the claimant's injuries. It was also found that the directors of the defendant company did not know of the unsafe system of working. However, the mine manager did know.

The claimant pursued a claim in the tort of negligence.

The dispute to be decided by the court was:

Was the defendant company liable for an injury suffered by its employee, even where it had delegated the technical management of the mine to a qualified mine manager?

Use these questions to analyse the legal issues:

- What is the scope of the duty of care owed by an employer to employees?
- What is the special nature of the employer's duty of care – can it be delegated?

The principle of law applied/established was:

The duty of care owed by an employer to employees, to take reasonable care for their safety, encompasses the following aspects:

- Safe place and safe system of working
- Safe equipment
- Competent fellow staff.

The duty of care owed by an employer to employees cannot be delegated. Although the employer may appoint someone to carry out the duty, the employer remains responsible for ensuring that reasonable care is taken. (So, the employer's duty of care is referred to as a 'non-delegable' duty.)

The outcome (the principle applied to the facts) was:

The defendant company, which owned the mine and employed the claimant, owed him a duty to take reasonable care to provide a safe system of work. That duty could not be delegated to the mine manager. Therefore, the employer remained responsible for the failure to provide a safe system. So, the claimant's claim against his employer was successful.

Notes:

The judgments in the case describe the employer's duty of care under three heads, but it is clear from subsequent case law that it covers four aspects: safe place of work, safe equipment, safe system of work, and competent fellow staff.

***

22.10 Vicarious liability

Various Claimants v Wm Morrison Supermarkets Plc [2020] UKSC 12, [2020] 2 WLR 941

The facts were:

The case concerned the liability of the defendant company ('Morrisons') for torts carried out by its employee. The employee was employed by Morrisons as an auditor. For the purposes of an audit of Morrisons' accounts he was given the task of collating payroll data. He was given access to data that contained personal information about Morrisons' staff (e.g., their names and addresses and bank details).

The employee had developed a grudge against his employer, Morrisons. So, he copied the payroll data and published it on the internet. The claimants were the Morrisons' staff whose personal information had been wrongfully published.

The claimants sought damages for misuse of private information, breach of confidence, and breach of statutory duty under the **Data Protection Act 1998**. The judge at trial found that Morrisons itself was not personally liable for any of those breaches. Therefore, the case concerned the vicarious liability of Morrisons for the actions of its employee, the auditor who had wrongfully published the information.

The dispute to be decided by the court was:

Was the defendant, Morrisons, vicariously liable for the wrongful disclosure of the claimants' personal data? The auditor was employed by Morrisons. He committed torts by wrongfully disclosing the data. However, were those torts committed **during the course of his employment** with Morrisons?

Use this question to analyse the legal issues:

- What is the test used to determine whether or not an employee who commits a tort was acting in the course of their employment?

The principle of law applied/established was:

An employer is vicariously liable for torts committed by its employee during the course of employment. The test to determine whether or not an employee was acting in the course of employment is:

Was the tort was **so closely connected** with acts the employee was authorised to do that it may fairly and properly be regarded as done in the ordinary course of employment?

In order to decide whether this 'close connection' test is satisfied the court must consider the following:

- What functions or 'field of activities' were entrusted by the employer to the employee (i.e., what was the nature of the employee's job)? and
- Was there was a sufficiently close connection between the position in which the employee was employed and the tort for it to be right for the employer to be held liable?

The outcome (the principle applied to the facts) was:

The court found that disclosure of the personal data was not part of the function entrusted to the employee. The close connection test was not satisfied, and the torts had not been committed during the course of his employment with Morrisons. Therefore, Morrisons was not vicariously liable for the wrongful disclosure of the claimants' personal data.

Notes:

In this case the Supreme Court applied the principles of vicarious liability set out in its previous decision, **Mohamud v Wm Morrison Supermarkets Plc** [2016] UKSC 11, [2016] AC 677.

For a further important decision on vicarious liability see also **Various Claimants v Barclays Bank Plc** [2020] UKSC 13, [2020] 2 WLR 960, on relationships capable of giving rise to vicarious liability. The case sets out the distinction to be drawn between a relationship with an **independent contractor** in business on their own account (which does not give rise to vicarious liability) and a relationship of employment or akin to employment (which may give rise to vicarious liability).

***

22.11 Occupiers' liability

22.11.1 Lawful visitors

Wheat v E Lacon & Co Ltd [1966] AC 552 (HL)

The facts were:

The claimant was the widow of a man who died when he fell from a staircase in a public house. The defendant company was the brewery that owned the public house.

The widow claimed damages arising from the death (under the **Law Reform (Miscellaneous Provisions) Act 1934** and under the predecessor to the **Fatal Accidents Act 1976**).

The claims depended on establishing that the defendant would have been liable to the deceased. The widow claimed that the defendant was liable to the deceased, as a lawful visitor, under the *Occupiers' Liability Act 1957* ('OLA 57').

The defendant employed a manager. The manager ran the ground floor of the premises as a public house. The first floor was used by the manager and his wife as their private living accommodation. The manager's wife was allowed to take paying guests in the private accommodation for her own profit.

The claimant and her husband were staying as paying guests. The husband fell from a staircase in the private accommodation and died. There were two relevant features of the state of the premises. First, the light at the top of the stairs had no lightbulb at the time of the accident. Second, the handrail on the staircase finished before the bottom of the stairs. The trial judge found that the husband, descending in the dark, probably fell because he reached the bottom of the handrail and stepped out, thinking he had reached the bottom of the stairs.

The widow had originally claimed against the both the defendant company and the manager and his wife. At trial, the claim against the manager and his wife was unsuccessful, and the appeal to the House of Lords concerned only the claim against the defendant company.

The dispute to be decided by the court was:

Did the defendant company owe a duty to the deceased husband to ensure that the handrail was safe or that the stairs were properly lit?

This involved considering: for the purposes of OLA 57, was the defendant company an occupier of the private part of the premises where the accident occurred?

Use these questions to analyse the legal issues:

- OLA 57 does not define the term 'occupier' other than to say that it has the same meaning as at common law. So, what is the test used to determine whether a person is the occupier of premises for the purposes of the Act?
- Where a person is the occupier of premises, what duty of care is owed to a lawful visitor coming on to the premises?

The principle of law applied/established was:

A person is the occupier of premises whenever they have a sufficient degree of control over premises that they ought to realise that their failure to take care could cause injury to a person coming on to the premises.

In order for a person to be an occupier it is not necessary that they have entire control or exclusive occupation of the premises. It is sufficient that they have some degree of control.

An occupier may share control of the premises with others, so two or more people may be the occupier. Where this happens, both occupiers owe a duty of care to visitors (the application of which will vary depending on their degree of control). So, both occupiers could be liable to the visitor.

The outcome (the principle applied to the facts) was:

The defendant company had a sufficient degree of control over the private part of the premises where the accident occurred. So, it was an occupier for the purposes of OLA 57. Therefore, it *did* owe the deceased a duty under the Act.

Under OLA 57, the duty owed by an occupier to a lawful visitor is to take reasonable care to see that they will be reasonably safe in using the premises. On the facts, the defendant was *not* in breach of that duty. As regards the staircase, no one had foreseen that the handrail was dangerous. As regards the lighting, it was reasonable for the defendant company to leave maintenance of lightbulbs to the manager and his wife (who were also occupiers).

Therefore, the widow's claim for damages was unsuccessful.

Notes:

During the appeal, the court expressed the view that the manager and his wife also had a sufficient degree of control over the premises to be an occupier. So, they had also owed the deceased a duty of care (though they may not have been in breach). However, the claim against them was not being pursued on appeal.

***

22.11.2 Trespassers

Tomlinson v Congleton BC [2003] UKHL 47, [2004] 1 AC 46

The facts were:

The defendant borough council was the occupier of a country park to which the public were allowed access. The park contained a lake which was known to be dangerous for swimming. Swimming in the lake was prohibited. The council had taken steps to warn the public of the dangers of swimming in the lake. However, it was aware that the warnings were often ignored, and that people continued to swim in the lake.

The claimant, aged 18, went to the park with some friends, and they decided to swim in the lake. The claimant waded into the water and then dived head first into the shallow water at the edge of the lake. The claimant's head struck the bottom of the lake and he suffered a very serious injury, resulting in paralysis.

The claimant claimed damages for his injury against the council as occupier of the park. Although the claimant was a lawful visitor to the park itself, he became a trespasser when he entered the lake because he was not permitted to be there. Thus, liability was governed by the *Occupiers' Liability Act 1984* ('OLA 84').

The dispute to be decided by the court was:

Did the council owe the claimant any duty of care under OLA 84 in respect of the danger posed by swimming in the lake?

Use these questions to analyse the legal issues:

- To what kind of dangers does OLA 84 apply?
- What conditions must be satisfied if the occupier of premises is to owe a duty of care to a trespasser who suffers injury on the premises?

The principle of law applied/established was:

Under OLA 84 s.1(1), an occupier may owe a trespasser a duty of care in respect of dangers due to the state of the premises.

Under s.1(3) such duty is only owed if all of the following are satisfied:

- The occupier is aware of the danger (or has reasonable grounds to believe that it exists).
- The occupier knows that the trespasser is in the vicinity of the danger (or has reasonable grounds to believe that he may come into the vicinity).
- It would be reasonable in all the circumstances to expect the occupier to offer the trespasser some protection against the danger.

The outcome (the principle applied to the facts) was:

The court held that the danger posed by swimming in the lake was **not a danger due to the state of the premises**. The danger was caused by the claimant's own decision to swim in the lake. The danger arose out of what he chose to do, not out of the state of the premises. This was sufficient to hold that the defendant did not owe the claimant a duty of care.

However, the court also considered the conditions in OLA 84 s.1(3) and held that (even if the lake had been a danger due to the state of the premises) it would *not* have been **reasonable in all the circumstances to expect the council to offer the claimant protection** against the danger. This was a further reason supporting the decision that no duty of care was owed.

Therefore, the claimant's claim for damages in respect of his injuries failed.

***

22.12 Product liability

Abouzaid v Mothercare (UK) Ltd [2000] All ER (D) 2436 (CA), [2001] CLY 920 (CA)

The facts were:

The claimant claimed damages arising from an accident caused by a product of the defendant company, Mothercare.

The claim was pursued under both the **Consumer Protection Act 1987** ('CPA') and in **negligence**. For the purposes of the CPA, Mothercare was the **producer** of the product, and so was a relevant defendant. In negligence, Mothercare owed a duty of care, as it had held itself out as the **manufacturer**.

At the time of the accident the claimant was 12 years old. He was helping to attach a fleece-lined bag to a pushchair. The fastening to attach the bag was two elastic straps fastened by a buckle. As the claimant was trying to fasten the straps, one of them slipped from his grasp. The buckle sprang back on the elastic and hit him in the eye, causing a serious injury. The claimant claimed damages for the injury.

The evidence showed that, prior to this accident, there had been no previous reports of similar accidents, so the risk posed by the elastic strap had not been appreciated.

The dispute to be decided by the court was:

Liability under the **CPA**: was the product defective within the meaning of the Act?

Liability in **negligence**: was the defendant in breach of the duty of care it owed to the claimant?

Use these questions to analyse the legal issues:

- Under the CPA, what is the test to determine whether a product is defective?
- In negligence, what standard of care is the manufacturer of a product expected to meet?
- What is the relevance to each claim of the fact that there were no previous reports of similar accidents?

The principle of law applied/established was:

Under the **CPA** a product is defective if its safety is not such as persons generally are entitled to expect.

In **negligence**, a manufacturer is expected to take reasonable care. Reasonable care would depend on the risk which could reasonably have been foreseen at the time of the accident.

The outcome (the principle applied to the facts) was:

On the claim in **negligence**, it was held that, although Mothercare owed a duty of care to the claimant (as manufacturer of the product), it was not in breach of that duty. Given that there were no reported accidents suggesting that the elastic fastening posed any risk to safety, Mothercare had not fallen below a reasonable standard of care.

On the claim under the **CPA**, the court held that the product (the fleece bag) was **defective**, since its safety was not such as persons generally were entitled to expect. The lack of any previously reported accidents alerting the defendant to the risk posed by the elastic strap was not relevant in determining whether the product was defective.

Therefore, the claimant's claim for damages under the CPA was successful and he was able to recover compensation for his injury.

Notes:

This case provides a good illustration of the difference between fault-based liability in the tort of negligence and strict liability under the CPA.

One of the issues in this case was whether or not the product was defective within the meaning of the CPA. For a more recent case, dealing with more complex issues regarding the existence of a defect under the CPA, you may wish to look at *Gee v DePuy International Ltd* [2018] EWHC 1208 (QB), [2018] Med LR 347.

***

22.13 Nuisance

Coventry v Lawrence [2014] UKSC 13, [2014] AC 822

The facts were:

The defendants carried out motor racing at a stadium. The racing activities had been taking place since 1976 and had planning permission. The racing caused noise.

The claimants moved into a bungalow near to the stadium in 2006. The claimants claimed that the noise from the racing at the stadium constituted a nuisance. The claimants sought an award of damages for the past nuisance already caused, and an injunction to restrain the defendants from continuing to cause a nuisance in future.

The dispute to be decided by the court was:

The defendant contended that there was no actionable nuisance because:

- The motor racing activities had planning permission.
- The motor racing had been carried on for more than 20 years.
- The claimants had moved into the bungalow when the motor racing was already taking place (i.e., the claimant came to the nuisance).

The defendant also wished to argue (on appeal) that, if the motor racing did amount to a nuisance, the grant of an injunction was not an appropriate remedy, and that damages in lieu of an injunction would be more appropriate.

Use these questions to analyse the legal issues:

- Where there is an unreasonable interference amounting to a nuisance:
  - Is this excused by a grant of planning permission?
  - Is it excused by the fact that the claimant came to the affected land when the nuisance was already in existence?
- What potential defence could arise where a nuisance continues for more than 20 years?

The principle of law applied/established was:

A grant of planning permission does not authorise the commission of a nuisance.

Nor does a grant of planning permission change the character of the neighbourhood. (This point arose because in a case of an intangible interference – such as noise – the court will consider the character of the neighbourhood as a factor in assessing whether the interference was unreasonable.)

The fact that a claimant came to an already existing nuisance is not a defence.

If a nuisance has continued for 20 years, it is possible for the defence of prescription to apply.

The grant of an injunction is a discretionary remedy. The starting point, where a nuisance has been established, is that an injunction should be granted. However, the court has a discretion to refuse an injunction and award damages instead. The court set out the principles for exercise of that discretion. In particular, it noted that public interest could be a relevant factor to be taken into account.

The outcome (the principle applied to the facts) was:

Although the defendant had been carrying on motor racing for over 20 years, the level of noise had not amounted to a nuisance for 20 years. So, on the facts, the defence of prescription did not apply.

The defendant's arguments about planning permission, and coming to a nuisance, had also not been successful. So, the defendant was liable in nuisance.

Thus, on appeal, the remedies granted by the trial judge were restored. These were:

- Damages for the past nuisance, and
- An injunction to restrain the defendants from committing a nuisance in future (by limiting the levels of noise that could be emitted by the motor racing).

Notes:

Should you wish to read further on this area, you may wish to look at *Hunter v Canary Wharf Ltd* [1997] AC 655 (HL) and *Fearn v Tate Gallery Board of Trustees* [2020] EWCA Civ 104, [2020] 2 WLR 1081.

For an important case on both private nuisance and the rule in *Rylands v Fletcher* see *Cambridge Water Co Ltd v Eastern Counties Leather Plc* [1994] 2 AC 264 (HL).

For the rule in *Rylands v Fletcher* see *Transco Plc v Stockport MBC* [2003] UKHL 61, [2004] 2 AC 1.

***

22.14 Defamation

The following case is just one of many that could have been chosen to illustrate defamation. However, it is useful because its facts illustrate each of the elements of defamation.

Byrne v Deane [1937] 1 KB 818 (CA)

The facts were:

The claimant, Mr Byrne, was a member of a golf club. On the club premises were some illegal gambling machines, which were used by the members. Someone reported the illegal machines to the police. As a result, the police required the machines to be removed. Somebody, whose identity was not known, placed a notice on the wall of the club. It contained a verse referring to the removal of the gambling machines, the last part of which read:

> But he who gave the game away,
> May he byrnn in hell and rue the day.

The defendants were the owners of the club. They would have been entitled to remove the notice but had failed to do so.

The dispute to be decided by the court was:

The claimant's case was that the words in the notice suggested that he had reported the matter to the police (and had acted dishonourably by doing so), and that this was **defamatory** of him. He claimed that the defendants had **published** the defamatory statement by failing to remove the notice when they became aware of it. The defendants denied that the words were defamatory and denied that they had published them.

Use these questions to analyse the legal issues:

- What elements must a claimant establish for a successful claim in defamation?
- When is a statement defamatory?
- Would it be defamatory to say of the claimant that he had reported illegal activities to the police?

The principle of law applied/established was:

For a successful claim in defamation a claimant needs to establish that the statement complained of:

- was defamatory
- referred to him
- was published by the defendant.

This case illustrates how a statement may **refer to the claimant** despite the fact that it does not directly name him.

There is no single definition of when a statement is **defamatory**, but the relevant principle here is that a statement is defamatory if it would lower the claimant in the estimation of right-thinking people. Applying this test, the court held that it could not be defamatory to say that a person had reported criminal activity to the police.

On the issue of **publication**, the judgments indicate that a person may be responsible for publishing a defamatory statement where they fail to remove it when they are aware of it, and have the right to remove it and could easily have done so.

The outcome (the principle applied to the facts) was:

The court held that the statement was **not defamatory** of the claimant. Therefore, his claim failed.

Since the claim failed, it was not strictly necessary to deal with the question of whether the defendants had published the statement by failing to remove it. However, the majority found that the statement had been published by the defendants.

Notes:

This case predates the provision of the ***Defamation Act 2013*** s.1: that a statement is not defamatory unless its publication has caused or is likely to cause serious harm to the reputation of the claimant. However, if the case arose today, the claim would still fail on the same grounds – that the statement did not have a defamatory meaning. So, it would not become strictly necessary to consider whether it had caused serious harm.

On the issue of serious harm under the ***Defamation Act 2013***, you may also wish to read ***Lachaux v Independent Print Ltd*** [2019] UKSC 27, [2020] AC 612.

***

22.15 Misuse of private information

Campbell v Mirror Group Newspapers Ltd [2004] UKHL 22, [2004] 2 All ER 995

The facts were:

The claimant was a well-known model. She had stated publicly that she did not take drugs. The defendant newspaper published a story about her. The story stated that she had taken drugs and was seeking treatment for addiction. It also contained a covertly taken photograph of her outside the treatment venue, and it gave details of her treatment.

After publication of the story, the claimant accepted that she had taken illegal drugs and had sought treatment for her addiction.

The dispute to be decided by the court was:

The claimant brought a claim against the newspaper for misuse of her private information.

It was accepted that the claimant could not make a successful claim in relation to disclosure of the information that she had taken drugs and had sought treatment because, given her previous denials, it was a matter of legitimate public comment for the newspaper to set the record straight on that issue. (On this issue, the claimant's right to privacy was outweighed by the defendant's right to freedom of expression.)

However, the claimant sought damages in respect of publication of the photograph and disclosure of the details of her treatment.

Use these questions to analyse the legal issues:

- *Considering the nature of the information disclosed, what is the first issue for the court to determine?*
- *In relation to the disclosure, identify the conflicting rights of the claimant and the defendant. In these circumstances, which was likely to prevail?*

The principle of law applied/established was:

The court first determined whether the information disclosed about the claimant was private. Was it information in which she had a **reasonable expectation of privacy**?

The court then considered the balance between the claimant's right to **privacy** under Article 8 of the European Convention on Human Rights ('ECHR') and the defendant's right to **freedom of expression** (under Article 10 of the ECHR).

The outcome (the principle applied to the facts) was:

It was held that:

- The photograph of the claimant and the details of her treatment were private information.
- In relation to this information, the claimant's right to privacy outweighed the defendant's right to freedom of expression.

So, the claimant was entitled to compensation for those disclosures.

Notes:

For more recent examples of claims for misuse of private information you may wish to look at **Richard v BBC** [2018] EWHC 1837, [2019] 2 All ER 105; and **Ali v Channel 5 Broadcasting Ltd** [2019] EWCA Civ 677, [2019] All ER (D) 128 (Apr).

Chapter 22 revision points

When reading and analysing a decided case:

Draw a clear distinction between:

- The facts of the case – established by evidence (or assumed for the sake of argument)
- The arguments put forward by the parties
- The legal principles applied by the court
- The outcome of the case for the parties – the principles applied to the facts

Ensure that you focus on the legal principles established or applied in the case

23 Problem questions

23.1 Chapter overview

This chapter provides a range of problem questions. You can use these to develop your skills of client case analysis, applying the legal principles to the facts in a clear, concise, and structured way.

These skills are useful not only for answering exam questions, but also in practice when advising a client on the merits of their claim or defence.

Suggested answer structures for each question are provided at www.routledge.com/cw/sqe.

23.2 Problem questions

Each question indicates the parts of this book that you should have studied before you attempt it. When planning your answer you should first identify the area of law concerned. A good starting point is to ask the following:

- What harm has the potential claimant suffered?
- What tort could provide a remedy for that harm?

Once you have identified the relevant area(s) of tort law, apply your knowledge of the principles of tort law to the facts, using the following structure:

- Identify the claimant – who has been harmed?
- Identify the defendant(s) – who is responsible for the harm?
- Identify the relevant tort – what harm has the claimant suffered?
- What are the elements of the tort – how do they apply on the facts?
- Does the defendant have a defence?
- If liability is established, what remedies may be available?

You may, of course, be considering a dispute from the defendant's point of view. However, you would still need to analyse the claimant's claim so as to be able to assess the strength of the defendant's denial of liability. So, the case analysis structure above remains a good starting point.

Problem questions

It is always a good idea to start by writing a plan – of your answer to an exam question or of your advice to a client. You should do this as you work through each problem question. Then compare your plan with the suggested answer structure provided for each question on the companion website.

Question 1

Before attempting this question, you should have studied:

- Part 3 – Negligence
- Part 4 – General defences

A father, mother, and daughter (aged six) prepared to travel in the father's car. The mother carefully strapped the daughter into her child-seat but forgot to wear her own seatbelt. The car was driven by the father carefully within the speed limit. At a junction, a car driven by Joe pulled into their path, suddenly and without warning, and caused a collision. The father was unhurt. However, the mother suffered a very painful impact to her chest. The daughter suffered cuts and bruises, and is now afraid to travel by car.

The mother attended hospital, where she was examined by a junior doctor, Sara. Sara said the chest injury was just bruising, and that the mother should go home and rest. Over the next ten days the mother suffered severe pain in her chest.

She eventually returned to the hospital, where she was seen by a different doctor. He diagnosed a broken rib and punctured lung. He said that if Sara had diagnosed the injury correctly at the first hospital visit the pain could have been substantially reduced with medication. However, he also said that Sara should not be blamed because she was only recently qualified and inexperienced.

The medical evidence shows that the mother's injuries would have been avoided if she had been wearing a seatbelt.

Advise Joe as to the claims in tort he is likely to face arising from the injuries suffered by the mother and daughter. Explain the extent to which those claims are likely to be successful. Outline any claim Joe should consider making.

Question 2

Before attempting this question, you should have studied:

- Part 5 – Negligence: limited duty situations

Milo recently inherited a large sum of money. Using half of the money, he set up a catering business. He secured an order to cater for a three-day music festival with 200 people attending each evening.

The festival was run by Events Ltd ('EL'). Whilst at the site Milo met a director of EL who told him that EL had obtained a substantial bank loan thanks to a report from Norman, a financial consultant. He showed Milo the report. It was addressed to EL's bank, and stated that EL was likely to make a substantial profit within 12 months. After reading the report, Milo decided to invest the other half of his inheritance in EL.

EL owned a marquee on site and allocated a space there for Milo to trade. The day before the festival, Milo purchased food for the first evening and stored it in the marquee. He intended to purchase fresh food for each day's trading. Unfortunately, that night the marquee caught fire and was completely destroyed, along with Milo's stock of food. As a result of the destruction of EL's marquee, Milo was unable to continue trading at the festival. Milo suffered the following losses:

- For the first evening's trading, he had spent £2,000 on food. He had expected to make a net profit (after costs and expenses) on sales of food of £5,000. So, his total loss was £7,000.
- For the remaining two evenings, he had not yet purchased supplies of food but had expected to continue trading and make a net profit of £5,000 each evening.

Evidence later showed that the fire had been caused by incorrect wiring installed by Lighting UK, a contractor engaged by EL to provide lighting on the site.

The rest of the festival was able to continue as planned. So, Milo expected to gain some profit from his investment in EL. However, shortly afterwards it was disclosed that EL had made huge losses and Milo's investment was worthless. The financial consultant, Norman, had carelessly underestimated the business costs in his report and, had Milo known the true state of the company, he would never have invested.

Advise Milo as to any claims in tort he may have arising from the above events.

Question 3

Before attempting this question, you should have studied:

- Part 5 – Negligence: limited duty situations

Tom, a self-employed heavy goods vehicle driver, was making a delivery to a supermarket. As Tom was reversing his wagon he was distracted by his mobile phone and failed to keep a proper lookout. He reversed the wagon into a bus standing at a bus stop outside the supermarket.

Aisha was just getting off the bus as the wagon collided with it. She was thrown to the floor and suffered a serious head injury.

Justin was a passenger on the bus. From his seat he did not witness the injury to Aisha. However, he was sitting close to the area of the collision, and was afraid for his safety as the wagon hit the bus. Since the accident he has suffered from anxiety and difficulties sleeping.

Aisha had been travelling with a work colleague, Renata. Renata had already got off the bus before the accident. She was some distance away, so in no danger herself. However, she witnessed the collision and heard Aisha's cries. Since the accident Renata has suffered from recurring nightmares and has been diagnosed as suffering from post-traumatic stress disorder.

Aisha was taken to hospital, where she was cleaned up after the accident and admitted for further treatment. At the time of the accident Aisha's husband, Harry, was away on business. As soon as he got home the next day, he rushed to the hospital to see her. When he arrived, Aisha was asleep in bed on a ward. Harry was deeply shocked to see his wife in hospital. He immediately collapsed and suffered a sudden recurrence of a previous medical condition, chronic fatigue syndrome. Amongst other things, this causes him to suffer from severe joint pain and frequent headaches.

Advise Justin, Renata, and Harry as to any claims in tort they might have against Tom.

Question 4

Before attempting this question, you should have studied:

- Part 6 – Remedies in tort

Helen and her friend Liyana were travelling in Helen's new expensive car. Suddenly, a lorry pulled into their path and a collision occurred. Helen was killed instantly and Liyana was seriously injured. The car was damaged beyond repair. The driver of the lorry has admitted liability for the accident in full. The damages will be paid by his motor insurer.

Helen was a single parent aged 40, with a daughter aged 15, whom she supported from her salary. Helen lived in a large house, so she rented out part of it to her mother, who has her own pension and is financially independent. Helen also allowed an old friend, Nadia, to live there rent free. Helen's funeral expenses were paid for out of her estate.

Liyana suffered an injury to her spine, and will need to use a wheelchair for the rest of her life. She has undergone several painful operations and will need further surgery in the future.

Liyana was employed as a teacher. For six months she was off work and received sick pay of half her normal salary. However, after six months her employment was terminated because it was clear she would never be fit to return. She immediately found alternative employment, working part time as a tutor, but her salary is substantially lower than in her pre-accident employment.

Before the accident Liyana was a keen mountain-bike rider. She can no longer do this, and she misses it a lot. She has paid for substantial alterations to her house to allow for wheelchair access and mobility.

Explain how the damages arising from Helen's death and Liyana's injury will be calculated.

Question 5

Before attempting this question, you should have studied:

- Part 7 – Employers' liability and vicarious liability

Stores Ltd ('SL') operated a supermarket. Richard was employed by SL as a delivery driver. James was his supervisor. Richard had arrived for work late on several occasions. Yesterday, Richard arrived ten minutes late again. As he was driving his van out of the supermarket garage, James asked him to stop and come into his office. James told Richard that he was to be subject to disciplinary proceedings because of the habitual lateness. Richard lost his temper and punched James in the face, causing him a broken nose. Richard then stormed out of the garage, leaving the van blocking the exit.

SL had engaged Peter, a self-employed mechanic, to visit the supermarket garage to service the delivery vans. Peter ran his own business working for several local companies, and was in a hurry to move on to his next customer. Therefore, Peter decided to move the van that Richard had left blocking the entrance. He was unfamiliar with manoeuvring such a large van but decided to give it a try. Unfortunately, as he did so, he lost control of the steering. The rear of the van collided with a parked car belonging to Nina, a customer of SL. The car was badly damaged.

After the collision Peter returned to his work servicing the other vans. He was in a hurry to get the work done. As a result, he made a mistake when re-fitting the brakes to one of the vans. When an SL employee, Martha, drove the van later that day the brakes failed, causing the van to crash into a wall. Martha was seriously injured.

Advise SL as to its liability in tort to James, Nina, and Martha arising from the above events. (Do not discuss any claims SL itself might make.)

Question 6

Before attempting this question, you should have studied:

- Part 8 – Occupiers' liability

An NHS Trust ('the Trust') recently engaged an independent contractor, Bridges Ltd ('Bridges') to design and build a bridge between two of the hospital buildings on the Trust's premises. Bridges had previously worked for other NHS clients, so the Trust was satisfied of its suitability for the job. When the work was finished, a site meeting took place and the Trust's site manager approved the works.

The bridge was then opened for use. A sign on the bridge read:

> This bridge is only for the use of visitors to the hospital. Use by all other persons is prohibited.

Shortly after the bridge was opened, five-year-old Anika was visiting the hospital with her mother. The mother allowed Anika to run ahead unsupervised. When Anika reached the bridge, she climbed on the railings and leaned over the handrail. Unfortunately, she lost her balance and toppled over, falling off the bridge and suffering serious injury. An engineer's report has since shown that the height of the handrail was too low and did not comply with building regulations. If the handrail had been at the correct height, it would have prevented Anika from falling. The Trust has not accepted responsibility because it had entrusted the design of the handrail to Bridges. It also says that the mother was partly to blame for failing to supervise Anika.

Later, a further accident occurred. Kevin, aged 16, was attempting to swing from the underside of the bridge when he lost his grip and fell to the ground, sustaining a very serious injury. The bridge had become an attraction for local teenagers in the evenings after the hospital was closed. They dared each other to cross the bridge by swinging beneath it. The Trust staff had warned the teenagers on several occasions that this was not allowed, but had not taken any further action. A report on this accident says there was no relevant defect in the bridge contributing to Kevin's fall.

Advise the Trust as to its potential liability in tort to Anika and Kevin.

Question 7

Before attempting this question, you should have studied:

- Part 9 – Product liability

You have been consulted by Jenny and Rob for advice on the following events.

Jenny was given a new electric hot brush for her birthday. The first time she used it to style her hair, the brush suddenly overheated and began to spark. Jenny dropped the brush, but it had already caused a nasty burn to her hand. She dropped it on to her dressing table, where it scorched the top. The dressing table was new and will cost £200 to replace. The brush itself no longer works. An expert's report shows that it had a faulty internal component which caused it to overheat.

Jenny has been unable to find out who manufactured the hot brush. She did manage to locate the shop from which it was purchased. However, the shop owner was unable to provide any further information on either the manufacturer or his own supplier. The shop owner also pointed out that the brush had been supplied to him in sealed packaging so that he had no way to inspect it prior to sale.

Rob is a self-employed painter and decorator. Recently, he was working at a client's premises using a pressurised paint-spraying machine. He took the machine outside to his van and refilled it with paint. As he re-pressurised the machine, it exploded. Rob suffered cuts from sharp fragments of the machine casing. Also, paint went everywhere, splashing over his van and causing substantial damage. Rob tried to contact the supplier from whom he had purchased the machine, but found that the supplier had ceased trading and can no longer be traced. Rob does, however, have details of the manufacturer. An independent examination of the remains of the machine showed that the pressure seal was broken. However, it did not determine with certainty why it had broken, so Rob is seeking further evidence on that point.

Advise Jenny and Rob as to their potential claims in tort arising from these incidents.

Question 8

Before attempting this question, you should have studied:

- Part 10 – Nuisance

Two householders – Martin and Tamsin – are each facing complaints from their neighbours, Julia and her boyfriend Steve. Six months ago, Julia became the tenant of a house in a quiet residential village. Steve moved in one month later. Although the tenancy remains in Julia's name, they both regard the house as their home. Steve works from home, so he converted Julia's spare room into his office.

Four months ago, Martin engaged a contractor to build an extension to his house. Martin moved out for the duration of the works and left the contractor to manage the project. The contractor warned Julia that the work would inevitably be noisy. The work took place between 9.00 am and 5.00 pm each weekday, and took three months to complete.

The noise made it impossible for Steve to work from home, so he had to rent an office elsewhere. Julia's job requires her to work at night. She needs to sleep during the day but was often unable to do so because of the noise. Now the work is finished, Julia and Steve have approached Martin and told him that they feel they should be compensated for the expense and inconvenience. However, Martin feels that the problem is nothing to do with him because he employed a contractor to manage the project.

Julia and Steve have also complained to Tamsin. Tamsin's house has a very large garden, in which she has constructed a smokehouse to produce smoked fish. Julia complains that the smoke drifts across her garden every weekend, making it impossible for her and Steve to sit in the garden. Tamsin runs a small business selling the smoked fish, and she was granted planning permission because the council were keen to encourage this. When Julia and Steve complained, Tamsin replied: 'I don't know why you are complaining. I have been doing this for five years. You only moved in recently, and your predecessors never objected.' However, Tamsin is worried that Julia and Steve may try to force her to limit her activities so that there is no smoke at weekends.

Advise Martin and Tamsin as to any claims in tort they may face arising from the above events, and the potential remedies.

24 Answers to multiple choice questions

24.1 Chapter overview

This chapter presents the answers to the multiple choice questions at the end of each part of the book. You can find a further set of ten such questions and answers at www.routledge.com/cw/sqe.

24.2 Part 2 – Trespass to land and to the person

Question 1

The correct answer is E. The developer has committed the tort of trespass to land. The neighbour can seek both damages for past loss and an injunction requiring removal of the fence. Having established liability, he is entitled to the remedy of damages. However, an injunction is a discretionary remedy, so he must request the court to exercise its discretion to grant the injunction.

A is not correct. Trespass to land is an intentional tort. However, the defendant only needs to intend to do the act that constitutes trespass (erecting the fence). He need not intend to trespass; so it is no defence to show that he did not intend to erect the fence on the neighbour's land.

B is not correct. The neighbour may seek both damages and an injunction.

C is not correct. An injunction cannot be demanded as of right.

D is not correct. It is not relevant that the land in question was uncultivated waste land, so that the neighbour has not suffered any loss. Trespass to land is actionable without proof of damage (actionable per se). Trespass to land protects the claimant's rights in land. So, if the relevant right is infringed, an action arises even if the claimant has not suffered any damage or harm beyond infringement of the right itself.

Question 2

The correct answer is D. By grabbing hold of the customer, the doorman intentionally inflicted unlawful force on him. This amounts to the tort of battery. By detaining the customer in the office, the doorman imposed an unlawful restriction on his freedom of movement. This amounts to the tort of false imprisonment, no matter how brief the detention; therefore, answer **A** is not correct.

B and **C** are not correct because the doorman committed both battery and false imprisonment.

E is not correct. Trespass to the person is actionable without proof of damage (actionable per se). It protects the claimant's rights to bodily integrity. So, if the relevant right is infringed, an action arises even if the claimant has not suffered any damage or harm beyond infringement of the right itself.

24.3 Part 3 – Negligence

Question 1

The correct answer is D. This gives the *best* explanation because it refers to each of the elements of a claim in negligence: duty of care, breach of duty, and causation of damage.

A is not the best explanation because it *only* refers to causation of damage.

B is not correct. The duty of care owed by a driver to a pedestrian is an established duty. So, it is not correct to ask whether it would be fair, just and reasonable to find that a duty was owed.

C is not the best explanation because it does not refer to breach of duty and causation of damage. Owing a duty of care does not by itself make the motorist liable.

E is not correct. It is not relevant to ask what the motorist himself foresaw because the standard of care he must meet is that of the ordinary reasonable motorist.

Question 2

The correct answer is E. The taxi driver owed a duty of care to his passenger, but was not in breach of duty because he was driving with reasonable care. Therefore, he is not liable.

A is not correct. Driver to passenger is an established duty situation. Therefore, it is not correct to ask whether it would be fair, just and reasonable to impose a duty of care.

B is not correct. The taxi driver's duty was to exercise reasonable care, meeting the standard to be expected of the ordinary reasonable taxi driver. The facts show that he met this standard, so was not in breach of duty.

C does not correctly explain why the taxi driver is not liable – he was not in breach of duty. (Also, *if* the taxi driver had been in breach of duty, the fact that the lorry driver was also liable would not exonerate the taxi driver.)

D is not correct. It is true that driver to passenger is an established duty situation, but the taxi driver did not breach the duty of care.

Question 3

The correct answer is D. This is the *best* explanation because it refers to the duty of care owed by the teacher to the motorist and explains how the duty was breached.

A is not correct. Although the teacher was guilty of an omission to supervise, a duty may be owed where the claimant is harmed by the actions of a party with whom the defendant has a relationship of control. So, the teacher, exercising control over the child owed a duty of care to the motorist.

B is not correct. The motorist's claim relies on the duty of care the teacher owed to him (not the duty she owed to the child).

C is not correct. A claimant's own actions will only break the chain of causation if they were *unreasonable*. It was reasonable for the motorist to swerve to avoid hitting the child.

E is not the *best* explanation. The explanation should refer to the duty of care owed by the teacher to the motorist because negligent behaviour is only actionable if a duty of care was owed.

Question 4

The correct answer is C. This is the *best* explanation because it correctly explains that the teacher is liable because she breached her duty of care to the pupil.

A is not correct. The teacher is in breach of her duty of care if she fails to meet the standard of care of a reasonable chemistry teacher, even if she personally lacks the necessary skill and experience to meet that standard.

B is not correct. The teacher's failure to require safety glasses is not properly described as an omission to act. She was engaged in the positive activity of teaching the class. Therefore, she did owe a duty of care to the pupil.

D is not the *best* explanation. It is true that a teacher owes an established duty of care to their pupils. However, liability only arises once that duty is breached. So, the answer needs to explain how the duty was breached.

E is not correct. The teacher owes an established duty of care to the pupil, which she breached by failing to meet the standard of care of a reasonable chemistry teacher.

Question 5

The correct answer is B. A doctor who acts in accordance with a responsible body of professional opinion is unlikely to have fallen below a reasonable standard of care, even where there are other doctors who would have taken a different view.

A is not correct. Simply doing what was best in her own opinion would not be sufficient to establish that the doctor took reasonable care.

C is not correct because it does not refer to the correct test to determine whether the doctor breached her duty of care.

D is not correct. The doctor is required to meet the standard of the ordinary reasonable doctor, not that of a lay person.

E is not correct. The standard of care in negligence is objective and impersonal. So, whether the doctor took reasonable care is measured not by her own level of skill and experience but against the standard of a reasonable doctor.

Question 6

The correct answer is E. The employer is not liable because, although it owed the employee a duty of care, it was not in breach. The employer did not fail to exercise reasonable care because the level of risk of ice was very low at the time, so it was reasonable not to put down grit.

A is not correct. It is true that the employer's control over the car park gives rise to a duty of care. (The employer owes a duty of care both as employer and as occupier of the car park.) However, the employer was not in breach of its duty.

B is not correct. It is true that employer to employee is an established duty situation, but the existence of a duty of care is not, by itself, sufficient to establish liability.

C is not correct. The employer did not fall below a reasonable standard of care, and so was not in breach of duty.

D is not correct. It is true that the employee may be guilty of contributory negligence if, by hurrying, she failed to take reasonable care for her own safety. However, the effect of contributory negligence is to reduce the claimant's damages, not to defeat the claim entirely.

Question 7

The correct answer is E. The claim is not likely to succeed because, although the doctor owed the woman a duty of care, and was in breach, the breach did not cause the damage. It cannot be said that 'but for' the doctor's negligence the woman would not have suffered the blindness; she would still have suffered it even of the doctor had not been negligent.

A is not correct. It is true that doctor to patient is an established duty situation, but the doctor's breach of duty did not cause the blindness.

B is not correct because the doctor is in breach of her duty. It is true that the claim is not likely to succeed, but for a different reason – that the breach did not cause the harm.

C is not correct. The 'but for' test applies to the blindness rather than the original fall and injury.

D is not correct. It is true that, by not meeting the standard of a competent doctor in diagnosing the injury, the doctor was in breach of her duty. However, the breach did not cause the blindness.

Question 8

The correct answer is B. There are multiple causes of the passenger's injury. Taking each driver individually, the passenger cannot show that 'but for' their negligence her injury would not have occurred. However, the passenger can establish causation against each driver by showing that they each made a material contribution to her injury.

A is not correct. Between themselves, the taxi driver and the bus driver can rely on the ***Civil Liability (Contribution) Act 1978*** to each seek a contribution from the other to the damages payable to the passenger.

C is not correct. Although the 'but for' test is not satisfied against each driver individually, the passenger can establish causation by showing that each made a material contribution to her damage.

D is not correct. Both drivers are liable for the same damage, and the passenger can pursue her claim against both of them. (This does not increase the award of damages – she will not recover damages twice for the same injury.)

E is not correct. The Law ***Reform (Contributory Negligence) Act 1945*** is not relevant. The Act applies where the claimant has failed to take reasonable care for their own safety, which is not the case here (and it is a partial defence, not the basis for a claim).

Question 9

The correct answer is C. Since the decorator's actions were not a reasonably foreseeable result of the engineer's negligence, they are likely to amount to a new intervening act, breaking the chain of causation between the engineer's negligence and the residents' loss.

A is not correct. A duty owed to the building owner cannot be the basis for a claim by the residents.

B is not correct. It *can* be said that 'but for' the heating engineer's negligence the residents' possessions would not have been destroyed. However, the decorator's negligence is likely to break the chain of causation.

D is not correct. Although the engineer's negligence caused the residents to vacate their flats, the subsequent careless actions of the decorator broke the chain of causation.

E is not correct. The fact that the decorator is liable would not prevent the engineer from also being liable. (In fact, the engineer is not liable; but this is because causation cannot be established against him.)

Question 10

The correct answer is B. Under the 'egg shell skull' rule, provided the type of harm was reasonably foreseeable, the employer is liable for the full extent of the damage, even though the extent of the damage was not foreseeable. The defendant must take its victim as it finds him. So, **A** is not correct.

C is not correct. An employer owes an established duty of care to its employee, so it is not relevant to consider whether imposition of a duty would be fair, just and reasonable.

D is not correct. Liability does not depend on what the defendant employer itself foresaw.

E is not correct. The employer is liable for the full extent of the employee's injury despite the fact that it was not reasonably foreseeable to a reasonable employer.

24.4 Part 4 – General defences

Question 1

The correct answer is A. The employer can rely on the partial defence of contributory negligence. The employee failed to take reasonable care for his own safety (by following the dangerous practice of riding on the truck), and this contributed to the damage he suffered. Under the ***Law Reform (Contributory Negligence Act) 1945*** the employee's damages will be reduced to reflect his share in responsibility for the damage.

B is not correct. The employee's failure to take reasonable care for his own safety is measured by an objective standard, not by what the employee himself foresaw.

C is not correct. The employee's contributory negligence is only a partial defence to the claim.

D is not correct. For the partial defence of contributory negligence to apply, the employee's failure to take reasonable care need not contribute to causing the accident. It is sufficient that it contributed to causing the injury.

E is not correct. For the defence of voluntary assumption of risk to apply, the employee must have known of the risk of harm and voluntarily consented to it. On the facts, it is unlikely that the employee appreciated, and consented to, the risk of the truck malfunctioning and crashing.

Question 2

The correct answer is B. The instructor is liable for the woman's injury (because she owed the woman a duty of care, which she breached causing the woman's damage). As a defence, the instructor seeks to rely on a clearly worded exclusion notice which was brought to the woman's attention. However, she cannot rely on the exclusion notice because the lesson was to promote her *business*. Liability for death or personal injury caused by negligence cannot be excluded if the defendant **acts in the course of a business** (*Consumer Rights Act 2015*). So, **A** is not correct.

C is not correct. Although the instructor provided the ride for free, she did so in the course of her business.

D is not correct (although it correctly states that the instructor is liable). It is not correct to say that liability for personal injury can *never* be excluded in any circumstances. If the instructor had *not* been acting in the course of business, her liability could have been excluded.

E is not correct. The woman may be guilty of contributory negligence (if a reasonable person in her position would have appreciated the need for a helmet). However, contributory negligence is only a partial defence, resulting in a reduction in damages.

Question 3

The correct answer is A. For the defence of illegality to apply, the claimant must have been engaged in serious wrongdoing, such that it would be viewed as offensive and unfair for him to receive compensation. This would be satisfied on these facts.

B is not correct. The ***Road Traffic Act 1988*** s.149 prevents the driver of a motor vehicle from relying on the defence of voluntary assumption of risk against passengers. (Moreover, for the defence of voluntary assumption of risk to apply, the claimant must know of the risk and voluntarily consent to it. There is nothing on the facts to suggest that the youth knew of, and consented to, the risk of the friend's negligent driving.)

C is not correct. The court found the friend not liable. This cannot have been because the defence of contributory negligence applied since this is only a partial defence, resulting in a reduction in damages.

D is not correct. To avoid the claim becoming statute barred, the claimant must issue proceedings within the limitation period. In a personal injury claim the limitation period is three years. The proceedings were issued within that period, so the defence of limitation does not apply. (It is not relevant that the trial did not take place until four years later.)

E is not correct. The ***Road Traffic Act 1988*** s.149 prevents the driver of a motor vehicle from excluding liability to passengers.

Question 4

The correct answer is C. The engineer owed a duty of care to the injured man because he engaged in a positive act (undertaking the maintenance of the train) that caused foreseeable physical damage to the claimant. He was in breach of duty, the breach caused the injury, and no relevant defences apply.

A is not correct. The mere fact that the injured man volunteered to work on the train does not give rise to the defence of voluntary assumption of risk.

B is not correct. For the defence of voluntary assumption of risk to apply, the injured man must have *known of the risk* from the valve and voluntarily consented to it. There is nothing to suggest this on the facts.

D is not correct. The injured man may have failed to take care by failing to wear overalls, but this did not contribute to the harm he suffered to his hands.

E is not correct. In the circumstances, there is nothing to suggest that a duty would not be owed because of the engineer's status as an unpaid volunteer.

24.5 Part 5 – Negligence: limited duty situations

Question 1

The correct answer is C. The supplier has suffered pure economic loss. No duty of care is owed in respect of this loss unless there is a special relationship between the bank and the supplier, involving *both* an assumption of responsibility by the bank *and* reasonable reliance by the supplier. There was no assumption of responsibility because the bank was not aware of the identity of the supplier. (The supplier did not disclose its identity, and instead used an agent to obtain the reference.) Therefore, **A** is not correct.

B is not correct. It is not correct to say that a duty of care is never owed in respect of pure economic loss.

D is not correct. Although the bank was negligent, is it is not liable because no duty of care was owed.

E is not correct. The bank did not undertake a responsibility towards the supplier by agreeing to provide the reference because it was not aware of the identity of the supplier.

Question 2

The correct answer is B (therefore, the other answers are incorrect).

Alison and Bernard have suffered psychiatric harm without physical injury. They each need to show that the restaurant owner owed them a duty of care (and that the duty was breached, causing damage).

Alison suffered a recognised psychiatric illness. She was a **primary victim** because she was in the actual area of danger. So, she was owed a duty of care because she was placed at a foreseeable risk of physical injury. (She can also show that the restaurant owner breached his duty, so causing the damage.)

Bernard suffered a recognised psychiatric illness. He was a **secondary victim** because he was not in the actual area of danger. He is owed a duty of care because:

- His PTSD was caused by a sudden shocking event.
- It was reasonably foreseeable that a person of ordinary fortitude would suffer psychiatric harm.
- He had close ties of love and affection with the immediate victim, Alison.
- He was in proximity to the incident and saw it with his own senses.

(He can also establish breach of duty and causation.)

Carol was a **secondary victim**. However, **no duty of care** was owed to her because she did not have close ties of love and affection with Alison.

24.6 Part 6 – Remedies in tort

Question 1

The correct answer is C. At her death, Amelia had a claim against the driver of the lorry in negligence. That claim survives for the benefit of her estate (save that there can be no claim for loss of income in the period after death) – *Law Reform (Miscellaneous Provisions) Act 1934*. The Act also allows for recovery of funeral expenses paid by the estate. Therefore, **A** is not correct.

B is not correct. Amelia's parents cannot make a claim for bereavement damages. They are not on the statutory list of persons eligible to make such claim – *Fatal Accidents Act 1976*.

D is not correct because Amelia's future loss of earnings are not recoverable.

E is not correct. Although Amelia's parents do fall within the statutory list of persons eligible to make a claim for loss of dependency, they are not financially dependent on Amelia.

Question 2

The correct answer is E (therefore, the other answers are not correct).

The claimant's injuries have reduced his life expectancy. His claim for future loss of earnings can cover:

- earnings for the period he is now expected to live (10 years), *and*
- earnings for the 'lost years' in which he would have lived had it not been for the accident (20 years).

Therefore, the calculation is based on his pre-accident working life expectancy of 30 years. For the first ten years his loss of wages is claimed in full. For the remaining 20 'lost years' a deduction is made for his own living expenses.

The calculation is based on *net* earnings (not gross as in answer **B**).

24.7 Part 7 – Employers' liability and vicarious liability

Question 1

The correct answer is B. The employer owed the employee a non-delegable duty of care. So, the contractor's failure to exercise reasonable care in designing the production line means that the employer was in breach of duty. The contractor, as designer of the production line, also owed a duty of care to persons using it and was in breach. The design defect caused the injury. Therefore, both employer and contractor are liable, and the employee should claim against both of them. (Of course, the employee can only recover damages once for his injury.)

A is not correct. The fact that the employer took reasonable care to select a competent contractor does not mean that the employer was not in breach of its duty, because the duty is non-delegable.

C is not correct. Although the employer is not vicariously liable for the negligence of its independent contractor, it is in breach of its own non-delegable duty of care to the employee.

D is not correct. The fact that the employer is liable does not absolve the contractor from liability.

E is not correct. Although the employer delegated the task to the contractor, performance of the employer's own duty of care cannot be delegated.

Question 2

The correct answer is D. The employer owed the employee a duty to take reasonable care to provide safe equipment and a safe system of work. The duty extends to taking care to ensure that the system is operated properly. So, provision of gloves and replacements by itself is not sufficient because there was no system for ensuring that worn-out gloves were replaced. Therefore, **B** is not correct.

A is not correct. There is no breach of the employer's duty to provide competent fellow staff. Although the failure to provide safety training means that the injured employee himself is not competent, this is a breach of the employer's duty to provide a safe system of work.

C is not correct. For the defence of voluntary assumption of risk to apply, the employer must show that the employee was aware of the risk of being burnt and voluntarily consented to such risk. This is not satisfied on the facts.

E is not correct. Where work equipment is defective, statute may attribute the fault of a third-party supplier to the employer. However, the equipment provided by the employer was not defective.

Question 3

The correct answer is A. The employee did not commit a tort against the customer, so the supermarket owner does not incur vicarious liability. The employee did not commit the tort of battery because he can rely on the defence of necessity, having pushed the customer to save her from being run over (therefore, **B** is not correct). He did not commit the tort of assault. An assault causes the claimant to anticipate unlawful force, but the force was not unlawful because necessity applied (therefore, **D** is not correct). He did not commit the tort of negligence because he did not fall below a reasonable standard of care (therefore, **C** is not correct).

E is not correct. The employer does not incur vicarious liability because the actions of the employee did not amount to a tort. (*If* the employee's actions had amounted to a tort, it would have fallen within the course of his employment because his actions were closely connected with the work he was employed to do.)

Question 4

The correct answer is D. The tanker driver is an employee who has committed a tort during the course of his employment. Therefore, the employer is vicariously liable.

A is not correct. The tanker driver's tort was committed during the course of his employment. His job was to deliver the fuel, and his negligence was closely connected to this task.

B is not correct. Vicarious liability arises without fault on the part of the employer, so it is not relevant that the employer could not reasonably have foreseen the tanker driver's negligence.

C is not correct (though it correctly states that the employer is liable). The employer did *not* owe a non-delegable duty of care to the petrol station owner. (An employer's duty is only non-delegable when owed to employees.)

E is not correct. Although the employer itself took reasonable care, it is nevertheless vicariously liable for the negligence of its employee.

24.8 Part 8 – Occupiers' liability

Question 1

The correct answer is E. The parent suffered damage caused by the state of the premises. The LA is the occupier of the school; the parent is a lawful visitor. So, the *Occupiers' Liability Act 1957* ('OLA 57') applies. The LA owed the parent a duty to take reasonable care to see that she would be reasonably safe. It gave a warning about the carpet; but a warning is only sufficient to discharge the duty if it would enable the visitor to be reasonably safe. That is not satisfied because the parent still had to pass over the dangerous area. Therefore, the LA breached its duty, causing damage. However, by not looking where she was going, the parent failed to take reasonable care for her own safety, and this contributed to causing her damage. So, under the *Law Reform (Contributory Negligence) Act 1945*, her damages are likely to be reduced.

A is not correct. The duty owed to the parent is not a common law duty. It is the statutory duty under OLA 57 explained above.

B is not correct. The OLA 57 imposes a *positive* duty on the occupier to take reasonable care to ensure that the visitor will be reasonably safe.

C is not correct. The warning was not sufficient to discharge the duty of care, as explained above.

D is not correct. It states that the LA is liable to the parent *in full*, whereas the partial defence of contributory negligence applies.

Question 2

The correct answer is C. The occupier owed the teenager a duty of care under the *Occupiers' Liability Act 1984* ('OLA 84') because the statutory conditions for duty of care to arise were met: he was aware of the danger and knew that trespassers were likely to come into the vicinity, and it was reasonable to expect him to offer them some protection (therefore, answer **B** is not correct). The occupier's duty is to take reasonable care to see that the trespasser does not suffer injury. OLA 84 recognises that this may be discharged by taking reasonable steps to warn of the danger or to discourage them from incurring the risk. The occupier did this with the warning notice and the fence. So, the occupier was not in breach of duty (therefore, answer **E** is not correct).

A is not correct. Entering the land without permission makes the teenager a trespasser, but this does not mean that no duty of care was owed.

D is not correct. The mere fact that a person enters land as a trespasser does not give rise to the defence of illegality. (Also, since the occupier was not in breach of his duty, he does not need to rely on a defence.)

Question 3

The correct answer is D. The son suffered damage caused by the state of the premises; the company is the occupier of the shop. Once the son goes under the cordon, into an area where he is not permitted to be, he ceases to be a lawful visitor. The *Occupiers' Liability Act 1984* ('OLA 84') applies (therefore, **A** is not correct). The conditions for a duty of care to arise under OLA 84 were met: the company was aware of the danger (because it created the danger); it knew that trespassers were likely to come into the vicinity (the toy department); it was reasonable to expect it to offer them some protection (therefore, **E** is not correct). So, the company owed a duty to take reasonable care to see that the son did not suffer injury. That duty was breached because reasonable care was not taken when the fitting was left partially secured (therefore, **B** is not correct). The breach made a material contribution to the damage suffered by the son, so the company is liable to him. The father also owed the son a duty of care, which he breached, also making a material contribution to the son's damage. Since both the company and the father are liable in respect of the same damage, the company can recover a contribution from the father under the *Civil Liability (Contribution) Act 1978*.

C is not correct. The fact that the father is liable does not exonerate the company.

Question 4

The correct answer is A. The damage to the friend's car was caused by an *activity* carried out by the householder on his premises (driving his car). The householder owed the friend a duty of care, which he breached, causing the damage.

B and **C** are not correct. Neither the ***Occupiers' Liability Act 1957*** nor the ***Occupiers' Liability Act 1984*** applies because the damage was *not* caused by the *state of the premises*. (**C** is also incorrect in referring to the 1984 Act because the friend was a lawful visitor, having been permitted to enter by the householder.)

D is not correct because this is not a case of occupier's liability. (Also, an occupier's duty of care to lawful visitors *does* cover damage to property.)

E is not correct. Damage is recoverable provided the type of harm was foreseeable, even if the full extent of the damage was not. The defendant must take his victim as he finds him.

24.9 Part 9 – Product liability

Question 1

The correct answer is C. The claim should be pursued in negligence. The manufacturer of a product owes a **duty of care** to the end consumer where it puts the goods into circulation intending them to reach the consumer in the same form as they left the manufacturer, and with no reasonable expectation of an intermediate examination. This is satisfied since the component was inside the sealed body of the machine (therefore, **D** is not correct). The duty is **breached** if the manufacturer falls below a reasonable standard of care. This is satisfied since the component had been negligently assembled. The breach clearly **caused** the damage. So, the manufacturer is liable for damage to the glass counter top.

A is not correct. The damaged counter is used by the café owner for his business. The **Consumer Protection Act 1987** ('CPA') does not provide a remedy for damage caused to business property. (Under s.5(3) the CPA does not impose liability for damage to property unless the property is both intended by the claimant for their own private use and of a type usually intended for private use.)

B is not correct. Although the café owner had a contract with the supplier, he also has a claim in negligence against the manufacturer as explained above.

E is not correct. The manufacturer's duty of care in negligence does cover damage to business property.

Question 2

The correct answer is E. The ***Consumer Protection Act 1987*** ('CPA') applies where damage is caused by a defect in a product. A product is defective if its safety is not such as persons generally are entitled to expect (so the pasta was defective). The manufacturer is a defendant under the Act as producer of the pasta. Liability is strict, so it is not necessary to show that incorporation of the stone during the manufacturing process was caused by the manufacturer's lack of care.

A is not the *best* explanation. Causation of damage is not, by itself, sufficient to give rise to liability.

In **B** it is not correct to say that strict liability arises where a product causes injury. For strict liability to arise the product must be *defective*.

C is not correct. Foreseeability of damage is not, by itself, sufficient to give rise to liability.

D is not correct. The manufacturer is liable because the product was *defective*. Although an 'own brander' is a potential defendant under the CPA, merely putting a brand on the product is not, by itself, sufficient to give rise to liability.

Question 3

The correct answer is D. The ***Consumer Protection Act 1987*** ('CPA') applies where damage is caused by a defect in a product. A product is defective if its safety is not such as persons generally are entitled to expect. So, the bike was defective (and answer **C** is not correct). The manufacturer is a defendant as producer of the bike. Liability is strict, so it is not necessary to show that the defect was caused by the manufacturer's lack of care. However, under the CPA it would be a defence for the manufacturer to show that the **state of scientific and technical knowledge** meant that no bike producer could have discovered the latent weakness.

A is not correct. The burden is on the claimant to prove that the product was defective, not on the manufacturer to prove that the product was safe. (Also, proof of a defect does not ensure liability, where the manufacturer can rely on a defence.)

B is not correct. The 'state of scientific knowledge' defence depends on showing that producers generally could not have discovered the defect (not that the manufacturer itself was incapable of discovering it).

E is not correct. Although the CPA imposes strict liability, the manufacturer may have a defence if producers generally could not have discovered the defect, as explained above.

Question 4

The correct answer is A. The damage to the laptop was caused by the faulty handle on the bag. The manufacturer of the bag owed the woman a duty of care because it put the bag into circulation intending it to reach the consumer in the same form as it left the manufacturer, with no reasonable expectation of an intermediate examination. That duty was breached by the manufacturer's failure to exercise reasonable care. So, the damage to the laptop is recoverable in negligence. As regards the damage to the bag itself, no duty of care is owed since such damage is classed as pure economic loss. Nor can the damage to the bag be recovered under the **Consumer Protection Act 1987** ('CPA') since the Act does not impose liability for damage caused to the defective product itself (s.5(2)).

B is not correct. Damage to the bag is not recoverable under the CPA, as above. Damage to the laptop is not recoverable under the CPA because it is business property. (Under s.5(3) the CPA does not impose liability for damage to property unless the property is both intended by the claimant for their own private use and of a type usually intended for private use.) (Therefore, **E** is not correct.)

C is not correct. The woman cannot claim for the bag.

D is not correct. The woman can claim for the laptop.

24.10 Part 10 – Nuisance

Question 1

The correct answer is B. Private nuisance is an unlawful interference with the claimant's use and enjoyment of land. There must be a continuing state of affairs (the fumes). On the facts, this nuisance takes the form of tangible damage to the land (death of plants and soil pollution). The company can seek damages for its past loss (cost of replacing plants and remedying soil pollution), and can ask the court to exercise its discretion to grant an injunction to prohibit the emission of toxic fumes in future.

A is not correct. As a leaseholder, the company has the necessary interest in land required to bring a claim in private nuisance.

C is not correct. The company's claim in private nuisance does not depend on showing that the factory owner failed to take reasonable care.

D is not correct. The company can both claim damages for its past loss and seek an injunction for the future.

E is not correct. Where the nuisance takes the form of tangible damage to the claimant's land, the character of the neighbourhood is not considered.

Question 2

The correct answer is E. Private nuisance is an unlawful interference with the claimant's use and enjoyment of land. This may take the form of encroachment onto the claimant's land. (The leaning fence satisfies this and the requirement for a continuing state of affairs.) The neighbour has the necessary interest in the land affected.

A is not correct. A claim in negligence would require tangible damage to be caused to the land, which is not satisfied on the facts.

B is not correct. Trespass to land requires a direct interference with the claimant's possession of land. On the facts, the interference from the fence is indirect. The interference is also gradual and unintentional, which makes nuisance the more appropriate claim.

C is not correct. A claim under the rule in *Rylands v Fletcher* requires the claimant to establish that the defendant made a non-natural use of their land, bringing a dangerous thing onto the land that escapes and causes damage. On the facts, these elements are not satisfied. The erection of a fence is not a non-natural use of the land.

D is not correct. For a claim in private nuisance, it is not necessary to show tangible damage to the land.

Question 3

The correct answer is E. Under the rule in *Rylands v Fletcher* a defendant is liable, without proof of fault, if they make a non-natural use of their land, bringing a dangerous thing onto the land that escapes and causes damage. On the facts, this is satisfied by storing large quantities of a harmful chemical, which escaped. So, the company is liable for damage to the field. However, a defendant is not liable for damage which was too remote because not reasonably foreseeable. So, the company is not liable for the damage to the pond.

A is not correct. It is not relevant to consider the duty of care owed in the tort of negligence because the facts state that the company took all reasonable care. The relevant tort to apply on the facts is the rule in *Rylands v Fletcher*.

B is not correct. Where the rule in *Rylands v Fletcher* applies, liability is strict. So, the company cannot escape liability by showing that it exercised reasonable care.

C is not correct. Liability under the rule in *Rylands v Fletcher* arises from an isolated escape.

D is not correct. Although liability under the rule in *Rylands v Fletcher* is strict, the extent of the defendant's liability is limited to damage which was reasonably foreseeable.

Question 4

The correct answer is D. By leaving the skip on the highway for an unreasonable period of time, the restaurant owner has committed the tort of public nuisance by causing an unreasonable interference with the reasonable comfort and convenience of a class of the public. For the flower shop owner to claim damages, she must show that she has suffered particular damage, over and above that suffered by the public in general. Her loss of business profits satisfies this (therefore **C**, suggesting that no one can claim, is not correct).

A is not correct because it refers to a claim in the tort of negligence. The flower shop owner's loss of business profits is pure economic loss, in respect of which no duty of care would be owed in negligence.

B is not correct. An individual cannot claim in public nuisance unless they have suffered particular damage over and above that suffered by the public in general.

E is not correct. Although the flower shop owner's loss of business profits is pure economic loss, it is recoverable in public nuisance.

24.11 Part 11 – Protections for reputation and private information

Question 1

The correct answer is A. For a successful claim in defamation, the claimant must show that the defendant **published** a **defamatory statement** which **referred to the claimant**. A statement is published when it is communicated to someone *other* than the claimant. The secretary did not communicate her suspicions to anyone other than the manager *himself*. Therefore, the statement was *not* **published**.

Given that the claimant cannot establish the elements of a claim in defamation, it is not necessary for the defendant to raise a defence. Therefore, answers **B**, **C**, and **D** do not state the correct reason why the claim will fail.

E is not correct. The statement *was* defamatory. A suggestion that the manager was accepting bribes would lower the manager in the estimation of right-thinking people. It is also likely to satisfy the statutory threshold of seriousness: that a statement is not defamatory unless its publication has caused or is likely to cause serious harm to the reputation of the claimant (***Defamation Act 2013***).

Question 2

The correct answer is C. Although the manager can show that the secretary published a defamatory statement that referred to him, the secretary can rely on the defence of qualified privilege. The defence applies because the secretary had a duty to disclose the information to the chairman, who had an interest in receiving it (therefore, answer **D** is not correct).

A is not correct. Although the secretary cannot rely on the defence of truth, the claim is not likely to succeed because the defence of qualified privilege applies – as above.

B is not correct. The statement was published when the secretary spoke to the company chairman.

E is not correct. The defence of absolute privilege does not apply in these circumstances.

Question 3

The correct answer is E. A claim in defamation will not succeed. Although the journalist published a defamatory statement that referred to the politician, the journalist can rely on the defence of truth. A claim for misuse of private information is not likely to succeed. It is unlikely that the politician could establish that she had a reasonable expectation of privacy in relation to the information (and, even if that were satisfied, it is likely that this would be outweighed by the journalist's freedom of expression because it would be in the public interest for the information to be disclosed).

Therefore, answers **A**, **B**, **C**, and **D** are not correct.

Answer **D** also incorrectly states that the statement is *not* defamatory. The statement *is* defamatory, but the defence of truth applies.

Question 4

The correct answer is D. A claim for misuse of private information is likely to succeed. The sportsperson is likely to have a reasonable expectation of privacy in information about a personal relationship, particularly since they have never made their family life public. In the circumstances, this is unlikely to be outweighed by the journalist's right to freedom of expression. A claim in defamation will not succeed because the journalist can rely on the defence of truth. Therefore, answers **A**, **B**, **C**, and **E** are not correct.

In relation to answer **B**, the fact that the information was **true** would *not* give the journalist a defence to a claim for misuse of private information.

In relation to answer **E**:

In a claim for defamation, publication of a story on a matter of public interest can be a defence; but it is not relevant here because the journalist can rely on the defence of truth.

In a claim for misuse of private information, it would not be a defence to show that the story was on a matter of public interest *unless* this outweighed the sportsperson's right to privacy, which is unlikely on the facts.

Index

Abatement 191–192; *see also* Private nuisance
Actionable per se 21–22, 214; *see also* Defamation; Trespass to land; Trespass to the person
Assault, definition of 32; *see also* Trespass to the person

Battery, definition of 30; *see also* Trespass to the person
Bereavement 119; *see also* Death
Breach of duty in negligence 47–53
    children 51
    objective standard 47–48
    proving breach 51–52; *res ipsa loquitur* 52
    reasonable care 47–51
    reasonable person 47
    reasonable precautions 49
    risk 48
    skilled defendants 50–51
    under skilled defendants 49–50
    see also Employers' liability; Product liability; Psychiatric harm; Pure economic loss
Burden of proof *see* Causation of damage
'But for' test *see* Causation of damage

Causation of damage 55–68
    burden of proof 57
    'but for' test 56–58
    multiple causes: material contribution to harm 59–60; material increase in risk 60–61

    see also Contribution between tortfeasors; Intervening acts; Remoteness of damage
Client case analysis 12–17, 225–232
    elements of claim, establishing 226
    evidence 227–228; lay witnesses 227; expert evidence 227–228
    litigation risk 226
    parties to claim, identifying 226
    preliminary issue, trial on 213
    relevant tort, identifying 225
    settlement of claims 228–229
Common duty of care *see* Occupiers' Liability Act 1957
Consent 34; *see also* Trespass to the person
Consumer Protection Act 1987 170–172
    claimant – who may claim? 170
    damage 171
    defect, meaning of 170
    defences 171–172; state of scientific knowledge 172
    defendant: 'forgetful supplier' 170; importer 170; 'own brander' 170; producer 170
    product, meaning of 170
    strict liability 170
Contract *see* Product liability
Contribution between tortfeasors 62
Contributory negligence 78–79, 119–120, 154, 160–161; *see also* Death; Defences; *Occupiers' Liability Act 1957*; *Occupiers' Liability Act 1984*

Damages *see* Death; Defamation; Personal Injury damages; Private nuisance; Remedies
Death 116–120
 benefits received on death 120
 bereavement 119
 contributory negligence of deceased 119–120
 dependency, loss of 118–119
 estate of deceased: claim for 117–118; survival of cause of action 116
Defamation 209–216; elements of claim 209
 claimant – statement referring to 210
 damage: libel – actionable per se 214; slander – special damage 214
 defamatory statement 210; serious harm 210, 214–215
 defences: honest opinion 211–212; limitation of actions 213–214; privilege 212–213; public interest 212; truth 211
 human rights – freedom of expression 216
 libel, definition of 214
 publication 210–211
 remedies: damages 215; injunction 215–216
 slander, definition of 214
Defences 77–84
 contributory negligence 78–79; children 79; reduction in damages 79
 exclusion of liability 80–81; statutory controls 81; death and personal injury 81
 illegality 83–84
 limitation of actions 79–80
 voluntary assumption of risk 82–83
 see also Trespass to land; Trespass to the person; *Consumer Protection Act 1987*; *Occupiers' Liability Act 1957*; *Occupiers' Liability Act 1984*; Private Nuisance; Defamation

Dependency, loss of *see* Death
Duty of care in negligence 41–46
 established duty 42–44
 novel duty 44–46; foreseeability 44; proximity 45; fair, just and reasonable 45–46
 omissions to act 42–43
 police 43
 see also Employers' liability; Product liability; Psychiatric harm; Pure economic loss

Economic loss *see* Pure economic loss
'Egg shell skull' rule 65–66; *see also* Remoteness of damage
Employers' liability 127–130
 defective equipment – fault of third party 128
 employer's duty – scope of 127–128
 non-delegable duty 129
Established duty *see* Duty of Care in negligence
Evidence *see* Client case analysis
Exclusion of liability 80–81, 154–155, 161; *see also* Defences; *Occupiers' Liability Act 1957*; *Occupier's Liability Act 1984*

False imprisonment, definition of 33; *see also* Trespass to the person
Freedom of expression *see* Misuse of private information

Honest opinion 211–212; *see also* Defamation
Human rights
 alternative remedy 121
 freedom of expression 216, 217, 218, 220
 private life 217, 218

Illegality 83–84; *see also* Defences
Injunction 2, 120–121, 190–191, 215–216, 219–220; *see also* Defamation; Misuse of Private

Index 309

Information; Private nuisance; Remedies; Trespass to land
Intervening acts 62–64
   acts of claimant 64
   acts of third party 63–64
   see also Causation of damage

Land see Trespass to land
Lawful arrest 35–36; see also Trespass to the person
Licence 25; see also Trespass to land
Limitation of actions 79–80, 213–214; see also Defences; Defamation
Limited duty of care see Psychiatric harm; Pure economic loss
Litigation risk 226; see also Client case analysis

Manufacturer's duty of care see Product liability – negligence
Material contribution to harm see Causation of damage – multiple causes
Material increase in risk see Causation of damage – multiple causes
Misuse of private information 217–220; elements of claim 218
   freedom of expression 218–219
   human rights 217, 220
   privacy, reasonable expectation of 218
   remedies: damages 219; injunction 219–220
Mitigation of loss 112; see also Remedies
Multiple causes see Causation of damage

Necessity 25, 34–35; see also Trespass to land; Trespass to the person
Negligence see Duty of care in negligence; Breach of duty in negligence; Causation of damage; Defences
Non-delegable duty 129 see also Employers' liability

Novel duty see Duty of Care in negligence
Nuisance see Private nuisance, Public nuisance, *Rylands v Fletcher*, rule in

Occupiers' Liability
   Trespassers see Occupiers' Liability Act 1984
   Visitors see Occupiers' Liability Act 1957
Occupiers' Liability Act 1957 147–155
   children 151
   common duty of care 150
   defences: contributory negligence 154; exclusion of liability 154–155; voluntary assumption of risk 155
   independent contractors 152–153
   occupier, meaning of 150; duty owed by 150
   premises, liability for state of 149
   visitor, meaning 149–150
   warnings 152
Occupiers' Liability Act 1984 157–162
   Defences: contributory negligence 160–161; exclusion of liability 161; voluntary assumption of risk 161; illegality 161
   limited duty of care 158; conditions for duty to be owed 159
   premises, liability for state of 158
   scope of occupier's duty 159–160
   trespasser, meaning 157–158
Omissions to act see Duty of care in negligence

Personal injury damages 113–116
   care – cost of 115–116
   loss of earnings 114–115
   medical expenses 115
   pain, suffering, and loss of amenity 113
   special damages and general damages 116
Police see Duty of care in negligence
Premises, liability for see Occupiers'

Liability Act 1957; Occupiers' Liability Act 1984
Primary victim *see* Psychiatric harm
Privacy *see* Misuse of private information
Private Nuisance 179–193; definition of 179–180
  act of nature 182
  adopting a nuisance 182
  claimant – interest in land 180–181
  coming to a nuisance 186–187
  continuing a nuisance 182
  continuing state of affairs 183
  damage, proof of 187, 188
  defences: consent 189; prescription 189; statutory authority 189
  defendant: creator 181; landlord 183; occupier 181
  encroachment 187–188
  independent contractor creating nuisance 181
  intangible damage – reasonableness factors 183–187; abnormal sensitivity 184–185; character of neighbourhood 184; intensity and duration 184; malice 185; substantial interference 184
  negligence, effect of 182, 185
  planning permission 186
  remedies: abatement 191–193; damages 190; injunction 190–191
  remoteness of damage 188
  tangible damage 187–188
Privilege 212–213; *see also* Defamation
Product, defective; *see* Consumer Protection Act 1987; Product liability; Pure economic loss
Product liability 167–173
  contract 167–168
  negligence, manufacturer's duty of care 168–169
  strict liability – *see* Consumer Protection Act 1987
Psychiatric harm 97–103
  limited duty of care 91; consequential psychiatric harm distinguished 97–98
  medically recognised condition 98–99
  primary victim: definition of 98; duty owed to 100
  rescuers 102–103
  secondary victim: definition of 98; duty owed to 100–102
  sudden shock 99–100
Public interest, publication on a matter of 212 *see also* Defamation
Public Nuisance 201–203; definition of 202
  claimant: Attorney General 202; individual 202–203
  class of the public 202
  personal injury 203
Pure economic loss 91–96
  definition of 92; defective product 92–93; property not belonging to claimant 93; statements and services 93–95
  limited duty of care 91; consequential economic loss distinguished 91–92

Reasonable care *see* Breach of duty in negligence; Employers' liability; Occupiers' Liability Act 1957; Occupiers' Liability Act 1984; Private nuisance – continuing a nuisance; Product liability – manufacturer's duty of care
Remedies 8–12, 111–121
  Damages: lump sum 112; purpose 111
  death, damages on *see* Death
  injunction 120–121; *see also* Defamation; Misuse of private information; Public nuisance; Trespass to land
  mitigation of loss 112
  personal injury *see* Personal injury damages
  property damage 112

Remoteness of damage 64–66
  'egg shell skull' rule 65–66
  reasonable foreseeability of harm 65
  'similar in type' rule 66
Res ipsa loquitur *see* Breach of duty in negligence – proving breach
Rylands v Fletcher, rule in 195–199
  damage 197–198
  dangerous thing 196–197
  non-natural use of land 197
  parties to claim 196
  strict liability 197

Secondary victim *see* Psychiatric harm
Self-defence 35; *see also* Trespass to the person
Settlement of claims *see* Client case analysis
'Similar in type' rule *see* Remoteness of damage
Statements, negligent *see* Pure economic loss – definition of
Strict liability *see* Consumer Protection Act 1987; *Rylands v Fletcher,* rule in

Trespass to Land 21–27; definition of 22
  actionable per se 21–22
  defences: lawful justification 25; licence 25; necessity 25
  land, meaning of 23
  possession 22
  remedies: damages 26; declaration 25; injunction 2; order for possession of land 26
Trespass to the Person 29–36
  actionable per se 21–22
  assault 32
  battery 30–32
  defences: consent 34; lawful arrest 35–36; necessity 34–35; self-defence 35
  false imprisonment 33–34
  medical treatment 31–32, 34
  remedies 36
Trespasser *see* Occupiers' Liability Act 1984; *see also* Trespass to Land
Truth 211; *see also* Defamation

Vicarious liability 133–140
  close connection / course of employment 137–139
  independent contractors 136–137
  relationship – employment or 'akin' to employment 134–136
Visitor *see* Occupiers' Liability Act 1957
Voluntary assumption of risk *see* Defences; *Occupiers' Liability Act 1957; Occupiers' Liability Act 1984*

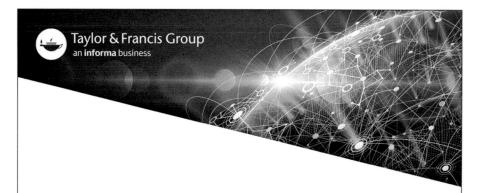